SEEING AND BEING SEEN

Seeing and Being Seen

THE Q'EQCHI' MAYA OF LIVINGSTON, GUATEMALA, AND BEYOND

Hilary E. Kahn

UNIVERSITY OF TEXAS PRESS
Austin

A version of Chapter 8 and sections of Chapter 4 previously appeared in 2001 as "Respecting Relationships and *Día de Guadalupe:* Q'eqchi' Mayan Identities in Livingston, Guatemala." *Journal of Latin American Anthropology* 6(1):2–29.

A version of Chapter 9 previously appeared in 2003 as "Traversing the Q'eqchi' Imaginary: The Conjecture of Crime in Livingston, Guatemala." In *Crime's Power: Anthropologists and the Ethnography of Crime,* edited by Stephanie Kane and Phillip Parnell, New York: Palgrave Macmillan, 2003, 33–54.

Requests for permission to reproduce material from this work should be sent to:
    Permissions
    University of Texas Press
    P.O. Box 7819
    Austin, TX 78713-7819
    www.utexas.edu/utpress/about/bpermission.html

⊗ The paper used in this book meets the minimum requirements of ANSI/NISO Z39.48-1992 (R1997) (Permanence of Paper).

LIBRARY OF CONGRESS CATALOGING-IN-PUBLICATION DATA
Kahn, Hilary E., 1966–
    Seeing and being seen : the Q'eqchi' Maya in Livingston, Guatemala, and beyond / Hilary E. Kahn. — 1st ed.
        p.   cm.
    Includes bibliographical references and index.
    ISBN-13: 978-0-292-71348-2 (cl. : alk. paper)
    ISBN-10: 0-292-71348-7
    ISBN-13: 978-0-292-71455-7 (pbk. : alk. paper)
    ISBN-10: 0-292-71455-6
    1. Kekchi Indians—Guatemala—Livingston—History.
2. Kekchi Indians—Guatemala—Livingston—Ethnic identity.
3. Kekchi Indians—Guatemala—Livingston—Social conditions.
4. Video recording in ethnology—Guatemala—Livingston.
5. Motion pictures in ethnology—Guatemala—Livingston.
6. Indians in motion pictures.   7. Livingston (Guatemala)—Social life and customs.   I. Title.
    F1465.2.K5K34   2006
    305.897'42072813—dc22

                                                   2006015717

This book is dedicated to my son
Noah Alexander Kahn Johnson and godson
Eduardo Martín Xol Chub for linking us all
through time and space.

CONTENTS

ACKNOWLEDGMENTS

My deepest thanks and respect go to all the people from Livingston, Guatemala, who are my friends, ethnographic subjects, and collaborators. While I cannot possibly mention everyone who shared their lives and smiles with me, I send my most heartfelt thanks to Juliana Tiul Coc, Alberto Sub, Santiago Caal, Manuel and Lenora Ical, Matilde Pop, Jose Gerardo Caal, Ricardo Quib Xo, Oscar Armando Tec Icó, Felipe Col Sagui, Manuela Chubac, Concepción Choc Pop, Venancio Pop, Agustin Caal Macz, Patrocinia Chocooj, Paulina Pop, Juana de León Pop, and Liverio Gamboa. For their kindness and support, I also greatly thank Ana, Herlinda and Bex, Chico, Tekla, Natalia and Juan, Pedro, Marcos, Hilaria, Javiér, Irma, Santos, Juan, Agusto, Maria, Estevan, Juan Carlos, Henry, George the Baker, Father Tomas, Father Ricardo, the Sisters at the Catholic church, Arturo, Omar, Gringa, Maria, Marcos Sanchez Palacio, Agnes and Hermalindo, Julio and Carmen, the hombres de agua, Walandra, Natty, and Keepish. I also want to thank Saida and Alvaro Sub Maquin, who are all grown up now but whose smiles and hugs as children made my days in the field full and joyful. Of course, their mother, Lola, means the world to me. Her friendship and laughter keep me drawn to Livingston and to her family. My neighbor Blanca, her husband René, and their entire family are my extended family. We shared a lot, even a church fire and an earthquake, and I thank them all for taking me and now my whole family into their house and hearts. Two close friends have passed away since I began conducting this research. Martín and Mariano were so very helpful with my work. I can only hope that they envision this book as part of the respect I have for them. I am the godmother of Martín's son, Eduardo, and I consider him and Martín's entire family part of mine. To all of you in Livingston, I say thank you. *Gracias. Bantiox.* I cannot possibly express how much I respect all of you and appreciate all your kindness, acceptance, and generosity through the years. Because of you, Livingston will always be home.

I would also like to thank the small contingent of outsiders who either reside in Livingston or were passing through. I thank Kathy Lopez, Manolo (may he rest in peace), Gerardo, Andy, Conrad, Ken Wood, Annie Lorrie, Norma, and Erik. Thanks are also due to Marcos Tiul from the Movimiento Nacional de Resistencia Maya, Garifuna, y Popular, whose knowledge and concern for the Q'eqchi' people of Izabal deserves recognition.

Others in Guatemala that I would like to thank are Carmen Foncea and Mike Stanton at the U.S. Embassy in Guatemala City, who were exceptionally helpful during my initial year in the field. I am also grateful for the assistance provided by Centro de Investigaciones Regionales de Mesoamérica (CIRMA) in Antigua, who allowed me the use of their library, their copier, and their message board. My original year of fieldwork was funded by the J. William Fulbright Scholarship Board and I am grateful for their initial support of what has become a life journey. Subsequent years of travel and related research were funded by a junior faculty travel grant from the Center for Latin American and Caribbean Studies at Indiana University, Bloomington, and the University of Illinois at Urbana-Champaign and University of Chicago Joint Center for Latin American Studies Summer Visiting Scholarship.

Many individuals who do not reside in Guatemala have helped me along this journey and have provided invaluable assistance with this manuscript in its various stages. I sincerely thank Bridget Edwards, Bruce Jackson, Gary Gossen, Peter Hervik, Bette Moscowitz, Stephanie Kane, Donald Pollock, Leah Shopkow, David Stoll, Barbara and Dennis Tedlock, Jim Thrasher, Rick Wilk, and the anonymous reviewers of the manuscript for their advice, encouragement, and critical viewpoints. I would also like to thank the Sound and Video Analysis Lab (SAVAIL) at Indiana University Folklore and Ethnomusicology Department for use of their video editing and imaging facilities. Alan Burdette, John Fenn, Zsuzsa Cselenyi, Anthony Guest-Scott, Paul Schauert, and Patrick Feaster always offered their technical expertise. Linda Lamkin and Louise O'Connor also deserve my gratitude for assisting me with the still video captures and other assorted last-minute tasks for this book. I would also like to thank everyone at the Office of International Affairs and the Department of Anthropology at Indiana University Purdue University–Indianapolis (IUPUI). I am particularly grateful for the support of Susan Buck Sutton, who continues to inspire me to be an ethnographer with heart. I owe much to Theresa May, Allison Faust, Leslie Tingle, and other members of the editorial staff at the University of Texas Press, for providing me with this opportunity and the time and guidance to make it happen. I am also beholden to Cathie Carrigan for her indexing.

My family mean everything to me. They have been by my side throughout this endless journey. I have unlimited gratitude, love, and respect for my parents, Eunice and Jack, for supporting me in so many ways throughout these years. I could not have completed this book without their guidance. My sister, Joy, and her husband, Rick, have always encouraged my work, and fed me in earlier years, and I sincerely thank them for that. My own family have also been there throughout and at times lost me to this book. From deep in my heart I would like to pay my sincerest appreciation to my husband, Jahdee. He keeps me grounded and supported and I am so grateful for his clarity and strength. He, our sons Noah and now newborn Skylar, and our step-daughter Tashi have shown me that anything is possible with respect, love, patience, understanding, and laughter.

SEEING AND BEING SEEN

One   INTRODUCTION

ASH WEDNESDAY 1996

I can see but not be seen. From a lofty window I observe a standoff. Two masses of young people are facing each other in the street below. *Ladinos* versus *Garifuna*. Armed with buckets, bags, and boxes, all brimming with white flour, the youths are determined not only to catch the opposing team's banner, but also to blanket their opponents with sticky white "ash." When an individual becomes separated from their group, he or she is tugged and shoved until covered in flour by the opposing team. Without receiving physical injury, but symbolically transformed through ethnic bleaching, these individuals are always pushed safely back to their home team. Whitened and sweaty bodies, sounds of conch shell horns and screaming youths, and tempered aggressions merge in this battle of identities.

An Australian couple, wondering what the commotion is about, stroll through town on their first day in Livingston. Ambushed by both teams and enveloped in "ash," they run to escape the ethnic conflict. As they emerge, whiter than white, from the orgy of bodies, the flour accentuates their already pale skin, marking and ridiculing their outsiderness. Tourists have no recourse but to run back to their hotels, where they hide from the roving youths who have marked them as prime targets for Ash Wednesday whitening. I remain in my second-story roost. Although I am known by many in town, I have been warned to lay low. Only elderly people within the youths' ethnic group are spared whitening.

From my haven above I see a surreal apparition. A Q'eqchi' woman and her two children glide out from the riotous crowd and pass the ethnic battle lines without so much as a dusting of flour or a hair out of place. I feel as if I am having a vision. The mass of youths becomes a background blur, while the woman and her two children appear in hyper-focus, as though levitating out of this chaotic space. I am shocked and mesmerized. The little Q'eqchi' boy looks around curiously. His mother grabs his hand and yanks him away to run her errands. I am jolted out of my trance. I realize that this is not a dream at all. Although initially appearing untouched and unfazed, this Q'eqchi' family is quite aware of its surroundings.

Unlike the white tourists who pass by and who are labeled transgressors, Q'eqchi' Mayans are perceived stereotypically by Garifuna and Ladinos, among others, as being culturally traditional, unchanging, and opposed to modernization; and therefore, I surmise, immune to the re-creation of their identity through whitening. However, while this may be what the Garifuna ascertain, Q'eqchi' do not envision themselves as so unalterable. In fact, they consider themselves part of an enduring, yet ever-changing, network of relations—social and cosmological linkages that connect them to deities, outsiders, owners, and other beings who constantly shift back and forth between positions of power, personae, visibility, and meaning. The Q'eqchi' categorize themselves and others through this dynamic structure that defines morality as action and categorizes behavior into acts of respect and disrespect. Visuality and its political differentials—whether one is the object of sight or the subject of seeing—support the practice and codification of this imaginary model. Individuals and institutions are organized into a social and cosmological taxonomy of visible and invisible, selves and others, and benevolent givers and criminally oriented takers.

Because of the model's porosity—the ability to structure and be structured—cosmological, historical, and economic exchanges are embedded and mirrored in intimate, familial, community, ethnographic, and interethnic networks. Thus, like the family who emerged unblemished from the mob on Ash Wednesday, Q'eqchi' Mayan perception and behavior surface from historical and cultural imaginaries. And, like the little Q'eqchi' boy who remained ash-free on his exterior, Q'eqchi' people look around, internalize, and recreate themselves from within webs of relations that they themselves have spun (Geertz 1973:5).

Ash Wednesday in Livingston is neither solemn nor religious. It is a performance of ethnic identities demonstrating the dynamic strata that intersect in multicultural Livingston. Like many other local rituals, this event mirrors the antagonism between the Ladinos—Hispanic people of mixed European and Indian descent—and the Garifuna—the Afro-Amerindian population that makes up the majority of this small Caribbean town. Ash Wednesday also provides us with a glimpse of the usually unobservable moral logic embedded within the Q'eqchi' imaginary. Because they do not see reciprocity or any form of active respect, but rather fruitless frivolity,

Q'eqchi' people work during this day, considering the ethnic contest lavishly wasteful and unproductive.

According to Catholic doctrine, ash smeared on the forehead symbolizes the body's inevitable transformation to dust. The showering of flour in Livingston, by controlling the manifestation of identities, challenges cultural and historical structures. Participants of this ethnic battle mock the histories, unequal power relations, and color-coded hierarchies that maintain animosity between the Garifuna and Ladinos and that bolster Q'eqchi' understanding of this ritual as a frivolous waste of time. The Ash Wednesday competition cumulates in all the flour-coated participants jumping off the pier in a social ablution, again assuming their original identity.

People create identities, whether self or collective, from within a shifting network of personal, social, cultural, economic, historic, and political relationships. Identities are thus articulations emerging from motion. Selves, communities, ethnicities, foreigners, and images are "be-ings" (i.e., movements rather than things) in process (Spanos 2000). Academic and experienced categories of object and subject, home and field, self and other, insider and outsider, method and theory, and image and word are reified through practice and tentatively given meanings through active exchange. Significance is positionally assigned to people, inanimate entities, images, and spiritual and mythical beings within fields of action. This research itself becomes one of these fields of motion, allowing us to peek into the flexible yet durable linkages that provide meaning to social exchange.

Articulations are likewise amassed within the Q'eqchi' imaginary, an internalized model that guides perception of self and other in various social fields. It is a mental trope used by the Q'eqchi' to understand neofeudalistic economies, colonial oppression, capitalism, and pre-Columbian and contemporary ritual payment to deities, as well as crime, tourism, transnational relations, community construction, ethnic relations, and ethnographic image-making. Within the Q'eqchi' imaginary, visibility, respect, reciprocity, ownership, and consumption are actions utilized to reinforce positions of power and maintain the integrity of the model. The role of foreigner is vital, and there exists a general orientation to the external, although the Q'eqchi' use this tendency to recreate more internalized concepts of community. External and internal, and outsider and insider, are thus, in many ways, one and the same, both being transitions rather than coherent entities.

This is where I, the foreign ethnographer, enter the picture. In 1995, I initiated a collaborative video project that became one of these social fields. Through participation in the project, we—Q'eqchi' individuals, myself, and the camera—unknowingly created a context in which long-standing structures guided not only the relationships we formed, but the way the Q'eqchi' participants appreciated what we were doing, the significance of the imagery we produced, the problems we encountered, and the way I, an outsider, was perceived and categorized. This collaborative methodology provided much more than qualitative data and video footage; it became a field of practice that revealed how a culturally modeled imaginary guides social action and processes of perception. Because of historic precedence and the project's inherent metaphors of sight, reciprocity, action, and foreignness, the Q'eqchi' seamlessly fit the project and me into their imagined world.

A cultural model of practice and perception is meaningless unless it is considered contextually, in coordination with a particular field where relations between people, institutions, nature, mythical beings, deities, and images are the structures embodied as internal dispositions. In this book, we (the reader, the Q'eqchi', and I) explore these linkages of the Q'eqchi' imaginary. I consider this a multi-sited ethnography (Marcus 1995), because it traverses the structure of a cultural script and it contextualizes the sites of contact within their particular fields of action. The video methodology helped me to accomplish this. An embedded set of codes guided the structural constitution of the project through a process of misrecognition—that what we saw as naturalized, personal behavior was actually the result of logic. The nature of our exchanges, the production of imagery, the decisions we made, the conflicts that arose, and the positions we occupied were ordered by a cultural script. Our collaboration became a form of ethnographic vérité, creating a third eye of deep cultural insight (Rony 1996:4). As protagonists, our methods brought unobservable culture within tangible reach, ultimately leading to the fortification of my own theoretical understanding of Q'eqchi' social action as guided by an internalized imaginary.

Because this is a multi-sited ethnography, it is vital that you, the reader, shift positions and maintain mobility—as does the practitioner of ethnographic vérité—if you, too, will access the insight provided by a third eye. You must be subject and object, observer and participant, insider and outsider, and simultaneously in the field and in your home. This intercultural slippage between categories and identities is what provides insight into unobservable culture. In this type of engaged ethnography, gazes are diverted, thwarted, and challenged; objects find voice; and the local melts into the global. In this book, therefore, not only will you look upon the members of the project and the community, but you will also step into their gazes as they look at (and sense) others. It was no chance occurrence that during Ash Wednesday I was in my lofty position above the street, invisible to the youth below, but free to gaze upon their moving bodies. Outsiders, like archetypal overseers, maintain positions of power through metaphors of vision: through the ability to see but not be seen (Foucault 1977). Q'eqchi' mountain spirits and other deities, for example, are invisible until a lack of respect is displayed or a wrongdoing occurs. Their authority to govern is based on their own intangibility and simultaneous ability to gaze upon constituents. Visual surveillance reproduces the Q'eqchi' imaginary, in a way akin to how anthropology and other academic disciplines gain knowledge and authority through visual dissection and investigation (or even the way globalization increases revenue through invisible outsourcing).

Our collaborative video project reverses the visual paradigm of Westernized knowledge production, which epistemologically originates from a distant, objective, and singular point of view. By providing multiple people the opportunity to see and to share their visions and other sensory experiences, we produce a montage of gazes, voices, and meaning. We thus deny the invisible, omnipresent social science viewpoint by sharing sight with subjects, by questioning our means of representation, and by likening our method to a bastion of theory. By breaking down differences between self and other, method and theory, word and image, insider and outsider, home and field, and object and subject, we peek through the third eye that provides insight into social mediation from multiple positions (Pink 2001:117–119; Rony 1996:4).

An additional and critical reason you see faces, witness gazes, and hear individual voices is that this research focuses on relationships and collective dispositions. I tend to reinforce the structures rather than the heterogeneity that exists within this Q'eqchi' community. I de-emphasize, but I do not deny, the vast range of cultural, social, and idiosyncratic means individuals use in the formation of their self-images. Hence, it is vital that you hear and see the people who represent this collective process. In this way, I hope to balance individual voices and localities with shared ideas, histories, and relations.

CHAPTER DEVELOPMENT

Social scientists have been criticized for extracting their research findings from the processes that lead to their academic theorizing (Agar 1996:59–63; Bourdieu and Wacquant 1992:8). Ethnographers have been rightly accused of stripping away the methods and personal dialogues that form the basis of inquiry. The research reported here represents a more reflexive, sensory-orientated, and phenomenological trend in anthropology (Behar 1996; Stoller 1992; Ruby 1980) and film (Minh-ha 1991), where product and process are collapsed into one, where histories and cultural scripts are embodied in perception and practice, and where the intricacies and inadequacies of method are given their rightful position next to theory and qualitative results.

In Chapter 2 I introduce the methodology I employed, which was vitally important to the project as a whole. By initiating a collaborative video project, the participants and I created a secondary field—a situation where the act of collaboration was itself a reflection of the complex set of social structures that are embodied in the Q'eqchi' imaginary. Through this active engagement, relationships were formed between individuals, the community, and representative outsiders—the camera and me. I began to understand how Q'eqchi' identify themselves and others, and how appropriate moral behavior emerges from the internalization of real and metaphoric exchanges that transcend time and space. I also realized how important sight and visibility are to the reproduction and maintenance of the imagined landscape of morality (Harvey 1989).

Chapter 2 thus provides a description of Livingston, the location of my ethnographic research, and Proyecto Ajwacsiinel, the field of action reproduced through collaborative video. The chapter begins with a historical sketch of Livingston, from its founding by the Garifuna people in 1802, through its transition from a thriving Atlantic port at the turn of the century to an economically depressed town, highly dependent on outward migration and tourism, by the 1960s. I then provide a portrait of Livingston today and an account of the social and economic lives of its residents, before turning to a discussion of the intricacies of the collaborative methodology we used in the field.

Chapter 3 is an "official" historical background of the Q'eqchi' people of Livingston, who are originally from Alta Verapaz, a northeastern department in the highlands of Guatemala. I begin immediately before Spanish contact in the early sixteenth century, and continue through the colonial period, with its reordering of indigenous models of autonomy. I then discuss the oppressive governments of the nineteenth and twentieth centuries whose onerous tactics provided indigenous labor to large *fincas* (sp. plantations),[1] which in Alta Verapaz were owned and operated mainly by Germans.

These pre-Columbian and historical contexts are the fields that have contextualized the incipient reproduction of an internalized framework that, although drastically reformulated through time, is still embedded in contemporary practice and perception. The Q'eqchi' imaginary has been maintained through socioeconomic and cosmological exchanges that for centuries have placed Q'eqchi' people in an obligatory cycle of reciprocal debt with outsiders: deities, leaders, and landowners. Pre-Columbian exchanges, followed by colonialism, Catholicism, coffee exportation, and now globalism and tourism, are the cosmological, socioeconomic, and political fields where outsiders are merged and internalized as metaphoric units. Q'eqchi' people situate themselves within these contexts, fortifying their structural links to and between outsiders. Foreign entities are envisioned either as benevolent providers and quasi-kin or as malevolent bodies that fail to reciprocate and through coercive means strip away labor, individuals, knowledge, cultural and political autonomy, and currency. Or, more commonly, outsiders can be both: the ambiguous foreigner. The way in which Q'eqchi' people categorize outsiders within each social context is pivotal in the moral reading of the exchange.

In Chapter 4, I investigate contemporary Q'eqchi' exchanges with the *Tzuultaq'a*—mountain spirits, both male and female, who reside within caves and are said to own and control nature. These sacred deities are typically personified as outsiders—most often Ladinos or Germans, but occasionally ancestors or ancient Mayans. Individual and community relationships with these spirit entities embody the moral metaphors of consumption, sight, reciprocity, and respect that bolster the Q'eqchi' imaginary. Q'eqchi' people and communities are obligated to pay respect to (and feed) these hungry deities through reverence and sacrifice. If the Q'eqchi' fail in this duty, Tzuultaq'a shift from invisible, benevolent providers of crops, water, and animals to visible nefarious forces that cause illness, drought, poor crops, and even death. Tzuultaq'a provide an archetypal model that illustrates how exchanges with outsiders (who are not only categorically foreign, but also familiar—self and other) form the basis of Q'eqchi' practice, perception, and processes of identification. Foreignness is also bolstered by and conflated with ownership and visibility, as many of the deities and outsiders, whether actual owners or not, are conceived as invisible owners, controllers, and masters of time and space. Their control of sight and gazes is directly related to their powerful positions within the Q'eqchi' imaginary.

The Q'eqchi' imaginary is reproduced by people and made tangible through the practice of morality. Following, though somewhat altering, the work of Mary Douglas, I find it most appropriate to theoretically conceive morality as action-in-place, rather than matter-in-place (Douglas 1966:35). I also apply the theoretical framework of practice theory (Bourdieu 1977, 1990; Ortner 1989) and more cognitive-oriented explanations of cultural continuities and discontinuities (Strauss and Quinn 1997; Holland et al. 1998) in this investigation into what are cultural dispositions, their endurance, malleability, and role in social action and discernment. However, Q'eqchi' people are not passive recipients of their imagined models; they actively create and maintain, and potentially alter, their framework of dispositions.

Chapter 5 demonstrates how foreignness and kinship are not opposing entities, but mutable constructions in flexible relations. Here I focus on private rituals, where individuals and the community actively respect (and/or feed) outsiders/owners and each other through collaboration, sacrifice, ritual, and consumption. We see how, by paying respect to foreigners, the Q'eqchi' community is reified.

At the wedding ritual of *uk'iha* (q. drinking of the water), the community consumes as one and simultaneously feeds Tzuultaq'a. This social and sacrificial act binds the two families, recognizes the new couple, and respects Tzuultaq'a in order to sanctify the union. *K'ajb'ak* is another ritual that structurally adheres to codes of community, collaboration, and consumption. Through communal feeding and respecting of Tzuultaq'a, the owners are granted permission to sow their corn fields, and because of this reverence and their adherence to ritual taboos, they are ensured a healthy and bountiful yield. These two rites of consumption introduce kinship as another taxonomic framework that magnifies structuring relations. Gender, age, and marital status are used to position individuals within the family hierarchy, which too is based on moral concepts of ownership and paying.

Like morality and ownership, respect is an action—a process rather than a thing—and the Q'eqchi' often practice it through forms of sacrifice and consumption. Occasionally, individuals, families, and communities forget to feed the deities, or outsiders fail to follow the rules of reciprocity. *Q'eq,* for example, is a mischievous, mythical entity who robs the poor to bring his bounty to his owners, the rich, foreign *finqueros* (sp. finca owners). He has a voracious appetite and he flies through the sky on midnight sprees, whistling and consuming food, household items, and money. This allegory of globalism is the antithesis of Tzuultaq'a, although both are active consumers who embody the moral framework. Q'eq is the symbolic outsider who breaks local rules of respect, but who, if treated appropriately, can be rehabilitated and made into kin.

In Chapter 6, we again encounter Q'eq when I turn from private to public performances. Both public and private acts are guided by an imagined model though they differ in the way they gain meaning through visual politics: private rituals are kept away from community gazes, whereas public performances are intentionally displayed. The two public dances I discuss in this chapter—the Deer Dance and the Devil Bull Dance—involve a socioeconomic struggle between foreign landowners, who take without permission, and local representatives, who struggle to maintain autonomy. These dances mimic the structures of morality and also turn them on their head, which leads me to question whether they magnify the socioeconomic field or resist it. After a discussion of these publicly viewed performances in terms of visual politics, I initiate an analysis of the different conceptions of *costumbre* (sp. custom) and *tradición* (sp. tradition), which are categorized respectively as invisible and visible, intangible and tangible, and, for some more orthodox thinkers, godly and worldly (i.e., the work of the Devil). These "opposing" labels are relatively defined and used by different individuals to designate the same object or practice. This reinforces the dynamic flexibility of the Q'eqchi' imaginary and its transient attachment to meaning. These distinctions also provide an opportunity to probe further into the meaning and potency of public and private ritual, to briefly address distinctions and non-distinctions between forms of faith, and to introduce vision as a key element in positioning selves, giving meaning to practice, and maintaining power. Objectifying gazes and ocular metaphors of knowledge are inherent components of anthropological investigations and the production of photographic and videographic images. Yet centralized gazes can be challenged and distorted through collaboration, multiplicity, and more intimate and sensory forms of ethnographic production (Marks 2000).

Whereas so far the discussion focuses primarily upon how families and communities are bound to a network of exchanges of respect with outsiders and among one another, Chapter 7 narrows (and broadens) the frame of reference from collective identities of community to more bodily conceptions of sensory realization and spiritual selves within cosmological realms. By building a sensorial and phenomenological picture of the Q'eqchi' imaginary, I conceptualize the hyperspace where selves arbitrate the moral structures linking individual to the community and beyond. The imagined landscape of morality is deeply embodied in Q'eqchi' personhood, in sensory perception, in bodies, and in the social processes of death—when ancestors transform into a type of outsider. As groupings of "lived-through meanings" (Merleau-Ponty 2002 [1945]:177), bodies link the past to the present through practice and perception. Ancestors (and their clothes) are likewise linkages; they are anachronistic mediators who traverse the external regions of the Q'eqchi' universe, actively demand exchange, and embody the relations from which they emerge. Ancestors actively keep the community. They demand respect and reverence, and they will come to haunt or cause illness if kin fail in this obligation.

The discussion of ancestors and spiritual selves begins with the annual ritual of *Todos Santos* (sp. All Saints' Day), when ancestors return home to be respected and fed. The Q'eqchi' use inconsistent terminology to describe their inner selves, a multiplicity that is also reflected in more external forms of Q'eqchi' identity (which I return to in Chapter 8). Yet the entire social process of death—particularly how the spirit *mu* (q. shadow) becomes separated from the deceased and lodged in their possessions—is guided by rules of respect and reciprocity. Spiritual selves are not only linked to human bodies or bound by human flesh; they are sheltered in personal items, such as clothes, beds, and canes, which are either buried with the deceased or subsequently burned, boxed, or stored. It is terribly disrespectful to wear a dead person's clothes or to sleep in his or her hammock. If one does so, the ancestor may appear in dreams or knock during the night until he or she is satisfied that the living descendent is practicing the appropriate form of morality. Possessions, like selves, are active mediators of time and space within cosmological universes.

The deeply ingrained structure that molds Q'eqchi' morality and perception also guides sensory discernment. Sight, space, and time, for example, are intricately linked to the ability of transcendental owners to maintain their positions of power. Tzuultaq'a, the mythical *Ch'olwiinq* (q. wild men), and ancient Mayans are powerful, quasi-foreign entities that have the capacity to control visual, temporal, and spatial processes. They are timeless and spaceless mediators who have the ability to oversee, govern land, and control time while they themselves are only visible during immoral breaches in reciprocal respect, when action is out-of-place.

Sight is thus not the only sense guiding perception and social practice. Muteness, for example, is a common symptom of soul loss, which tends to be a physical manifestation of an inappropriate action. Sensory perception of time and space is linked as well to how the past is conceived and is equally relevant to the successes and problems encountered in the video project, particularly since I introduced a foreign technology that, like ancestors and illness, distorts the senses. I thus conclude this chapter by considering the appropriateness of our visual methodology and the role of the Q'eqchi' participants who appear to link time and space through tangible action, and fear and desire through anachronistic mediators. Although video replicates temporal processes of life, it also distorts them by capturing and reifying these processes within the bounded space of videographic technology. However, the collaborative video project stirred up and brought unobservable culture "in-sight" and within sensory reach.

Chapter 8 focuses on *Día de Guadalupe,* a festival that takes place on 12 December in which Q'eqchi' identities are borrowed, exchanged, and confirmed. In Livingston, this day centers on the dance of the Pororo in which some Q'eqchi' women participate by renting their indigenous dress to the Garifuna performers. That these women commodify what is considered a key component of their ethnicity may seem peculiar, particularly considering that Q'eqchi' women frown upon the way the Garifuna disrespectfully handle their clothing. However, the practice of renting their clothing is about controlling acts of consumption.

This festival also demonstrates how Q'eqchi' people identify themselves as montages of internal selves and external identities. Like the spiritual selves internalized in practice and possessions, identities are hybrid processes that emerge from the encounters between cultural imaginaries, individual wills, and various fields imbued with power and difference. Q'eqchi' identify themselves through local, interpersonal, cosmological, and even transnational linkages where institutions and individuals are intertwined, related, and in a constant process of producing, reproducing, and redefining social and cognitive structures. I will argue that identities, subjectively constructed and objectively reproduced, semiotically parallel photographic and videographic images, as well as most every form of social reification.

Q'eqchi' identities and images are composites formed through and reinforced by a variety of relationships within diverse fields of action where exchange and production are as symbolic as they are material. Lastly, the categorical distinctions between self and other, foreign and familiar, internal and external, and subject and object are more the results of a Westernized fascination with bounded sites of knowledge than with Q'eqchi' perception and processes of identification. These dichotomies dissipate when morality, selves, and research are considered as relational and always in motion.

Chapter 9 elaborates upon those whom the Q'eqchi' categorically define as non-reciprocating criminals, which allows me to delve further into the means by which the Q'eqchi' perceive their Garifuna neighbors. Simply and crudely, the Garifuna are completely misunderstood by the Q'eqchi', who see them as wasteful criminals who do not labor for the fruits they receive. This is far from true. In fact, Garifuna social networks and rituals adhere to rules similar to Q'eqchi' practices, but because the Garifuna seem to fall between categories, I argue that the Q'eqchi' have a difficult time marking them. They inscribe them—along with tourists, guerrillas, and the state—as non-producers and criminals. It is estimated that one quarter of the entire Garifuna ethnic group are emigrants to New York City (Jenkins 1998:152), and kin who stay behind are heavily reliant on remittances sent from abroad. It is likely this linkage to the United States, the greater contact with foreign tourists, and the mythical Q'eq that ensures this Q'eqchi' misconception of the Garifuna in Livingston.

Chapter 10 brings us to the pulse of ethnographic vérité. Three ethnographic vignettes reveal how I—as an intimate friend and professional cohort—and my ethnographic methods were drawn into the Q'eqchi' imaginary. Through collaboration, the camera, the participants, the ethnographer, and even our methods were involved in a form of ethnographic vérité. We were catalysts to action and for the revelation of what exists below observable surfaces. We recreated a field for the emergence of the Q'eqchi' imaginary. Like the film genre of *Cinéma Vérité,* where cameras and filmmakers are protagonists that stimulate subjects to reveal themselves, collaborative image-making was a radically empirical anthropology that went beyond the visual ability to record and see (Stoller 1992:213–215).

The phenomenological method of ethnographic vérité challenges academic constructs. It dismantles the epistemology of Western-centered knowledge as originating from singular, objective points of view. In its place are multiple articulations that return temporality, spatiality, emotions, and the senses to ethnographic endeavors. Meaning emerges from movements and transitions rather than things (Merleau-Ponty 2002 [1945]:320–321). Collaborative methods and the effortless shifting of the ethnographic viewpoint open a third eye that explores deeper and more intimately what is deemed invisible. The intangible becomes tangible. With this roving third eye, movement, and self-awareness, ethnographic vérité also probes into the porosity between home and field, subject and object, and self and other (Rony 1996). Significance cannot be discerned without the entanglement of the ethnographer.

I conclude, in Chapter 11, by returning to beginnings. More importantly, I pay my respects to Lola, Eduardo Martín, Juana, Blanca, Mariano, and the entire Q'eqchi' community in Livingston, who shared their lives, homes, and smiles with me, and who extended their families to include me. I am forever indebted to them. I can only hope that this book is something they will cherish, as I envision it as an active process of respect that fortifies and pays reverence to the relationships we formed. The Q'eqchi' are the true authors. They are the ones ultimately responsible for the methods and theories discussed in this book. They are the ones who allow us to traverse their imaginary worlds. Because of them, we have insight into the invisible undercurrents of culture. I share my authorship with them and I bow before them with a heart full of respect. Selves are already becoming others, objects are merging into subjects, methods shift to theory, and distinctions between home and field are collapsing. Endings lead to beginnings as the Q'eqchi' in Livingston, Guatemala lead us within and far beyond.

Two   FIELD(S) OF ENGAGEMENT

Livingston and Proyecto Ajwacsiinel

Fieldwork—the keystone of ethnographic uniqueness and a fountain of qualitative data—is often overshadowed by anthropological theory, particularly at the point when field experience is compressed into ethnographic text. Conversely, ethnographic film tends to have its analytical theory stripped away from the intricacies of methodological practices that, because of the tangible (and technical) means of photographic representation, seem fundamentally embedded in film and video. Physicality marginalizes film and other visual products within academic arenas where palpable methods are subordinate to the intellect of theory (Prosser 1998:97–99). This ethnographic product attempts to reverse this trend. Method and theory are equal partners. Without collaboration and personal interactions in the field(s)—the field of Livingston and the field reproduced through the video project—a theoretical understanding of Q'eqchi' culture would not have had such a dynamic context in which to surface.

LIVINGSTON: TODAY AND YESTERDAY

I first came to Livingston in 1991. Arriving on the midday ferry from Puerto Barrios, I found the town hot and humid compared to the highlands I had left. The bright sun was burning not only my skin, but also my eyes, as the light bounced off the reflecting water. I was met at the *muelle* (sp. pier) by a group of Garifuna boys who were hoping, for a small tip, to show me to my accommodations for the night. I allowed myself to be led to an inexpensive little hotel on the river. Although I had intended to spend only one evening in Livingston, I stayed a full week, enraptured by the cultural diversity, the Caribbean food and music, and the incredible beauty. Lush green jungle, slow-moving salt-water rivers, waterfalls, and crystal-clear swimming holes are all within walking distance of town.

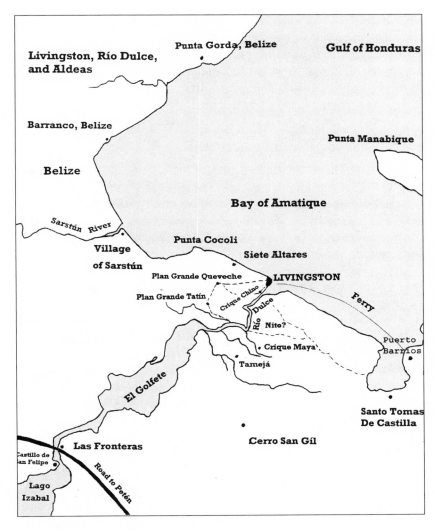

FIGURE 2.1. *Map of Livingston area*

The small town of Livingston (covering a mere 5.5 square kilometers [a little more than 2 square miles]) is located on the northwest bank of the Río Dulce where the river widens into the Bay of Amatique. The river is particularly gorgeous, with its limestone cliffs and thick green walls.[1] Herons, egrets, and pelicans fly between the steep palisades. Trogon nests and bromeliads dangle weightlessly from branches. Long-tailed iguanas rest stoically on trees jutting from cliffs, and groups of playful dolphins swim up the winding river towards the Golfete, where the river broadens before reaching Las Fronteras. The area is so stunning and idyllically tropical that early Tarzan movies were filmed there. The nineteenth-century explorer John Stephens wrote: "It was, as its name imports, a Rio Dolce [sic], a fairy scene of Titan land, combining exquisite beauty with colossal grandeur" (Stephens 1856:33).

The town of Livingston is the *cabecera* (sp. head administrative town) of the *municipio* (sp. area under local government—somewhat equivalent to a county in the United States) of Livingston, which is situated in Izabal, a northeastern department of Guatemala that surrounds Lago Izabal and the Río Dulce.[2] Most locals consider Livingston an island because it is surrounded by water, although it is actually the tip of a peninsula. One can only reach the town via water because no roads lead to the area. Motorboats running from Las Fronteras or Puerto Barrios and the daily ferry carry passengers to the town.

Before the Spaniards came to the New World, the area around Livingston was probably inhabited by a group of Chol Mayan people.[3] Nito, a Mayan trading center said to have been visited by both Gil González de Ávila and Hernán Cortéz[4] (Chang 1995:6), is believed to have been located on the southern bank of the mouth of the Río Dulce. Although some Chol escaped resettlement by fleeing into the dense bush, by the seventeenth century most were rounded up by the Spaniards and shipped off to highland *reducciones*[5] (Jones 1989:100–101). There they eventually mixed with the Acala, Lacandón, Pocomchí, and Q'eqchi' Maya (Thompson 1938:84–102). Others were taken to lowland settlements. According to Sapper (1985 [1936]:35), eighty-five "heathen Indians" were gathered together in what is now Livingston as part of the Chol mission. Here and elsewhere, these lowland settlements were unsuccessful because of the rapid spread of epidemics in the tropics (Schackt 1986:13–14).

While "recalcitrant" Indians were under partial control, English, Dutch, and French pirates posed a threat in the area. The Río Dulce and Lago Izabal were major trading routes, and Bodegas (now called Mariscos) was an important commercial port on Lago Izabal. In 1595, the Spanish built a tower at the point where the Río Dulce meets Lago Izabal in order to protect the lake from the intrusion of pirates. In 1651, at the same location, they began constructing El Castillo de San Felipe de Lara, a fort that was occupied until 1825. Unthreatened, pirates still hid at the mouth of the Río Dulce to plunder the supply ships heading to Bodegas. The first colonial town in Guatemala, San Gil, was founded by Gil González de Ávila at this time. Cerro San Gil, the now-vacated hilltop settlement, is south of Livingston.

Locally, the history of Livingston is debated. I do not know how long the so-called Indian reducción of Livingston existed. I never heard anyone speak of it during my stay, nor is there mention of it in 1802, when the Haitian Marcos Sánchez Díaz arrived with a group of Garifuna people from the island of Roatan in Honduras. Marcos Sánchez Díaz is credited as the founder of Livingston, but he and his followers left soon after they arrived, only to return again on 15 May 1806. This latter group stayed and named their new home *La Buga,* the Garifuna term for "the mouth." The Garifuna are thus the official founders of Livingston.

According to official history, the Garifuna originate from shipwrecked African slaves who ended up on the Caribbean island of San Vicente (Saint Vincent) between 1625 and 1667, although they could also have been runaway slaves from plantations on nearby islands (Arrivillaga Cortés 1989:2). On San Vicente, these African Maroons mixed with Arawak and Carib groups, also referred to as Yellow and Red Island Caribs (Gonzalez 1988:16), and their descendents were known as Black Caribs. During the seventeenth and eighteenth centuries, ownership of San Vicente alternated between France and Great Britain, until 1796 when the island was firmly in Great Britain's hands. In 1797, the British began relocating the Black Caribs to the island of Roatan off the coast of Honduras.[6] From Roatan, the Black Caribs migrated to the Atlantic coast to what is now Belize, Honduras, and Guatemala. These Black Caribs became the people we today know as the Garifuna, or the *Garinagu.*

Many Garifuna people now deny that their ancestors ever spent time in San Vicente or Roatan, instead claiming that they came directly from Africa or even South America. Some say they were indeed slaves; many say they were not. Certain locals informed me that the Garifuna did not arrive in Livingston until 1832 (and according to Chang Sagastume [1995:15], 150 Black Caribs did arrive in La Buga that year). Furthermore, Livingston natives tell me that the Garifuna language incorporates a variety of languages including African, Dutch, English, Fon, French, Portuguese, Spanish, Taino, and Q'eqchi' Mayan. According to linguistic investigations, Garifuna is an Amerindian language derived mainly from Arawak and Carib language branches with French, English, Spanish, and minimal African influence (Drummond 1987:30).

In 1821, Guatemala gained independence from the Spanish empire. In 1831, the government designated La Buga as the cabecera of the department, renaming the town Livingston in memory of the North American legislator Edward Livingston.[7] When a fire engulfed most of the town in 1835 (Drummond 1987:16–19), the government moved the cabecera to the town of Izabal, near present-day Mariscos. After that, the title of department head reverted to Livingston and then back again to Izabal, until Puerto Barrios became the capital of the department of Izabal in 1920.

During the nineteenth century, Livingston grew into a substantial commercial port. On 1 January 1883, President General Justo Rufino Barrios inaugurated Livingston as a free port with an import and export license (Mejía 1997:98; Wagner 1987:94). It soon became the most important Atlantic port in Guatemala. After Livingston was declared a duty-free zone, foreigners came to the area. A North American and British company ran two steamships from Lago Izabal to Livingston (King 1974:32). The United Fruit Company (UFC, also known locally as *La Frutera*) transported bananas through the water routes in Izabal, and Compañía Ferrocarril Verapaz y Agencias del Norte Limitada, a German-owned and -operated export company, located its shipping headquarters in Livingston. Called *Ferropazco* locally, the company controlled the railroad from Polochic to Cobán in the department of Alta Verapaz and owned most of the steamships that carried products down the Río Dulce. It had control over much of the coffee, cacao, and lumber that was shipped from Alta Verapaz through the port of Livingston (Brigham 1887:34–35). Along with its steamships, Ferropazco constructed a line of ferries, one of which still runs between Livingston and Puerto Barrios. Because of the high volume of export goods from the UFC and Ferropazco flowing out of the area, both the United States and Germany had consulates in town.

During the First World War, the Guatemalan government constrained German fincas by allowing them to sell their produce only under government supervision (King 1974:35). After the war, Guatemala returned control of the fincas to the German owners, although many of the returned assets, including Ferropazco, were united into a new company with its seat in New York. Central American Plantation Corporation (CAPCO), formed in 1921, allowed the Germans to continue running their companies in Guatemala (Wagner 1987:120). In 1942, during the Second World War, the Guatemalan government unconditionally expropriated the German property and assets of Ferropazco. Although German owners had much of their land returned once the war ended (Sieber 1999:22), Ferropazco remained a possession of the Guatemalan government.[8]

Puerto Barrios had already replaced Livingston as the most important port of exportation on the Atlantic coast. In 1904, during the regime of Manuel Estrada Cabrera (which lasted from 1898 to 1920), the Guatemalan government gave the UFC the contract to complete the railroad between Puerto Barrios and Guatemala City, an arduous task that the government had been unable to complete for thirty years (Stanley 1994:16–21). The UFC completed the railroad in 1908. Along with the concession to operate the railroad, the Estrada Cabrera regime also granted the UFC the wharf at Puerto Barrios (Schlesinger and Kinzer 1982:65–77). Lago Izabal and the Río Dulce were no longer optimal transportation routes, even though the UFC still used the waterways to buy from small plantations. In 1939, La Frutera discontinued the practice of buying from small producers and used only bananas from its large plantations, those through which the railroad ran. Using rail rather than river transport, the UFC shipped fruit to Europe and North America from their wharf in Puerto Barrios.[9] Then, when Guatemala ousted Ferropazco during the Second World War, the Río Dulce's role as a major shipping route came to an abrupt end. Even so, the river remained, until fairly recently, an important route for zinc, lead, copper, and nickel (Mejía 1997:101).[10]

The UFC employed many Garifuna from Livingston, although the export industry enticed numerous newcomers to the area. Chinese, Middle Easterners, and East Asian Indians arrived, often as indentured servants. Belgians came to build the port at Santo Tomás. Ladinos,[11] North Americans, Belizeans, and the British and other Europeans also took up residence in Livingston. More recently, K'iche', Tz'utujil, Kaqchikel, and Mam Mayan people have migrated to this Caribbean town.

No one agrees upon how many people live in Livingston. I have heard estimates ranging from 5,000 to 10,000, the disparity most likely arising from poor census counts and migration. I estimate the permanent population closer to 5,000, while I acknowledge the extensive number of immigrants in the United States who still consider Livingston home. The official count for the entire municipio in 2004 was 48,591, comprising 23,322 Indigenous, 20,407 Ladinos, 4,376 Garifuna, and 486 persons of East Asian descent (referred to locally as *Hindoos*). Garifuna people tend to live directly in town, while only 500 or so indigenous people do, the majority of whom are Q'eqchi' Mayan.

Some thirty or forty years ago, the *barrios* (sp. neighborhoods) were still segregated, with the Garifuna in one area and *Hindoos* and Ladinos in another. The Q'eqchi' lived only in the *monte* (sp. the bush). Today, there is less segregation in Livingston, although Barrio Marcos Sánchez, down by the river, is predominantly populated by Ladinos and East Indians. Garifuna people tend to live in barrios along the bay, and Mayan people live scattered throughout the town.

Although there are no roads to Livingston, there are roads in town, most of which have now been paved. Trucks, brought over on barges, deliver

cigarettes, batteries, bottled water, Coca-Cola, Gallo Beer, Bimbo bread, and other goods. Pick-up trucks to transport materials around town and various taxis are now in use. Bicycles are common. Most people, however, walk from place to place, and the pace is a slow amble. Only tourists, and young children playing, walk fast.

Unlike other towns in Guatemala, Livingston does not have colonial roots. The Catholic church is not the center of town, and there is no town square or permanent market. K'iche' vendors from the highlands bring their vegetables and fruit on Tuesday and Saturday mornings to sell in front of the municipal building. If you miss the early morning vegetable market, you must rely on the stores, which sell vegetables at higher prices. The gymnasium and the Catholic boys school are community meeting houses.

During the majority of my fieldwork and follow-up, the mayor was a well-liked Ladino from Zacapa, a neighboring department.[12] Livingston has access to only one national newspaper, *La Prensa Libre,* which is delivered on bicycle to subscribers. Non-subscribers can buy the paper *only* if they can find the delivery boy after he has picked up the load from the noon ferry and begun his regular route. News is learned by word-of-mouth or from a radio station in Puerto Barrios. For years, a Garifuna man named Bibi was the local *noticiero* (sp. newsman). Like a town crier, he rode around on his adult-sized tricycle with an attached speaker, notifying the people of Livingston of local news, upcoming events, sales, and community meetings.[13] Private telephones have recently become somewhat affordable in Livingston, although cellular phones are the least expensive and most common means of communication.

During the early mornings, Garifuna and Ladina women sell fish along the road. They obtain their product by meeting the fishing boats at dawn, or by way of their men who fish at an early hour. Later in the morning, Garifuna women sit in the shade selling sweet potatoes, yucca, tomatoes, and bags of noodle chow mein. Because of the scorching sun, the town is very quiet from noon to three, when only Q'eqchi' women and girls sell tortillas and empanadas. By late afternoon, Garifuna women and girls are selling coconut bread, banana bread, coconut oil, pineapple pastry, and coconut candy on the side of the street. In the evenings Garifuna women sell hot *atole* made from bananas, *arroz con leche,* or flour tortillas with beans and fish. Rosaria, a K'iche' Mayan woman, fries vegetarian tacos in front of her husband's store nightly.

Locals tell me that the Garifuna used to cultivate cassava, yucca, bananas, and plantains, and dominated the fishing industry in their small *cayucos* (sp. canoes). While they still practice these occupations, now it is mainly for personal consumption or for extra pocket money. Today, the East Indians dominate the shrimping and fishing industry for export. Ladinos, Chinese, K'iche' Mayans, and foreigners control most of the local commerce. Fewer Garifuna and Q'eqchi' people own businesses. Many are dependent on a stagnant tourist industry. The Garifuna more than others rely on monthly remittances from relatives who have emigrated to the United States.

Foreigners have been coming to Livingston for some time. A few North Americans and Europeans have made their homes in town. While many of the younger outsiders make a minimal income by selling jewelry made from seeds, shells, rocks, and bones, a handful have established successful businesses, hotels, and restaurants. Tourists tend to be young backpackers from Europe, Australia, and South and North America. Most are following the "gringo trail" and are on their way to Tikal, Belize, or Honduras. Wealthy Guatemalans from the capital come for weekends and holidays, and Livingston is a popular vacation spot for Guatemaltecos during Easter and Christmas.

Soon after the decline of Livingston as a port town, the Garifuna began emigrating to the United States. Most head towards New York City (specifically Brooklyn) and Los Angeles. This flow of people, ideas, money, values, and objects has had a substantial impact on the people of Livingston. Significantly, and somewhat ironically, González (1988:110–11) presumes that this migratory process was secured when the Q'eqchi' began moving toward the Livingston area. By occupying untitled lands that were once used by the Garifuna for agriculture, González claims, the Q'eqchi' became an economic plug, forcing the Garifuna to maintain migration as their primary economic resource.

THE Q'EQCHI' IN LIVINGSTON

The majority of the 23,000 or so Q'eqchi' who reside in the municipio of Livingston live in small rural hamlets known as *aldeas*. There are also a growing number of Q'eqchi (roughly 1,000) who live directly in town or who occupy the outer limits (approximately 500). Thus, when I discuss the Q'eqchi' people in Livingston, I am including people who live in town as well as those in Crique Chino Barrio Nuevo, a neighborhood on the outskirts of town, and Crique Chino, an aldea that is a twenty- to thirty-minute walk from town. Most of the men and many of the women in these areas work in the town itself on a daily basis. These people are dependent on Livingston for employment, material necessities, provisions, churches, medicine, and doctors. I will also discuss, although not at length, the Q'eqchi' who reside in Plan Grande Tatín and Plan Grande Queveche, two aldeas much further from Livingston. While Tatín was founded some sixty years ago, Queveche has existed for perhaps forty or fifty years. The people in these towns are also dependent on Livingston, but to a lesser extent. Both of these towns have churches and simple stores that diminish the need for travel to Livingston. They lie much further into the bush than Crique Chino; it takes as least two hours to walk the arduous paths from town. The residents are predominantly subsistence farmers (planting on communal land) rather than day laborers, although when possible men obtain work in Livingston. The people in these two aldeas come to Livingston

to sell their produce, buy materials and food, visit friends, attend baptisms, or perhaps to vote in an election.

Most Q'eqchi' people live in one-room, thatched-roof structures with dirt floors. Women cook on wood-fire hearths, which are the central features of Mayan homes, and light is often provided by kerosene lamps, although electricity is becoming more common. Furniture typically is sparse, consisting of a table, some stools, hammocks for sitting and sleeping, a wooden bed or two, a corn bin, and an altar, assuming the family is Catholic. Clothes and other personal belongings are stored in cardboard boxes or strung over hammock ropes and ceiling rafters. Walls are usually bare, although locally produced calendars (often with scenes of foreign women or snowcapped mountains) are common wall coverings. Doors remain open during the day, so dogs, chickens, and turkeys are frequently shooed out of Q'eqchi' homes, whether in town or on the periphery.

Three decades ago, only two Q'eqchi' men lived in Livingston proper. Most families preferred to stay in the aldeas where they grew corn in their *milpas* (sp. cornfields). Within the past two or three decades, Q'eqchi' people have started taking up residence in town, with a considerable increase in the 1990s. As with the initial causes of migration (see Chapter 3), reasons for the final leap to Livingston are complex. Many see residence in Livingston as an improvement in their lives, as a step upward. Most people move from the aldeas to Livingston so that family members, male and female, can find wage labor. Many are tired of what they see as risky milpa agriculture as their primary means of subsistence. Some lost their land in the aldeas when individuals from Guatemala City appeared with newly obtained titles. Claiming ownership to the land, these wealthy *capitalaños* (sp. people from the capital, Guatemala City) remove the local residents from their land or force them to pay rent.

Education is another reason people move to Livingston. Parents have high regard for formal education and they want their children to have opportunities they did not have themselves. They consider schools in the aldeas to be inadequate, and if children want to continue with their education beyond primaria (the sixth grade), they must attend school in Livingston.[14]

Once in town, most Q'eqchi' families rent houses or take care of one for someone who lives in the capital, the United States, or Europe. Few Q'eqchi' people own the land where they have their houses. Most of those who do are the same handful who own small businesses. Many who move from the aldeas to reside in Livingston maintain their corn milpas in the aldeas. Generally, this corn is not sold but used for personal consumption. In Crique Chino Barrio Nuevo, most of the Q'eqchi' have small parcels with usufruct property rights, which allows them to sell their land with the mayor's approval. On these parcels they build their homes, grow peppers, tend chickens and turkeys, and have small plots of corn. The majority of people in Crique Chino Barrio Nuevo are migrants from El Estor, and many rent milpas from wealthy landowners who, like those who own property in town, often live in the capital or out of the country. Many Q'eqchi' have milpas adjacent to the small lots where they build their houses, though again their harvested corn is not sold but rather used to complement the income from day labor.

Many Q'eqchi' men work for the *municipalidad,* constructing roads, painting buildings, cleaning the cemetery for Todos Santos (sp. All Saints' Day), putting in water pipes, loading sand, and doing other tasks of manual labor. Other men work for private individuals, constructing houses, clearing lots, fixing roofs, or doing whatever their patron needs done. A few work as conductors of the motorboats (sp. *lancheros*) taking tourists and passengers around the area or to Puerto Barrios. Most do not work for themselves, but for those who actually own the motorboats. I know of five Q'eqchi' families who own and run stores, although only one of them is noticeably successful. Many younger boys, girls, and women work in the numerous restaurants and hotels in town that cater to tourists. Some women sell tortillas and empanadas, which they spend all morning making and all afternoon selling. They also make various other street foods that they send their children out to sell. Yucca with salsa, fresh corn on the cob, young corn tamales, regular tamales, and even bread are sold throughout the streets by Q'eqchi' children.

PROYECTO AJWACSIINEL

After my initial weeklong visit in 1991, I returned to Livingston for three weeks in 1994 for preliminary research and then again in September 1995 to conduct extended fieldwork.[15] The first Q'eqchi' woman I met was Lola. I had acquired some basic Q'eqchi', and I walked by Lola's home and tried it out on her. "Chan Xawil," I greeted her. She was impressed with my attempt to speak her native language and she immediately invited me in. I ended up spending the entire day with her and her family, learning how to prepare the tortillas she used to sell three times per day. It did not take long for us to become close friends. I spent countless hours in her home, helping her make tortillas, swinging in her hammock, playing with her children, and tending her crying baby. We would do errands together and I would often take her children out for ice cream and candy. Through Lola I was introduced into the Q'eqchi' community in Crique Chino Barrio Nuevo, where I later organized the video project. When I was in the field, Lola, her husband Alberto, and their seven children lived in the town of Livingston (where they took care of a run-down house for a Ladina woman and ran a tortilla business), although they also had a house in Crique Chino Barrio Nuevo, where they kept chickens and turkeys. They now reside full-time at the latter residence, and when I want to talk to my friend, I call her eldest son's cell phone or send him an e-mail.

I waited three to four months before seeking out participants for the video project. I wanted to learn more of the Q'eqchi' language, get people accustomed to seeing me and my camera, and spend some time doing basic participant observation.[16] For me, it was vital that I had a solid grasp of the cultural setting and attitudes, as I did not want to force an inappropriate methodology upon the Q'eqchi' people. When I was confident that the video project could work, I went to the Catholic church in Crique Chino Barrio Nuevo, where I addressed the congregation. They had already gotten to know me. I had previously attended a wedding and a few Masses there, including one on Todos Santos.

It was dark, and kerosene lamps and candles sat on the table altar at the front of the church, bouncing light off the textured thatched-roof ceiling and walls. I stood before the seated congregation and explained who I was (an anthropologist investigating Q'eqchi' culture, history, and identity), what I wanted to do (teach them how to use a video camera), why I was interested in this project (because I thought that it was important that they do the recording of their own culture and I believed that their culture was something to respect and which could educate), and what they would get out of it (I would leave them copies of videotapes and start a small library, and with any proceeds, we would hopefully construct a cultural center in Crique Chino Barrio Nuevo).

Nine people said they were interested in learning video. The first thing we did was decide upon a name for our project. The congregation suggested two Q'eqchi' names: *Proyecto Ajwacsiinel* and *Proyecto Ajwaclisiinel*. *Aj wacsiinel* means "one that advances, lifts up, stirs up, rouses" and *aj waclisiinel* signifies "the sower." The agricultural metaphor of the latter option is clear: they saw the project as the sprouting of seeds, as a milpa that would need respect, tending, and patience if it was to provide a bountiful harvest. The message of the former centered on an idea of advancement, that the project, like a formal education, was a catalyst to progress. What I did not realize at the time was that these choices of names were unknowingly organized by a type of internal logic that saw collaboration and respect as a means to prosperity. Even at this preliminary stage of the project, the dialogue was prompted by socialized structures. We chose *Proyecto Ajwacsiinel* because the participants thought that a language project in El Estor had already used the other. The project was formed—Proyecto Ajwacsiinel—the one that advances, rises, lifts. What surfaced through the form of ethnographic vérité was the Q'eqchi' imaginary, an internalized framework of dispositions that guided this and many other social practices and perceptions.

We decided that lessons would be held at my house on Saturdays. Juana,

Matilde, Juliana, and Lenora were the four women who participated in the project. Agustin, Armando, Venancio, Santiago, and, occasionally, Manuel were the male participants. I think we were all nervous about the first class to be held, and it did not take long for me to realize I had made my first mistake. Men and women arrived together. However, the Q'eqchi' women felt intimidated by the men. Only when they were alone did they vocalize their opinions or ask questions. This is something I would continue to notice. In the presence of men, Q'eqchi' women were demure, quiet, and submissive. This bothered me, because I grew accustomed to our banter and to us laughing and giggling about footage, but this would cease as soon as the men arrived. After that initial lesson, during which I hooked the video camera to a monitor so that the participants could hold the camera and see themselves on screen, we held separate classes for women and men.

The men seemed to learn more quickly than the women, perhaps because they had some experience with electronics or guns. We started with the basics, such as putting on the battery pack, a task with which most of the women continued to have problems. Then we proceeded to turning on the power, recording, zooming in and out, focusing, and using microphones, which no one opted for, preferring the built-in microphone on the camera. I gave no formal instruction on how to frame a subject or fill a frame. My most instructive suggestion was that they should not shoot directly at the sun. I handed out copies of a pamphlet I had composed, which provided written explanations in Spanish alongside visual diagrams of the camera.

Lessons occasionally lasted for as long as three hours. I emphasized the importance of interviews as opportunities to hear viewpoints on specific aspects of their culture. We therefore held numerous practice interviews (they would interview me and one another and I would interview them); these training interviews were sometimes videotaped and sometimes not, but they always offered intriguing input on cultural matters. We also spent much time discussing what the participants wanted to videotape. They knew I was researching Q'eqchi' culture and that their choices would reflect how they viewed themselves. I had told them that they were free to borrow the video camera whenever they wanted to videotape something. The ways they were led to perceive the camera, the methods of taking video, and the choices they were to make regarding their subjects were open-ended. I offered minimal guidance; I wanted to see how they perceived their own options, aesthetics, and abilities.

The men often borrowed the camera when they were heading to a *Palabra de Dios* (sp. Word of God), a Catholic prayer meeting, which revealed the crucial position of religion in their lives. They also wanted to video-tape themselves when they collaboratively sowed their cornfields. They said this was a meaningful event that occurred twice a year, although on the intended day they were running late and were unable to pick up the camera before heading out to the fields. Instead, Matilde and I videotaped the ritual that is organized by the women while the men are sowing the fields. Everyone showed an interest in videotaping the making of tamales and other festivities during Christmas, which is celebrated on the 24th of December. Women videotaped food preparation, particularly tortilla-making, although they always appeared nervous and hesitant to borrow the camera without the men. Together, the men and women once took the video camera and taped themselves talking about the symbolic importance of candles and copal incense. The entire project also attended a Pan-Mayan Revitalization meeting in Tameja, where Armando and Matilde videotaped the proceedings.

Some members soon lost interest in the project, for two reasons: it con-flicted with work obligations and they failed to see rewards. The most active members from start to finish were Agustin, Armando, Juana, Juliana, and Matilde. These five members' interest never waned and they remained resolute in their commitment to the project. In the pages of this book, you will see their pictures and hear their words. I interviewed them at various times throughout my fieldwork, and they provided engaging and enlight-ening viewpoints on a wide array of topics.

I found it difficult and extremely time-consuming to teach Q'eqchi' people the basics of video. Most of the participants had no formal educa-tion beyond the sixth grade, if any at all, and little or no experience with cameras, televisions, microphones, tape recorders, VCRs, or video cameras. I never did teach all the required skills of video production. I fear that I may have betrayed the participants by falling back on my promise. I simply could not teach all of them the basic skills, and I occasionally wish I had ini-tiated the project as soon as I arrived in the field. Except for Armando, who was an excellent videographer, much of the Q'eqchi' footage was inchoate and revealed a lack of technical ability. For example, focusing was a problem throughout the extent of the project. I thus regret that I, rather than project members, authored many of the images located in this book, although project members instructed me as to what events I should videotape.

Even so, the video project's ability to mirror and recreate cultural struc-tures was what I consider its greatest contribution to this research. The project became a field where an internalized imaginary guided the for-mation of relations. Because I was developing social relations, discussing histories, teaching techniques, organizing classes, and working intimately with a group of people, the video project mimicked the organizing of "community." Through interaction and conversation that was more spontaneous than academic, I began to understand that video images alone do not represent cultural forces: so too do the social means and ways Q'eqchi' people form themselves into collaborative projects. By watching and listening to how they discussed and understood their relations to the project and to the foreign anthropologist, an entire, previously unseen layer of comprehension was revealed. By making mistakes, fumbling, and working through problems the project encountered, I observed and participated in Q'eqchi' culture as methodology became a bastion of practiced ideology.[17]

I also acquired a keen sense of the politics embedded in the use of this unique recording device. I remember being extremely nervous when I first pulled out my video camera on the street. I was scared that, as a foreign piece of technology, the camera would set me apart from the people of Livingston. I was full of theoretical notions about the invasive and violating properties of the camera. I was overly concerned about the ethical questions involved in "capturing" images; so much so that I postponed emerging with the camera until I felt comfortable with the surroundings and the residents of Livingston.

The first time I had the camera out on the street was for Día de Guadalupe. I positioned myself in front of my friend Mariano's store, where I had a good view of the street. I was getting comfortable with filming when I was suddenly yelled at by a Garifuna woman, who chastised me for taking video of the fly-covered meat she was selling from a blue, plastic washtub. She spoke in English. "Hey, stop that! You know in the United States people are paid for getting their picture taken!" She quickly covered her meat. I, quickly and defensively, responded that I was from the United States and I had never heard of anyone paying money to videotape someone's meat! Other Garifuna women who knew me told the meat seller that I lived there and that she should not be so tough on me. They explained to me that she thought I was a tourist. I was humiliated and ashamed, but I learned a few important lessons.

You cannot assume that you are free to videotape anything as long as it is not a person. I never considered the photographic capturing of non-animate objects as an ethical issue, but I learned that owned objects also contain people's sensitivities and ideas of self. I experienced how image production involves commodification and consumption and how image-producing subjects expect and deserve payment. Likewise, I learned the difference between being a tourist and being an ethnographer. Unlike tour-

ists, who remain distant and outside societal ties, ethnographers have social obligations. They become part of a community, whether they desire
such intimacy or not. However, the humiliation and shame reminded me
that even though I was bound to the community, I was far from being
part of it. Rather, I was straddling the porous boundary between the internal community and the outside world. I became acutely aware of how
this ambivalent position of native/outsider was a central part of being an
ethnographer. I was a professional voyeur, and my privileged position as
gringa allowed me fluid access across cultural, ethnic, and other imagined
boundaries.

Livingston is a multicultural town, with people and influences from all
over the world. Just as easily as I could make tortillas with Lola, I could go

hang out on the beach with tourists, or slip into a shady bar and rebelliously drink rum with elder Garifuna men. I could swing in a hammock and listen to reggae music or I could head down to a North American–owned hotel on the river to listen to jazz, drink margaritas, eat dolphin-free tuna sandwiches, and practice my Q'eqchi' with the women who worked in the kitchen. From Puerto Barrios, I was able to take a bus to Guatemala City, where I could have hot showers and watch cable television from the confines of my hotel room in Zone One. Once, I attended a Christmas party at the elite, Zone Ten mansion of Marilyn McAfee, the then United States Ambassador, where I felt much more like an outsider than I ever did in Livingston. As a gringa, I had access to many histories, cultural ideas, and social groupings (Nelson 1999:41–73), and while I was accepted into many social spheres, I realized that this was only because I was an outsider and would always be one.

Swallowing my pride, I continued to shoot videotape during the Día de Guadalupe. I entered the gymnasium to watch and take footage of the Pororo dance (see Chapter 8). I watched the footage the following day and numerous times alone and among others. Re-experiencing the festival through the video images was a priceless ethnographic method. While analyzing my research stateside, I returned again to the footage, which provoked emotion far beyond the capacity of my field notes. An ethnographer is capable of remembering only a slice of what occurs at a particular moment in the field, and video allows one to see more than what would normally be viewed through one's own eyes. This capacity for reanalysis—to be able to return again and again to the field experience—furthers ethnographic engagement and reduces emotional distances between home and field.

Although I spent much of my time working with the video project, I also interacted with numerous members of the community who were not project participants, many of whom you will hear from in this book. I resided alone in a house located on the highest point in town, in a neighborhood called La Loma (sp. the hill), where Mayan and Ladino families also had homes. No Garifuna people lived in La Loma. Interestingly, it was in this neighborhood that the German export company, decades earlier, had their administrative seat, and I often found old hand-blown German beer bottles behind my home. My house was made of cement, with glass windows and tiled floors, and it had electricity and running water when the tank above the house was full. Both electricity and a theft-proof home were necessary for the video project, because of the value of the video monitor, video camera, tape recorders, still camera, microphones, computer, and printer I carried as my ethnographic tools. Crime is not uncommon in Livingston and thatched-roof houses are easily broken into. I washed my clothes and myself in the public area I shared with the house next door. Blanca, the woman of this house, was East Asian; her great grandmother immigrated from India at the beginning of the century. We became quite good friends as we often drank coffee together, shared recipes, and borrowed sugar, hot peppers, and oil. We remain close friends.

Lola did not have much time to participate in the video project as a cameraperson, although I shot hours of footage of her and her family. I did show her some basics of videography during her spare time, and she would occasionally take the camera and shoot things, although only in my presence. I informally interviewed her on a daily basis, and formally interviewed her husband, Alberto, once. Another person who was a great support to me but who did not participate in the project was Mariano, one of the few Q'eqchi' store owners in town. I spent hours speaking with him in front of his small shop, and I often assisted him in the store when he was not feeling well or when he had to run an errand. I was tremendously saddened to hear of his death in 2002. Felipe, an elder who lived in the aldea Plan Grande Tatín, but who effortlessly walked the rugged four miles to Livingston three times a week, was also a close friend. When he came to town to sell oranges or corn, he often stopped to visit at my home. I would always reciprocate his gifts of tortillas, fruit, or fresh young corn by fixing him sweet coffee and food. He was a kind man who shared much knowledge and laughter with me. I would visit him and his family in Plan Grande Tatín and stay at his house on occasion. Martín, a catechist with the Catholic church, also shared his bountiful wisdom and wit with me before his untimely death in 1997. I am now godmother to the son he never met. Alma, Chico (who has also since passed away), Javiér, Manuel, Líve, María, and Patrocinia were invaluable as both friends and ethnographic subjects.

Numerous other families and individuals allowed me access into their homes to share their culture and lives. On the days when I did not have an interview, video class, or other obligations, I would visit my friends and help them tend their stores, make tortillas, shuck dried corn off the cob, or fetch water. I always tried to do something in return for them sharing their cultural knowledge and personal insights with me. After these informal conversations, I would often run home to scratch the details down on a piece of paper before I forgot what I had been told. I carried a notebook with me, although I tried to keep the use of this ethnographic tool to a minimum when I was just *paseando,* a Spanish term best translated as "hanging out," something that many of my Q'eqchi' friends believed was all I did.

I hired Juan as a language teacher for the first three months of my field-work, although I never acquired a full proficiency in the Q'eqchi' language. While many people were impressed with my ability to hold simple conver-sations, I resorted to Spanish when topics became complicated. Practically all interviews were held in Spanish. I gathered Q'eqchi' translations for significant ideas and terms and I present both Q'eqchi' and Spanish trans-lations for important words and phrases.[18]

Three

CYCLES OF DEBT

Colonialism, Coffee, and Companies

We can only speculate as to how the pre-contact Q'eqchi' conceptualized their social and cosmological universe, although they likely were engaged in a paternalistic, quasi-contractual relationship with invisible deities. Archaeological and epigraphical research reveals that pre-Columbian Mayan gods were ritually and regularly fed with the blood of sacrificial human victims, animals, and kings (Freidel et al. 1993:201–207). Supernatural beings had their ravenous appetites satisfied so that the universe was maintained in equilibrium, crops grew, and rain fell (Sharer 1994:539). Deities wavered between positional identities of outsider and ancestor, capable of both benevolent and malicious deeds (McAnany 1995:81).

Similarly, indigenous leaders—the civil and religious governors of the land—were perceived as foreign recipients of tribute and paternalistic providers of welfare and land (McAnany 1995:128). In the Yucatan, the Postclassic indigenous lineage head Ah Kuch Kabob gathered taxes and distributed land. In Alta Verapaz, aj pop (q. the leader; called *cacique* by the Spanish) maintained minimal autonomy (Sieber 1999:20), controlled land allotment, and even sold slaves to the Spanish (Jones 1994:94). The relatively independent Q'eqchi' chiefdoms may have been paying tribute to Utatlán, the center of the K'iche' Maya in what is now the western highlands of Guatemala (Ivic de Monterroso 1995:6). Deities external to the community, ancestors no longer among the living, rulers from afar, and local indigenous leaders were quasi-foreign (and partial-kin) recipients of respect and other forms of payment.

Although today the 400,000 to 500,000 Q'eqchi' language–speakers in Guatemala and Belize have the largest geographical extension of all Mayan groups (Cahuec del Valle and Richards 1994:1),[1] before European contact they were concentrated in what are now Guatemala's northeastern departments of Alta Verapaz and Baja Verapaz. Q'eqchi' people first inhabited the hills surrounding the Polochic and Chixoy rivers during the Preclassic era (King 1974:13–14; Parra Novo 1993:15–17), and they soon settled Chamá, now one of the most recognized archaeological sites in Alta Verapaz (Villacorta 1929:59–60). Although concentrated in this specific area, the pre-Columbian Q'eqchi' were already engaged in foreign networks. Influences were felt from the area that is now Mexico,[2] and the Q'eqchi' also were traders, moving between highland and lowland regions via water (Butler 1940:250; Wilk 1991:43).

When the Spaniard Pedro de Alvarado entered Guatemala in 1521, the Q'eqchi' were living in large sites controlled by caciques, although few Q'eqchi' lived within these political centers, preferring scattered hamlets in the mountains.[3] Juan Rodríguez Cabrillo directed the first Europeans into the region, and then in 1528 Sancho de Barahona led another group of Tz'utujil Maya from Atitlán to Chamá. This latter group captured the cacique of Chamá, imprisoning the Q'eqchi' ruler in Santiago de Guatemala, the first capital of Guatemala, and forcing him to work in the mines. For this apparent colonial success, Rodríguez Cabrillo and Sancho de Barahona were granted Cobán as an *encomienda*.[4]

In the silver mines outside of Santiago de Guatemala, the Q'eqchi' cacique died. In 1529 there was an election for a supreme indigenous leader who when elected would govern the entire Q'eqchi' region with an absolute hand. The election of Aj Pop'o Batz created a unified and invincible region that the Spanish were never able to successfully conquer, even though they tried three times (Parra Novo 1993:20). Because of the fierce resistance they encountered from the Q'eqchi' and their Pocomchí neighbors, the Tlaxcalan soldiers named this area Tezulutlán, "the land of war" (Estrada Monroy 1979:21).

Bartolomé de Las Casas played a momentous role in the history of the Q'eqchi' of Alta Verapaz when he began to question the "inhuman savagery" with which the Indians were treated (Las Casas 1992 [1552]:362). This Dominican friar believed that the military methods of conversion were abusive and cruel. In 1537, he petitioned the governor of Guatemala, Licenciado Alonso Maldonado, for permission to peacefully convert the Indians of Tezulutlán (Estrada Monroy 1979:39–51). Las Casas was granted permission with three conditions—that the agreement would remain secret, that the indigenous inhabitants would not be submitted to encomiendas, and that no Spanish would enter the area for five years. With this agreed, priests began entering the area in 1539. They were to respect existing land rights, and Spanish colonization would be prohibited. Indigenous leaders would maintain their positions and any remaining encomiendas would be rescinded.

Initially, they kept these promises. The Dominicans ousted a military camp, Nueva Sevilla, populated by Spaniards from the Yucatan, and they prohibited outsiders access to the area until the nineteenth century (King 1974:27; Parra Novo 1993:20). The Dominicans made their first reducción in the K'iche' area of Rabinal in what is now Baja Verapaz. There, they began to learn the Q'eqchi' language from relocated Indians in order to facilitate the conversion of others (King 1974:20–21; Pedroni 1991:12). As the caciques were easily converted to Christianity, Tezulutlán fell under the control of the Dominicans who, in 1547, renamed the area Verapaz: "true peace."

Although the Verapaces did not suffer the repressive brutality of the encomienda system as encountered in other regions of Guatemala (Lovell 1985:75–94), the Indians were nonetheless gathered up, resettled in reducciones, baptized, and obligated to pay tribute or taxes.[5] Conversion to Christianity appeared fairly successful, although the resettlement program was not. Few Q'eqchi' lived in the resettlement towns, which mostly served as markets, religious centers, and residences for the elite (Wilk 1991:45). Census numbers for the region dropped from 7,000 tribute-paying subjects in 1561 to 3,135 ten years later (King 1974:22). Although epidemics and disrupted agriculture added to this drop in population (Wilk 1991:46), it is likely that the Q'eqchi' simply refused confinement. Their milpa agriculture favored a broader settlement pattern, and they preferred to live near their cornfields. Some moved to the lowlands in order to grow cacao, pataxté (a wild form of cacao), and plantains (Sapper 1985 [1936]:17), and the excessive taxation and exploitation further stimulated migration. The Catholic Church was extremely frustrated by the Indians' refusal to submit to the reducción system, and the Dominicans eventually betrayed Las Casas' agreement by calling in the military to bring fleeing individuals back to reducciones.

Resettlement had varying effects. King (1974:26) stresses the deep association between the Q'eqchi' and their milpa, and the subsequent emotional breakdowns as a result of resettlement. Wilk (1991:46) demonstrates how the cycle of displacement and resettlement had a severe impact on social and economic relations. Schackt (1986:14) writes that the Q'eqchi' created ties to their new municipio town centers as a sort of spatial marker of communal identity. Conversely, by emphasizing that the Q'eqchi' were not congregated to the extent found in other parts of Guatemala, Cahuec del Valle and Richards (1994:3) claim that Q'eqchi' identity became based on language rather than municipio.[6] I would like to contribute that the Q'eqchi' maintained power by making themselves invisible through migration, thus removing themselves from the colonial gaze.

Throughout the eighteenth century, the reducción policy declined and the Q'eqchi' population began to grow. Urban populations at Cobán and San Pedro Carchá became centers of weaving and trading. Dominicans set up sugar, cotton, and cochineal[7] plantations and used Q'eqchi' as slave or forced labor (King 1974:26). The Q'eqchi' also began producing cash crops on their private or community land.[8] By the beginning of the nineteenth century, as a result of Dominican corruption and overtaxation, most reducciones had disappeared (Wilk 1991:47). On the eve of Independence, tax deficits were at their highest and Q'eqchi' migration from Alta Verapaz was at its most elevated (Escobar 1841:96–97; King 1974:27).

During the eighteenth century in Spain, the Bourbon kings were "emphasizing commercial reforms to increase production and trade between Spain and the Indies, while attempting to eliminate contraband and competition with Spain's rivals, particularly Great Britain" (Jones 1994:153). These ideas, in response to the industrial revolution in Northern Europe, led to the Crown's increased desire for control and intervention in its New World colonies. For Guatemala, this meant the promotion of capitalist growth by emphasizing plantation rather than individual subsistence agriculture (Woodward 1990:53). However, the extensive *control* of rural areas by the Church rather than the government left the Crown unable to regulate taxes and contraband trade (McCreery 1993:21). The Bourbon Reforms ultimately backfired on Spain, leading to depression, unrest, and, eventually, to Guatemala's break with the Crown.

Independence came to Central America in 1821. During the next four decades in Guatemala two factions would vie for political power. The Conservatives, who were descendants of the Spanish oligarchy, clung to a more traditional, neo-feudal ideology. The Liberals, followers of the Bourbon reforms and obsessed with modernization, were emerging capitalists who took the United States as their model (Wilk 1991:48; Woodward 1990:59). They were the first to gain power after Independence, and they pushed for the exportation of agricultural goods. For the needed labor, the government passed the first *mandamiento*—a law that forced Mayans to work on plantations or public projects (Cambranes 1985:99). Landlessness, drunkenness, and vagrancy were now punishable by forced labor.

In 1824, the Dominicans lost their jurisdiction in Alta Verapaz when Ladino merchants entered the area for the first time. Ladinos immediately bought tracts of land and the Guatemalan government desired more of this type of investment. For example, the government sought a foreign company to construct a highway between the Río Dulce and the port of Santo Tomás de Castilla. To this end, fifteen million acres in Verapaz and Izabal, many of which were occupied by Q'eqchi', were offered as usufruct to the Eastern Coast of Central America Commercial and Agricultural Company (EC) of London. For twenty years, the EC harvested lumber and monopolized navigation of the river systems in the region. The British company, however, could not comply with all the government's conditions, and a smaller parcel of land surrounding the port of Santo Tomás de Castilla was purchased by a Belgian company, which soon after went bankrupt (Mejía 1997:96–97). Although the entire fifteen million acres were not sold to foreign investors, this period marks the beginning of the Liberal policy of expediting access to land for foreigners and wealthy plantation owners (Wagner 1987:88–89; Wilk 1991:49).

In 1839, the Conservatives took over again and repealed the mandamiento laws, although other forms of forced labor continued. Titles for communal lands were offered and, perhaps as a result of the influx of foreigners and Ladinos, many communities united to receive land rights. For an annual return tax of 3 percent of the land's value, communities received titles to communal lands. But these titles were granted only if the property was not prime agricultural land desired by finqueros (Wilk 1991:49).

During the middle of the nineteenth century, coffee came to Alta Verapaz. For the region's capitalists, the timing was perfect. Artificial dyes had recently been invented in Europe and a new export crop was needed to replace cochineal and indigo. Lumber had lost its prominence on the world market and coffee promised higher and more secure returns (Cambranes 1985:59–60; Stanley 1994:5–6; Wagner 1987:95–99; Wilk 1991:49). In addition to setting up a model coffee farm, the government gave loans, seeds, and advice. With government assistance, the Q'eqchi' were able to grow coffee on their communal lands. Active encouragement was particularly directed at the municipio of Cobán where the Verapaz government claimed that it was providing the way for the impoverished to become coffee planters. By 1862, there were thirty-nine coffee fincas in Cobán, 70,000 bearing plants, and another two million plants in various stages of cultivation in the department (Woodward 1990:69).

Even with government subsidization, the Q'eqchi' were no match for the Ladino and foreign plantation owners who, upon discovery of prime agricultural land, often forced the indigenous to rent them their communal land. The government supported the outside occupation of community land in Alta Verapaz by exempting Ladino coffee growers from military service. As a result, Ladinos were able to exploit the government's offers of seedlings, loans, and land (Cambranes 1985:61–85). The Q'eqchi' people could not compete; many had to drop the production of other cash crops that they had established during the eighteenth and nineteenth centuries. Subsistence agriculture became the definitive economic model for the Q'eqchi' (Wilk 1991:49). Further, once a migratory pattern was established, the Q'eqchi' would encounter difficulties making a shift from subsistence to cash crop agriculture (Swetman 1989:106). Resistance increased as Mayans destroyed coffee plants on foreign-owned plantations or refused to appear for labor drafts. In 1864, a Q'eqchi' man named Melchor Yat began an uprising against the local government and foreign plantation owners (King 1974:29).

Even so, it was not until after the death of Conservative President José Raphael Carrera in 1865 that the major assault on indigenous land and labor occurred (Woodward 1990:67–69). Between Carrera's death and the Liberals' taking power in 1871, many of the community "rentals" had already become privately owned. Coercion and trickery left many Indian communities without land to cultivate while forcing others to flee to the mountains (Woodward 1990:68–69). When the Liberals took power, coffee accounted for half the country's exports (McCreery 1990:105) and the Liberal leader, Justo Rufino Barrios, not surprisingly, was a wealthy coffee grower himself. He wanted to develop Guatemala through the production of cattle, bananas, tobacco, wheat, and, most importantly, coffee. In order to do so, he reinstated the mandamiento that forced all men to carry a document attesting to their integrity, production, and solvency. Although he did not abolish indigenous rights to communal land outright, as many believe, under Barrios private property tended to take precedence (King 1974:30; McCreery 1990:106; Pedroni 1991:14). The Barrios regime confiscated "unused" land from the Catholic Church and made at least one million acres available at extremely low prices.[9] Indians lost even more of their land because they did not have the capital to purchase it, and much of the unclaimed and uncultivated land was sold to individuals with connections to the government (Smith 1990:84). Foreigners were attracted to the bargains of fertile land and cheap labor. One group who began buying up large tracts of property in Alta Verapaz would have a dramatic effect on more than just the economy of Guatemala and the Q'eqchi' people. Their name would become synonymous with foreign intervention during the neo-Liberal regime. Coffee became their product and Alta Verapaz became their colony. Germans flooded into Guatemala.

Although German immigrants had been entering the country since the middle of the century, an 1887 treaty ensured their continued immigration to the area. The treaty promised government protection, complete liberty to live and travel, and freedom to buy or rent land to all German citizens. German citizenship was guaranteed to all legitimate children born to German nationals in Guatemala and young German men were excluded from military service (Stanley 1994:8; Wagner 1987:97, 1996:100). Germans brought their skills, capital, and European culture. They constructed opera houses, parks, and theaters, organized chamber orchestras, and brought kerosene street lamps from New Orleans (King 1974:31). In order to assist them in their business, the Guatemalan government built roads, completed railroad networks, and opened up communication by installing a telegraph system. By 1897, Germans owned 1,420 square kilometers (548 square miles) of land in the municipio of Cobán. They produced one third of Guatemala's coffee, controlled two thirds of the trade (King 1974:33), and owned 75 percent of the businesses in Alta Verapaz (Mejía 1997:99).

President Barrios wanted a modern nation. Through incentives such as tax exemptions and cheap land and labor, he encouraged private and foreign investors to furnish his vision. Decrees opened up unused land in Alta Verapaz and Izabal for cattle, chicle, rubber, and lumber. However, President Barrios saw indigenous people as an impediment to his ideals. He conceived of the Indians only as a labor supply, and he used coercive and hostile means to secure them as such. For example, when he learned that Indians were claiming exemption from the mandamiento system by running for local office, Barrios got rid of these offices, thus providing 15,000 more men to the labor force. A special court was set up in Cobán to force Indians to work on the fincas (King 1974:31) and a military militia was sent to the highlands to enforce the mandamiento policy and to uphold Ladino, German, and state authority (McCreery 1993:23). Indians were forcibly recruited for military service, although they were not allowed to join the predominantly Ladino-served militia but rather ordered to serve in the army as defenders of the nation. After centuries of relative isolation from the nation's domination, this period marked the beginning of the state's supremacy and control in rural areas of Alta Verapaz.

By demanding work, labor, land, and money from indigenous populations, the mandamiento rules of the late nineteenth and early twentieth century made debt an institutional obligation. What facilitated enforced labor was that most of the land in Alta Verapaz had been bought by Germans, and the Q'eqchi' were no longer able to flee to their homes in the mountains because this land was now owned by foreigners or Ladinos.

Even German entrepreneurs complained of being unable to find uncultivated and ownerless land and labor (Cambranes 1985:305). In 1898, the political boss of Alta Verapaz wrote:

> Agriculture is the patrimony of the majority of inhabitants in this Department. They are devoted to growing coffee on a large scale and the results are gratifying because this product is doing particularly well on the European market. . . . In order for the growers to be able to harvest the coffee without any difficulty, the Jefatura in my charge has ordered the local authorities to procure the necessary help and has forced unwilling laborers to fulfill their responsibilities, punishing those who fail to comply with Regulations. (Cambranes 1985: 234)

Only if a Mayan man lived on a finca would he avoid being rounded up for military service or forced labor, and the conditions on many of these coffee fincas were horrendous. Finqueros treated their workers inhumanely, forcing them to work seven days a week, beating them with whips and machetes, and raping women. Nourishment was far below average needs, and vitamin deficiency diseases such as rickets were common. Because the military was there to protect the landowners, Mayans had little room for retaliation.

Even so, there was overt resistance. In 1885, an uprising in Alta Verapaz led to immediate repression from the state. In 1897, a community elder from Cobán, Juan de la Cruz, organized a rebellion against local Ladinos and foreigners and against agro-exportation, although it is suggested that he was interested in money more than political causes (McCreery 1993:26). In 1906, a nativistic uprising occurred in San Juan Chamelco (King 1974:34). There were also more subtle forms of resistance. Indians cut down coffee trees and avoided forced labor by manipulating the system. Grievances and complaints were written and submitted to local governments. The unequal economic relations between finquero and *mozo* (sp. serf) were defined, performed, and ridiculed through indigenous dances, folktales, and religious ceremonies (McCreery 1993:27). The Q'eqchi' people did not succumb, but rather asserted themselves in both open and discreet ways.

Migration was still a common solution. Escaping loss of land and slave-like labor, the Q'eqchi' fled south to the lowland areas north and east of Lago Izabal and also north to the Petén (McCreery 1993:33). Development in these areas and fear of forced labor caused some Q'eqchi' to move even further east into Belize, or south to El Salvador and Honduras.[10] The region around El Estor, located at the western end of Lago Izabal, was popular among the ancestors of many of the Q'eqchi' migrants now living in Livingston. However, not all movement at this time was made in search of land or in order to avoid plantation life. The United Fruit Company relocated many Q'eqchi' families to its fincas in Izabal, and others were relocated to coffee fincas in Senahú (Pedroni 1991:15).

With coffee markets in the United States and Europe expanding, labor became scarce. In order to halt self-initiated migration to Izabal, new laws were drawn up that offered Indian refugees exemption from taxes, military service, and labor upon their return to Alta Verapaz. Few took the offer (McCreery 1993:34). Thus in 1894, debt-peonage officially joined the mandamiento system as a method of acquiring and assuring a steady work force (Dessaint 1983:26). Finqueros offered *habilitaciones* (sp. cash advances) that roped individuals into future labor and cyclical debt (Cambranes 1985:152–160; Wilk 1991:51). Although individuals with debts were exempt from the dreaded mandamiento, debt-peonage dragged Q'eqchi' workers into an economic encumbrance that was difficult if not impossible to work off. A debt of at least fifteen cents to a finquero exempted an individual from the government work force (McCreery 1995:207), but it tethered one into a burdensome economic relationship with the (usually foreign) owner.

After 1920, the mandamiento policy was finally abolished. Debt-peonage and vagrancy laws began their reign as the new means of creating labor. Every man was required to carry a *boleto de trabajo* (sp. working papers) attesting to his indebtedness. If his papers were not in order he would be labeled a vagrant, fined, and transported to a plantation where he would stay until he worked off the new debt (McCreery 1995:220; Stanley 1994:12). Before a man could obtain employment on a plantation, he would have to receive a *boleto de solvencia* (sp.)—written proof that he had paid his debts to his previous finquero.

General Jorge Ubico, Justo Rufino Barrios' godson, came to power in 1931. Like his godfather, Ubico came from a wealthy family of coffee growers (Benz 1996:16). In 1934, Ubico issued a decree that halted debt-peonage, declaring long-term debt servitude and wage advances illegal. A few days later, however, he replaced it with *Decree 96,* the Vagrancy Law. Henceforth, the state enforced cheap labor by requiring a minimum number of days worked per year on the fincas. A vagrant was defined as anyone without sufficient land to provide an income, anyone who did not work the minimum days per year, and anyone who was neither working for a

finca nor producing a certain number of *manzanas*[11] of coffee, sugar, tobacco, corn, wheat, potatoes, and vegetables, among other products. An
appendix to the decree stated that those with more than ten square *cuerdas* of cultivated land would work 100 days, while those with less than ten
square cuerdas would work 150.[12] Men were still required to carry *libretas*
(sp. booklets) that recorded their work status (Adams 1990:142), and the
government made it difficult for rural people to obtain the documents that
certified their land holdings (McCreery 1995:221).

This era is still vivid in the memories of elderly Q'eqchi' men in Livingston.[13] They clearly recall General Jorge Ubico, who ruled Guatemala from
1931 until 1944. Both Felipe and Chico, for example, mentioned to me the
violent period of Ubico, when they had to carry with them boletos that
proved they were employed. Felipe told me that without his booklet, the
military forced him to work on the highways. Ubico clearly tightened the
governmental reins around Indians through Decree 96, which made it illegal not to own land. This placed the Q'eqchi' people in an onerous position,
since most had been displaced from their land or had never acquired titles.
Once completely dependent on the land for survival, the Q'eqchi' people
were now landless, labeled vagrants, and subsequently forced to work on
foreign-owned fincas.

A cyclical debt exchange became secularized. Now payment was owed
not only to deities, leaders, the community, and religious institutions, but
also to an invisible government and to finca overseers, all of which were
outside institutions to the Q'eqchi' people. Therefore, alongside a transmissible belief of paying debt or sacrificing to outsiders as a means of reinforcing community, Q'eqchi' payment became a civic duty to foreign
owners. By merging all these institutions of outsiderness, ownership took
on divine qualities, deities became powerful owners, and providing outsiders became peripheral, and often invisible, members of the community
(see Chapter 4).

Life during the middle of the twentieth century was difficult for most
indigenous Mayan people. Malnutrition was rampant and illiteracy reached
as high as 99 percent in indigenous areas. Life expectancy was a mere forty
years (Gordon 1983:48). Approximately 72 percent of the arable land was
owned by 2 percent of the landowners.[14] Three foreign [United States]
companies—United Fruit Company, International Railways of Central
America, and Electric Bond and Share—practically ran Guatemala by controlling the railroad, ports, and electricity. Unrest was growing. In 1944,
mostly under pressure from urban elites, intellectuals, members of the
middle class, and students, Ubico stepped down from power. General

Federico Ponce and his Progressive Liberals became the new political power, although young military officers and civilians shortly overthrew them (Handy 1990:166). Ponce was aligned with the Conservatives who had ruled a century earlier. In an effort to win votes in rural areas, he offered the German land, expropriated by Ubico only a few years before, to rural Indians (Adams 1990:142). This seemingly reformist action stirred up national sentiment against Ponce. As expressed in the *indigenista* writing movement of the 1930s and 1940s, Ladinos perceived Indians as distrustful, rebellious, lazy, and ignorant (Adams 1990:148). Ladinos saw Ponce's policy towards the indigenous as a potentially dangerous attack on their interests.

Juan José Arévalo Bermejo, a self-exiled philosophy professor, was voted into office in December 1944, thus beginning a ten-year long political and economic revolution in Guatemala. In addition to revoking Decree 96, he signed labor laws that created, among other benefits, equal pay for men and women, a minimum wage, social security, the right to strike, and severance pay. He decentralized the political system by allowing elected officials, rather than the military, to govern the rural areas. His government constructed schools and built hospitals. Private monopolies were banned and the government gained the power to expropriate some private property (Galeano 1967:50; Gordon 1983:50–51). Full-blown land reform, however, was a task left for Colonel Jacobo Arbenz Guzmán, the president democratically elected in December of 1950.

Arbenz was determined to free Guatemala from the world's economy and from the imperialist hands of the United States. His primary goal was to create a modern capitalist state through the development of a peasant-controlled economy. By building ports, hydroelectric stations, and roads, he directly challenged the hegemony of foreign—particularly United States—interests in Guatemala. He began to wrestle Guatemala out from its northern neighbor's economic grip, although it was the Agrarian Reform Law that had the most significant impact during Arbenz's time in office. Decree 900, approved by Congress in June 1952, promoted the development of a peasant-controlled capitalistic economy. It eliminated feudal-type property and abolished antiquated production relations such as forced labor and other relics of slavery. Land, means of production, credit, and technical support were offered to all farmers. The government expropriated idle land from fincas larger than 672 acres (Galeano 1967:51–52; Stanley 1994:179).

Some 20 percent of the nation's fertile agricultural land, or 1.8 million acres, was redistributed (Brockett 1992:3). Approximately 100,000 families were granted land under this policy. Land once owned by Germans was given to peasants, although titles remained in the government's name and individuals were given only lifetime usufruct privileges. In return, the new landowners paid the government 3 percent of their annual production. Other idle lands were expropriated and agrarian bonds with 3 percent annual interest rates were offered as compensation. Financing came from a newly established bank, the National Agrarian Bank, which had the sole purpose of extending credit to small farmers (Handy 1990:169). Expropriation was the result of local initiatives, such that individuals were to report unused land to local officials before laws could go in to effect. Large landowners reacted violently. *Campesino* (sp. peasant) and agrarian organizations were formed in the countryside in order to implement the law and confront opposition.

With the Red Scare growing in the United States, which was no longer caught up in the aftermath of the Second World War, North America became quite concerned about its interests in Guatemala. Strikes against the United Fruit Company had become more frequent, and at least 233,973 acres had been expropriated from Compañía Agrícola, the United Fruit Company's south coast subsidiary.[15] The CIA-supported coup that followed has been examined elsewhere, and for the purposes of this research only a brief mention is necessary.[16] In 1954, the United States State Department and the CIA ousted Jacobo Arbenz and handpicked and trained his replacement, General Carlos Castillo Armas, a move that established a string of military presidents (Schlesinger and Kinzer 1982:227–255). The United Fruit Company received all of its land back and many federal lands were privatized.[17] Over the next five years, fourteen million dollars in aid came from the United States. Most of this money was used to oust indigenous families living on UFC land (Brockett 1992:8).[18] The majority of land that was occupied by indigenous people during the revolutionary period was returned to those who claimed ownership prior to 1944. Campesino organizations, formed earlier to maintain land reform in Alta Verapaz, disintegrated. Not surprisingly, seasonal and permanent migration significantly increased.

For all of Latin America, the middle of the twentieth century was a period of migration to urban areas (Hamilton and Chinchilla 1991:81–85; Pedroni 1991:15). Q'eqchi' people went against this trend by migrating toward rural areas, sometimes from urban ones. Many Q'eqchi' moved to Guatemala City[19] though others went to Belize, the Petén, and the department of Izabal. El Estor and Panzos also became popular destinations. Foreign interests affected this migratory process. Besides the massive impact of the Germans, the UFC relocated some Q'eqchi' to its banana plantations in Izabal. Foreign-supported mineral and petroleum exploration in the Franja Transversal del Norte (FTN) also attracted Q'eqchi' to the departments of Izabal and Livingston. President Carlos Arana Osorio offered EXMIBAL (Empresa Exploraciones y Explotaciones Mineras de Izabal), a Canadian-owned nickel company, the rights to mine nickel in the FTN for forty years (Mejía 1997:84). EXMIBAL then found one of the largest sources of nickel in the world on the western end of Lago Izabal. Its extensive development plans for the area brought many Q'eqchi' to Panzos and El Estor in the 1970s (Carter 1969:5), and its abrupt end of production in 1981 devastated the local El Estor economy. Before its premature closing, the company had provided community services, amphitheaters, parks, and air-conditioned concrete accommodations to numerous Q'eqchi' families. However, it also destroyed the manatee habitat and the surrounding environment and eluded taxation through corrupt exemption laws (Mejía 1997:169–170). Its closing was a catalyst for much of the continued migration to Livingston.

Migration toward the aldeas of Livingston had already started decades before. The two primary Q'eqchi' villages near the town of Livingston, Plan Grande Tatín and Plan Grande Queveche, were founded in the 1940s and 1950s, respectively. Ferropazco brought workers from Alta Verapaz to load coffee on the docks, and a number of Q'eqchi' individuals told me that they came to the area because they had family working at the German company. Felipe, for example, was initially attracted to the area fifty years ago because his mother had accompanied a German man who worked with Ferropazco to Livingston. Chico also came from Cobán some fifty years ago to work at the company. Others told me that their families were tired of working so hard, that life in Alta Verapaz was like slavery (sp. *esclavitud*). Manuel, one of the initial members of the project, informally told me how the finca owners and the government of Alta Verapaz were one and the same and that his father had to work fifteen days for one and fifteen days for the other. He said that when his family grew tired of this, they migrated to Izabal in search of their own land for cultivation.

> [We came here] for work, because in El Estor there is practically no work. In comparison to here, one can always find work. Because when we were there in El Estor, we were dedicated to our work, but only away, we would have to go away, we would have to leave El Estor, for thirty days, we'd go find work on the fincas. There in the fincas is where they provide for us, they give us food, and not all the time do they

take good care of us because there you earn very little. And
there the food that they have to give to you is, it is only some
beans and rice, just a little bit of food, and because of this we
decided that we should come here where we heard there is
work. For this we came here. (Videotaped interview with
Armando)

Paulina: We came for work.
Hilary: Because in El Estor there is no work?
Paulina: No, there is no work in El Estor, only in *cuadrillos*
[(sp.) labor teams] could the men find work. Then we would
have to stay home alone. For this reason we came here.

Cuadrillo is, ironically, a vestige from the nineteenth century, when work
teams were recruited by the government to provide labor on foreign-
owned plantations (Cambranes 1985:97). People such as Paulina still use
this term to describe the practice of organizing teams of men to work for
perhaps one week or one month in the coffee and cattle fincas of Izabal,
where workers are provided with room and board. However, women and
children are left behind, the pay is minimal, the work arduous, and the conditions unfavorable. Although it is not exactly debt-peonage, this type of
work is still highly exploitative and provided, for many, the final impetus
for migration.

Migration toward Livingston has been and continues to be an incre-
mental process (Adams 1965:14–15), often beginning in Alta Verapaz, then
stopping in western Izabal, and heading east towards Puerto Barrios or
Fronteras, before finally arriving in the municipio of Livingston. Even
here, most Q'eqchi' live in the aldeas before moving into town. Lola and
Alberto came to Livingston from Senahú, an area in southern Alta Verapaz, where they lived on a coffee finca owned by German descendants.
They first moved to Tampico, and then to Crique Chino, before locating
themselves in town as caretakers. Manuel's family moved from Alta Verapaz, to El Estor, to an aldea near Puerto Barrios, to Plan Grande Queveche,
and finally to Crique Chino Barrio Nuevo, where they now live. This process of advancing toward Livingston continued slowly through the 1960s
and 1970s (Pedroni 1991:15–21), with bursts in the early 1980s and again in
the 1990s.

The various arrival dates reported to me, from fifty years to within the
past month, show that migration to Livingston was not simply a reaction
to turnover of land reform after 1954. Rather, it was a reaction to a complex

PAULINA

history of social and political systems that negate ties to land and means of subsistence. While land and labor continue to be the primary justifications of migration, as Paulina explained, these reasons are temporally defined. In agreement with Hamilton and Chinchilla's (1991:106) findings for the Central American region as a whole, I find that Q'eqchi' migration is a result of influences of national and international capital penetration, resulting structural changes, foreign intervention, and historical precedence.

Unlike other Mayan people in Guatemala (Morrison and May 1994:135), Q'eqchi' people in Livingston rarely offer violence as a reason for their migration to Livingston, even though by the end of the thirty-year civil war (in 1996), approximately 150,000 to 200,000 civilians throughout Guatemala were dead or "disappeared" (Jonas 1997:6). During the 1960s, a Ladino-led and Cuban-supported guerrilla movement began an insurgency that was quickly annihilated with assistance from the United States. Green Berets and Rangers trained counterinsurgency soldiers in the United States and assisted them on Guatemalan territory.[20] Fighting occurred throughout Izabal, mostly in the Franja Transversal del Norte, although there was little indigenous involvement. Extensive indigenous participation did not occur until the late 1970s and early 1980s, when the guerrillas resurfaced. Most of this latter fighting occurred in areas other than where the Q'eqchi' of Livingston then lived. People today tell me that they never witnessed any massacres, that they only heard of them secondhand. Only one man (whose anonymity I will maintain) told me that he came to Livingston because he had been a target of government death squads due to his involvement in labor unions. Although I will not discuss the violence of the 1970s and 1980s here, I am not downplaying its importance, but rather arguing that it does not explain the migration of the Q'eqchi' to Livingston.[21] Nonetheless, silence may be a survival tactic, a socialized code that I, as an outsider, may not fully comprehend (Green 1999:68–70).[22]

COLLAPSING THE CONNECTIONS

Meaning emerges from learned patterns between historic units (Strauss and Quinn 1997:82). For the Q'eqchi' people of Livingston, these units are their families, communities, and the vast array of often invisible (or intangible) individuals and institutions that shift between positions of outsider and kin. Historic (and contemporary) connections—with deities, ancestors, rulers, saints, Dominican friars, government officials, German finqueros, and industries of globalization—have been collapsed into the Q'eqchi' imaginary. They are registered and forged within an internalized scheme that perpetuates the perception of outsiders and deities as landowners, outsiders and owners (and thus ownership) as semi-divine, and outsiders as capable of both malevolent and benevolent deeds. An active practice of respect and payment reinforces this cultural scheme and a transcendental concept of ownership and visibility helps maintains it. But how exactly did this happen? I will present one hypothesis, though in no way do I suggest this is a firm and accurate depiction of how history became embedded in the contemporary Q'eqchi' imaginary. Further, I openly admit that my reading of history is based on tertiary sources rather than first-hand accounts that have the potential to challenge dominant narratives of Mayan history.[23]

During the pre-Columbian era, the Batabob of the Yucatan governed hereditary land and oversaw how people used it. The aj pop of the Q'eqchi' region were powerful rulers who controlled land and even owned and sold slaves to the Spanish (Jones 1994:94). These leaders were civil and religious governors of the land who demanded payment of respect, just as deities required sacrifice and reverence. Though Batabob and aj pop were human, not supernatural, within the Q'eqchi' imaginary it is likely that indigenous leaders slipped into the category of supernatural owners. We do, after all, have confirmation that pre-Columbian leaders were considered semi-divine (McAnany 1995:125).[24]

When the Spanish brought Catholicism to Guatemala, they furthered an already intact ideology that categorized deities and leaders as foreign owners, governors of the land, and givers and takers. The Crown attempted to position a vision of "proper" colonial relations upon still-intact pre-Columbian political and social structures (Sieber 1999:20). Yet, Europeans added a layer of significance and conflict—the concept of private ownership, which is not divine, kin-based, communal, or based upon laboring of land. And the Catholic Church became one of the largest landowners of the first half of the colonial period. By demanding tribute, taxes, and land, it became a recipient of not only ideological reverence but also material payment. Belief, payment, and sacrifice were united into one entity, reified into law and religious code.

Spaniards also altered the tangibility and accessibility of power, thus reaffirming vision and sight as an integral component in the maintenance of the social structure. Supreme deities, owners, and rulers were more fully invisible, no longer accessible through semi-divine rulers. Power—which colonists used to move, mark, torture, and tax indigenous people—emanated invisibly from afar, from a distant Imperial Spain or from out-of-sight Papal decrees. Likewise, powerful private rituals too became invisible, hidden from the Catholic authority. Both the divine God and sacred private ritual became invisible and internal (see Chapter 6).

The Church and local officials then implemented brotherhoods called *cofradías* (Foster 1953). Rather than emphasizing payment only to invisible outsiders and deities, these civil and religious organizations affirmed obligation to one's community. By paying, sacrificing, and demonstrating respect to outsiders, the Church, and the saints, social and religious cargo systems maintained and integrated the moral, religious, and economic structure of community (Cancian 1965:134–136). Everyone was connected through obligatory ties that enforced respect to saints, the Church, deities, and the community. Payment and respect to landowning outsiders (whether invisible deities or the landholding Dominicans) became civil, religious, social, political, ideological, and solidly symbolic in the everyday.[25]

The Dominicans provided the Q'eqchi' people with a new deity to revere—the Christian God—and a refurbished pantheon of revered beings—the saints. However, these entities did not efface the beloved pre-Columbian deities and indigenous leaders from their cosmological and political networks. Rather, supernatural and worldly controllers of land were wed into a composite. While Colonial Spanish and Dominican political and social structures slowly supplanted those of the Postclassic period, aj pop and other authority figures persisted in the Q'eqchi' imaginary as supernatural figures who maintained their control and governance of the land. They represented units of cosmological and political significance who were then merged with renascent outsiders who mastered the territory—i.e., the Dominicans and other foreigners who entered the region to seize available land and bodies.

This makes the death of the Q'eqchi' leader in the mines outside of Santiago de Guatemala even more significant. The Q'eqchi' of Alta Verapaz heard of their ruler's tragic ending (Estrada Monroy 1979:16), and news of his death inside the mountain could have assisted in the further conflation of indigenous rulers with supernatural deities, who were believed to govern the land from mountain caves (Bassie-Sweet 1991:77–126). Foreign occupation of land and of bodies paralleled the power of indigenous entities, and Tzuultaq'a, traditional mountain spirits, were refashioned as semi-divine and partially foreign beings that control land from cavernous homes inside recesses of the earth. The secular merged with the cosmological, and the hills became tangible liaisons to supreme invisible power.

Today, echoes of these divine and civil figures reverberate in meanings attached to the contemporary outsiders and globalized institutions. Henceforth, the Q'eqchi' people perceive outsiders—whether ethnographers, Canadian nickel companies, tourists, neo-Liberal regimes, or the local Garifuna—through a cultural and historical filter that links morality and power to ownership and visibility. "Owner" and "outsider" have been firmly and metaphorically wed in the Q'eqchi' imaginary as potentially benevolent and maleficent recipients of payment, respect, and fear.

Four

ENVISIONING POWER AND MORALITY

Tzuultaq'a, Germans, and Action-in-Place

When one says Tzuultaq'a, they mean hill. Even though it is Tzuultaq'a, he is sent by God. Or it is like you have your mother, and you are the daughter, then you always have someone who gives you orders. Well this is like Tzuultaq'a . . . They are always women and men . . . They are the owners of the lands where one is. Or rather each hill has its borders, then, when you pass through their borders, you pass into the region of another hill that receives you. Each hill owns its land.
—VIDEOTAPED INTERVIEW WITH ARMANDO

Q'eqchi' individuals and communities have intimate relationships with the hills, home to their beloved Tzuultaq'a mountain spirits.[1] Social exchanges with these deities actualize and reinforce the socioeconomic and cosmological structures that in the past and present have placed the Q'eqchi' in a position of laboring, respecting, and paying debts to fearsome outsiders. Tzuultaq'a deities manifest as mountains, animals, and natural objects. When made visible because of a breach in the moral code, they are seen as light-skinned male or female humans or serpents. Tzuultaq'a own and govern the land from their homes deep within the recesses of the earth.[2] They master the chickens, caves, corn, milpas, riverbanks, valleys, and hills from deep inside mountain caves where they have entire fincas and pens full of pigs, turkeys, cows, and hens. At night, you can hear their animals squawking alongside the thunder roaring from within caves. Corn, beans, yucca, and pineapples are stacked throughout their homes. Snakes hang from the rafters and coil around the hammock's cords where the Tzuultaq'a rest. Q'eqchi' people call their mountain spirit the "owner" (sp. *dueño*, q. *aj eechal*) of the natural world. They do not own only their homes and natural objects, but they are also the owners of specific regions. Like governors, Tzuultaq'a control the territory that surrounds their mountains. Natural features act as boundaries, separating one domain from the next. Typically, thirteen of these deities exist, most residing in the area surrounding Cobán in Alta Verapaz.[3] They are multifaceted exemplars of morality-in-action: invisible owners ruling from afar and foreign providers demanding respect.

MULTIPLICITY AND FOREIGNNESS

> It looks like a white woman, and a very pale man, they say. With fine clothes, well dressed and everything . . . They say he is Ladino, but they all speak Q'eqchi' too. (Audiotaped interview with Manuel)

A Tzuultaq'a is most often identified as a pale-skinned individual with light (blonde) hair—often a Ladino, German, or gringa—and occasionally an ancient Mayan. However, the Tzuultaq'a are not wholly foreign; there is a partiality involved in his/her identity. Tzuultaq'a are considered both foreign and familiar, as exemplified in their light skin and ability to speak Q'eqchi' as well as German, Spanish, and English. This multiplicity is also revealed through the fact that, depending on the size and shape of the mountain, the spirits are either male or female (Wilson 1995:54).[4]

> **Martín:** There are thirteen hills.
> **Hilary:** Do you know which ones [you recite in prayer]?
> **Martín:** Not all of them.
> **Hilary:** Are they hills around here or are they all from Cobán?
> **Martín:** It seems that they are all from Alta Verapaz, because you mention Coha, Xucaneb, Sumj'ab, Itzam, there are others that I can't remember, and you mention Cerro San Pablo. But they mention the thirteen, and they also mention the ones they know around here.

> **Manuel:** Yes, for example Tactic, Chixim, Santa María Itzam, there are others, Cachebeleju. Yes, there are four, Jo Cua Ixim. He is the boss, they say. These are the hills you have to mention when you are going to sow your fields. Like Cerro San Gil, Cerro La Vaca, Cerro La Virgen. They say there are twelve. . . .

ARMANDO

Hilary: And when you had your milpa, you asked permission? And you have mentioned these twelve, hills from here
and hills from there, from Cobán?
Manuel: Oh yes. There are twelve. You have to mention all
of them. Yes, from here and from Cobán.

Armando, Martín, Manuel, and others are reorganizing their divinity in
Livingston, adding local geographic features to the sacred hills of Alta Verapaz. This practice is different from other Q'eqchi' regions, where migration
tends to change the content but not the structural framework of prayers
to the Tzuultaq'a (Wilson 1995:224–229). Q'eqchi' people in Belize, for example, claim the existence of thirteen, and only thirteen, Tzuultaq'a, even

though they may substitute them with new localities (Schackt 1986:60–61). In contrast, the Q'eqchi' of Livingston vary in the number of Tzuultaq'a that they believe exist and in which ones they must revere and recite in prayer. Perhaps this is because they are more recent migrants, in transition, and undecided as to how many of the Tzuultaq'a, if any, moved with them. Some people, like Chico, say that Tzuultaq'a only exist in Alta Verapaz, that these deities own strictly the thirteen mountains surrounding Cobán. Others, like Juliana, Martín, Armando, and Manuel, believe that Tzuultaq'a now reside in the Livingston area, and most independently agree upon the locations of these mountain spirits.

ACTING MORAL

> Let's say, well they give us permission. If I'm going to use your bathroom, then I'm going to tell you. That's fine, "go ahead," you will say. If I don't ask permission, what are you going to say to me? "Why do you enter my bathroom? Who gave you permission?" It's the same with them. So it is with the Tzuultaq'a, because surely when I just enter your house, you will chastise me, right? Ahah, because I didn't ask permission. Perhaps I am going to rob something, you think. It's the same for our harvests. It's the same. Except when you ask permission, you pray, and the land gives to you. (Audiotaped interview with Patrocinia)

Q'eqchi' pay, respect, and feed Tzuultaq'a with *pom* (q. copal incense), candles, blood, tamales, respect, and liquor. When individuals want to build a house, cut down a tree, or plant a cornfield, they must first ask permission from Tzuultaq'a. People do not simply dig up rocks and trees; they "feed" and "pay" Tzuultaq'a in return for permission to use or alter the land. If a person avoids this mandatory obligation, a number of unlucky things can come to pass. A house may burn down, an individual may be bitten by a snake after stepping in a hole, or rats may come to the fields to eat the corn. Tzuultaq'a can also become visible, suddenly appearing and frightening disrespectful subjects. When a Tzuultaq'a becomes angry, s/he will make hens fall ill and die, ruin harvests, or cause a tree to fall on top of the pigs and turkeys. Many Q'eqchi' people, particularly the elderly, complain that young people today fail to ask permission and that they stir Tzuultaq'a into anger. They complain that people no longer show respect to each other, to God, to elders, and to the land. Sickness, poverty, crime, and poor crops result from this apathy.

> We say, that the corn doesn't turn out well anymore, that we don't have any more corn, that the corn is so small. Because we don't use anything anymore, because we don't burn copal pom anymore, that we are ashamed to burn our candles, to ask permission of God. (Videotaped interview with Agustin)

> A man was walking on a road. He was on a mountain where there were no people. He found a very small baby chick. He carried this little chick home and it started to grow. When the hen was big, the man found a rooster to mate with her. The hen gave his family a total of fifty eggs. The woman of the house took care of the eggs and they all began to grow into chickens. As they were growing bigger, the woman said that they should eat the hen because she was old and she could not give them any more eggs. "Let's eat her," she said. They killed the hen and ate her. A few days later, the woman's chicks began to die, one by one. Soon they all died. Not one survived.

>   The hen, you see, belonged to Tzuultaq'a and the people should have shown more respect. Tzuultaq'a did not like it when they killed his hen. This angered him. Tzuultaq'a wanted to help these people but they did not appreciate what he had given them. They should have kept the hen and burned some incense in order to show their thanks but they did not do this. They might have been able to eat the hen after all but they should have asked permission first. (Audio-taped interview with Mariano)

Requesting permission is the practice of paying respect at both the individual and community level. Permission is requested through community rituals, such as *mayahaac,* and within more personal or familial domains, such as during the sowing ritual (which has individual and community realms), or when an individual prays before a home altar. Prayer is almost always accompanied by more active forms of respect, with the payment of food, the burning of copal pom, and the observance of social norms and specific ritual taboos. Practically every Catholic home in Livingston has an altar where individuals and families pray to both God and Tzuultaq'a, burn pom and candles, and leave food as an offering. Although the Christian

God does not eat, Tzuultaq'a is always hungry. He loves to consume sweet copal, and this tree resin is burned at all Q'eqchi' rituals. Candles, cigarettes, tortillas, and liquor are also fed to Tzuultaq'a. Individuals must physically pay or feed the voracious appetite of Tzuultaq'a, which is a way of actively respecting and fortifying the relationship they and the community have with this quasi-foreign deity.

INVISIBLE MASTERS

The Q'eqchi' distinguish between the Judeo-Christian God and Tzuultaq'a, but at the same time, in narratives and prayer, they often blend God and Tzuultaq'a into one supreme figure. Both supernatural powers are referred to as God (q. *Tyox,* sp. *Dios*) and as owners. It often takes an ethnographer's inquiry for people to discriminate between the two, which they do by describing Tzuultaq'a as created by God to protect God's creations. While Tzuultaq'a is the owner of the land, the Christian God has ultimate power because God created Tzuultaq'a. Tzuultaq'a, then, is God's agent controlling the land his/her superior created.

> Sure, it is for sure that there are Tzuultaq'a, but they are like *mayordomos,* like an administrator. He handles all the things that God passes on to him. It is like if there was a patron who lived in the capital, and if he had his land here, then they would have an adminstrator that took care of the workers. And so, he is like the adminstrator, it's like having a servant here for his land, for his finca, right? (Videotaped interview with Agustin)

Mayordomo has many meanings, including an intermediary between a patron and workers, and a ritual office holder within a cofradía. In this case, Agustin is referring to the former. On fincas, mayordomos are the managers—the administrators—who run the finca for their, usually foreign, patron. Within their domains, mayordomos occupy positions of power, at least compared to the laborers, but in wider political fields they are merely one of the owner's mozos. While Tzuultaq'a govern the regions that surround their mountains, they are only following the orders of their patron— God. God created Tzuultaq'a to help in the governance of the land, so that the people on earth would be able to reach the intangible God through a tangible entity—the hills. Every individual with whom I spoke agreed to

AGUSTÍN

this—God made Tzuultaq'a and they are present in the hills to serve the almighty and invisible God.

Agustin also reveals how God is perceived as a *patrón en absentia,* referring to the supreme deity as an individual who owns a finca in the countryside but who resides in the capital. This perception implies abundant wealth, since all capitalaños, like all foreigners, are believed to be well-to-do. That God is intangible and invisible is also vital to understanding the relationship between Q'eqchi' and outsiders. Vision maintains the power of patrons. Absentee landowners, like God, are not viewable, but they have eyes in their intermediaries, means to oversee the workings of their fincas. (Sight and intangibility as elements of power in these relationships are discussed more extensively in Chapter 7.)

Q'eqchi' people unanimously believe that they cannot see God, that he is *en espíritu* (sp. in spirit). They often say the same thing about the Tzuultaq'a, even though the mountain spirits can manifest themselves visually. As hills they are more discernible, and as snakes and humanlike spirits they can reveal themselves to individuals, often doing so in dreams or when someone is alone in the jungle. Even so, Tzuultaq'a are only visible when an individual or community is doing something socially immoral or failing to practice respect. Agustin continues:

> Well, they say before, that before they used to see various ones. They would reveal themselves as a little old man, or as a woman, and everything. I mean that they are people, but they are invisible, they are invisible. They can appear, but only when someone is doing something bad, because if they personally arrive and appear to someone, when someone is good or healthy, they can make that person ill too.

Agustin's community in Tactic, where he lived before moving to Livingston, was forgetting to revere the hills. Three Tzuultaq'a appeared before him in a dream, manifest as light-skinned women. They were angry and hungry, so they made their presence visible to the irreverent followers. They arrived suddenly to reveal their wrath, to indicate that they were aware that the community failed to actively respect them.

> This happened one time in my dreams. Two women arrived before me, but they had hair like you, blonde too, all blonde. Ah, there were three of them . . . All right. "Well, look, excuse us, we came to ask you a favor, if you would please look for some three handfuls of corn *maza,*" they told me. "Because no one thinks of us anymore. No one, none of the people think of us anymore," they told me. "The people don't think of us anymore. Because in the past," they told me, "the people used to think of us, they would provide for us. But now no one gives us anything. Now we are hungry."

Tzuultaq'a love to consume and they get hungry when people fail to pay them with copal smoke, which is considered an essential food item for the mountain spirits. By feeding and respecting Tzuultaq'a, individuals and communities ensure bountiful harvests, safe travel, and health.[5] By providing for Tzuultaq'a, individuals and communities reproduce social and moral structures as they secure their positions as recipients of provisions from the benevolent mountain spirit. However, if they fail to show respect, Tzuultaq'a will appear and, if so, mountain spirits cause a number of predicaments. Visible mountain spirits can cause illness and sensory distortion (see Chapter 7). Tzuultaq'a can also create droughts, floods, snakebites, and dangerous plunges into caves or other holes in the ground. Tzuultaq'a are thus providers and takers; they are equally benevolent and malevolent.

PATERNAL PROVIDERS

Not only are the Tzuultaq'a considered fore(wo)men, but they are also conceived of as kin, as paternal providers of care and nourishment.

> Among us, the Q'eqchi's, when someone prays, they begin by saying "God—Mother God, Father God, Mother God, Father God." A feminine God and masculine God. And they also mention many Tzuultaq'a. Tzuultaq'a are the hills and valleys. This is because they say that we have a mother, and mothers feed us with milk, with breast milk, and with this we live. Tzuultaq'a gives us food too. They give us corn and beans, rice, everything that is grown. (Audiotaped interview with Martín)

That an outside entity can be considered simultaneously kin and commander further substantiates the hybridity involved when multiple connections are meshed into one multifaceted being. It also demonstrates the slippage between providing outsiders and kin members who form family and community. For example, in the quote above, Martín demonstrates that in prayer Tzuultaq'a (and also the Christian God) is *inna', inyuwa'* (q. my mother, my father). The thirteen Tzuultaq'a in Alta Verapaz are related by blood ties, as San Vicente and Xukaneb', two of the thirteen, are brothers (Wilson 1995:55). Likewise, at death, family members become ancestors who then take on certain characteristics of outsiders, such as being invisible and demanding respect and food on Todos Santos. Foreign patrons (and anthropologists) are often asked to be *compadres* (sp. godparents) of young indigenous children, thus formally and ritually making them family. In the Q'eqchi' imaginary, foreignness and kinship are not opposing essences, but merely mutable characteristics in ever-changing relations.

Foreign finqueros seep into the Q'eqchi' perception of Tzuultaq'a, as evinced in the numerous references to these outside owners in the above discussion on Tzuultaq'a. Exchanges between Q'eqchi' workers and their foreign patrons, like Q'eqchi' believers and Tzuultaq'a, embody some of the essential logics that reify these relationships and reproduce imaginary structures that guide morality. Both finqueros and Tzuultaq'a are invisible overseers who provide and impair; they are owners of their fincas/land; they are identified as cultural hybrids; their connections to the Q'eqchi' people follow similar semiotics of payment and consumption; and they are imagined as simultaneously foreign and kin.

THE GERMANS

More than fifty years ago, Antonio Goubaud Carrera (1949) wrote in his diary a description of a Q'eqchi' woman's dream, in which she encountered a pale, blonde German who turned out to be the owner of the hill—a Tzuultaq'a. The woman, instead of respecting and treating the foreigner kindly, was frightened, and screamed. Goubaud Carrera reports that, because of her disrespect, she would never receive the fortune carried on the German's mule.

I had been in Livingston only a few days when I first heard about *los alemanes* (sp. Germans). Lola's husband, Alberto, was helping me look for a house to rent, but we got stuck in a violent rainstorm. My field notes read:

> While we waited for the rain to stop, he told me about the Germans in Alta Verapaz. Because they came with no wives, they had to find wives in the indigenous population. For this reason, he says, there are many *naturales* who look German, with blonde hair and blue eyes. He tells me his two little children are light-skinned with light hair because his grandmother was *una cruz,* a mix between a German man and an indigenous woman.

While they ranged from narratives of foreign exploitation to tales of admiration, nearly everyone has stories about the Germans. Many have first-hand experience because a large majority of Q'eqchi' over the age of forty were born on fincas owned by German descendants. Germans are not only a force experienced by previous generations; they symbolize something very much in the present. Q'eqchi' people see and re-experience them everyday.

> The Germans love to teach the Indians how to work. They are not egotistical at all. They show them how to be mechanics, how to be blacksmiths, how to run the machines that grind the coffee, all types of work. . . . This is what I saw on the plantations in Alta Verapaz. This is where I learned too. (Audiotaped interview with Carlos [not his real name])

Although in Chapter 3 I emphasized the exploitative nature of the historic relationship between the Q'eqchi'-as-laborers and the Germans-as-patrons, the actual sentiment of the Q'eqchi' people regarding their German patrons is somewhat different. Many people praise the Germans, including Lola, who once spoke of her German patrons when I was visiting her after she gave birth to her youngest daughter, Sulma. At the time she was spending the traditional forty-day postpartum period of seclusion away from the community in her home in Crique Chino Barrio Nuevo. Lola was reminiscing about the German coffee and cattle-raising finca that she grew up on in Senahú. She told me how nice the Germans were to her and her family, and how they took care of all their workers, providing them with concrete-block houses and even helping young mothers without husbands. Eventually, the patrons sold the finca where she lived. The new, non-German owners reorganized; Lola and her husband then left for Livingston. Remembering them as kind and caring, Q'eqchi' people like Lola and Carlos respect and admire the Germans.

There is another side to this story, however. Manuel, for example, complains that he received only ten *centavos* a day on the German-operated fincas of Alta Verapaz, and children earned only two. They worked like animals, from six in the morning until five at night. "Who would like this?" he asks. Unfortunately, he tells me, they had no other option because they had no land (he and his family migrated to Livingston with the goal of obtaining land). Considering life in Alta Verapaz as slavery, Manuel remembers patrons who went to the government offices for assistance in forcing their indigenous laborers to work. Because the patron and the government were one and the same, he says, the finqueros had all the power. If they wanted land, they could remove you from yours. If they wanted labor, with support of the local and federal government, they had no trouble finding the needed bodies.

GERMANS: RESPECTING OWNERS

And my father, he is the son of Germans. Uhuh. Yes. This is why I speak some [Spanish] too. But I do not speak much in Spanish because we did not grow up with my father. We grew up alone because my father, because he had a finca. This is where he was. And my mother, well he didn't want her. This is because they say that he had lots of women, my father did. (Videotaped interview with Juana)

German finqueros share numerous similarities with Tzuultaq'a and the Judeo-Christian God. Finqueros are often invisible (through absence), and they are certainly perceived as givers and takers. Because they have assaulted laboring and female reproductive bodies, as well as been godparents to children of Q'eqchi' laborers, the Germans are "kin," related biologically and ritually.[6] Further, finqueros are highly respected and, like Tzuultaq'a, they are actively paid with the fruits of Q'eqchi' labor. In fact, the semiotic and linguistic means through which Tzuultaq'a and foreign patrons are provided respect is the same.

The Q'eqchi' language exhibits two kinds of respect—one for showing respect to outsiders like Tzuultaq'a and foreign patrons (*kehok sa snaq xpaab'ankil*), and one for expressing interpersonal respect within the living community (*loq'inkil*). The first, more externalized version of respect is from the verb *paab'ankil*, which means "to obey," "to believe," and "to serve one's religion." Because *kehok* means "to put into action" or "make worthwhile" and *naq* is "when," *kehok sa snaq xpaab'ankil* is roughly translated as "making it happen when you respect." This external-oriented respect one pays to Tzuultaq'a and finqueros is the same active type offered to other superiors, foreign anthropologists, ancestors, and God.

Interpersonal respect (*loq'inkil*) between kin and *paisanos* (sp. fellow country person, used generally to mean fellow Q'eqchi') is far more intimate and stems from the verb *lok'oc*, which means "to buy." The stem *lok'oc* is also the word for "regarded highly" and "revered," as in *loq'laj ch'och*, "the saintly world." Thus, it appears that you can buy prestige by actively respecting and maintaining one's community and kin. This form of respect is practiced through communal house construction, community-supported rituals, and through appropriate actions of respect to kin and community members.

Intimate (community and family) and extrinsic (deities, finqueros, ancestors) expressions of respect indicate that respect is a relationship and an

JUANA

action. Respect is not an object; there is no single noun in Q'eqchi' that translates into respect. Rather, respect is understood as an active process—as obedience, belief, labor, paying debts, and buying esteem. Respect is expressed and given meaning through relationships between people, land, deities, owners, and institutions.

> He is the owner of everything, first and foremost. God is the owner of everything in the world. This is why nothing turns out right without respect to him. You must ask God for permission so that he will give you chicks. (Audiotaped interview with Felicia [not her real name], an Evangélica who works for a North American–owned hotel)

Like most Mayan peoples of Central America and Mexico, the Q'eqchi' of Livingston are Christians, either Protestant (known throughout Guatemala as *Evangélicos*) or Catholic (*Católicos*). Differences certainly exist between their cosmological worlds, but so do similarities. Not all Catholics perform ritual to Tzuultaq'a, although nearly all, except those most heavily influenced by Catholic Action doctrine,[7] believe in their existence (Warren 1989:108–110; Wilson 1995:190). Yet, even the most fundamentalist Catholics and Evangélicos speak of mountain spirits, although they may claim they are the devil (sp. *el diablo,* q. *ma us*). Even so, Felicia, an Evangélica, and Juana, a Católica, say that the mountain lives (q. *yo' yo li tzuul*).

Ideas regarding ownership likewise cross the faiths, such as how both Catholics and Protestants refer to the Christian God as an "owner." I understood that Tzuultaq'a was considered an owner, but I was caught off guard by the fact that the Christian God, too, was defined by this economic term. This realization prompted me to go to the Catholic church in Livingston to talk to the priests and catechists, to see where their congregation learned the concept of God-as-owner. The priests, so they told me, do not refer to God as an owner. While perhaps calling him creator or maker, the priests and Martín, the catechist, denied ever calling God an owner during Mass or Bible Study. I also inquired about this issue to an Evangelical pastor, who as well responded that he did not refer to God as an owner, either in Spanish or in Q'eqchi'. Why then, do so many Q'eqchi' people tell me that God is the ultimate owner? If they did not learn it through their religious communities, then where was this understanding of God-as-owner acquired? What exactly are the internalized moral codes that guide behavior and how do they actively bolster practice and perception?

PRACTICING MORALITY

> For the collective force is not entirely outside of us; it does not act upon us wholly from without; but rather, since society cannot exist except in and through individual consciousnesses, this force must also penetrate us and organize itself within us; it thus becomes an integral part of our being, and by that very fact this is elevated and magnified. (Durkheim 1976 [1915]:209)

Q'eqchi' practice and perception is guided by an internalized script that is formulated by an active history. This imaginary is a historical subject that produces, structures, and reveals itself through a deeply ingrained social consensus that has been so naturalized that its historical component is denied. Through everyday socialization and practice, extrapersonal world structures are internalized as an intrapersonal, culturally maintained imaginary (Ortner 1989:127; Strauss and Quinn 1997:6). This internalized model, which is reinforced through practice, is a *cultural scheme* that embodies and solves political and economic contradictions (Ortner 1989:196).[8] "Instituted differences," are embedded into this imaginary, and "transmuted into natural distinction" (Bourdieu 1990:152). Meanings are then attached by individuals to "all interpersonal and institutional relations" (Holland et al. 1998:26–27).

As a means of categorization, internal imaginaries are not hard-wired blueprints, but imprecise knowledge that allows individuals to be flexible within a variety of contexts. The moral codes that reify the imaginary are not "hard-and-fast rules," because they are learned and reproduced everyday through practice that varies (Strauss and Quinn 1997:44). The structures of this imagined model consist of categorical relations that are realized within different social fields and are alterable and adaptable.[9] They are invented "spaces of representation" or "imagined landscapes" that guide but do not overrule perception and practice (Harvey 1989:218).

For centuries, the economic and religious fields of the Q'eqchi' people have been governed by moral codes involving acts of respect, consumption, and debt to outsiders. The economic and religious fields, as well as associated social structures, have been conflated in an imagined landscape of morality. Religious ideas about reciprocity, nature, and exchange with deities/outsiders, and economic interchanges that involve paying respect to landowners and tribute to institutions, have merged into a field of morality with a broad scope—i.e., the Q'eqchi' imaginary. Driven by the semiotics expressed within religious and economic contexts, rules of conduct and structural linkages have transcended their original meanings. Moral codes, although originally structured through religion and economics, have become meshed and so intricately connected through the centuries that they have become an imagined field of perception that can be expressed in links not necessarily religious nor economic, but more broadly cultural and social. As noted, morality is a historical consciousness that is not confined to one expressive mode; "it may be created and conveyed—with great subtlety and no less 'truth'—in a variety of genres" (Comaroff and Comaroff 1992:159).

Morality is a broad set of categories that socially bind groups of people who use their moral codes to explain who they are and who they are not,

how they should act, and how they should think.[10] Morality is a base component of how all societies organize relationships (Howell 1997:9). Moralities are flexible and fluid through time and space, and always within personal and wider realms of power. Yet, while flexible, they are still shared
by many who adhere to them, consciously and unconsciously. Supplied
with these shared moral codes, individuals are actors who interpret specific
fields of action and then attach meaning to the relationships that structure that field. With moralities in motion, people interpret and sustain
differences.[11]

To understand morality, I borrow from Mary Douglas, who applied her
understanding of *matter out of place* to material actions, taboos, and societal
structures (1966:35). While Douglas conceded that moral codes are more
difficult to pin down than pollution taboos, she concluded that moral in-
justices go hand in hand with defilement and dirt. She views immorality
as being created when something is found to be out of place, when something does not fit into a constructed idea of what is moral or "in place."
Because she defines purity as matter in place, or as following a positive
structure that must not be negated, she claims that purity is the enemy
of ambiguity and change. "When there is no differentiation, there is no
defilement" (1966:169). Like pollution, which only occurs when there is
difference, immorality surfaces through an encounter with the unknown
and foreign.

Morality and immorality among the Q'eqchi', however, are not about
matter as much as they are about action. Individuals, for example, practice
their morality through acts of respect, and respect itself can only be interpreted as a process of doing. Thus, I replace Douglas' *matter* with *action*.
Q'eqchi' morality is *action-in-place*, active adherence to a socialized and
moralized imaginary. Conversely, immorality, emerging from displaced
and nonproductive conduct, is *action-out-of-place*.[12] Because society consists
of "people joined or separated by lines which must be respected" (Douglas
1966:138), a breach in moral codes ensues when these relationships are not
actively maintained.

As a symbolic ordering that emerges from action, the guiding moral
framework is the Q'eqchi' imaginary, employed by the Q'eqchi' to define a
wide spectrum of social activity and perception, including crime, sexuality,
identity, and illness. It is their imaginary that defines who acts appropriately, to whom one should pay respect, who should be feared and labeled
a criminal, and who is kin. Because of the conflation of religious and economic fields, which position people in exchanges with outside owners,
the Q'eqchi' imaginary tentatively categorizes subjects into insiders and

outsiders, and subsequently into "owners" and "non-owners." Thus, God is an "owner," parents act as masters of their children, and ethnographers are positioned as figurative possessors of collaborative endeavors. Outside owners, however, are only reconfigured and positioned as recipients of respect and payment if their actions are indicative of moral practice—in other words, if they act-in-place.

IMAGINING THE GLOBAL STRUCTURE THROUGH LOCAL VISION

A transnational network that links individuals to social relations, communities, and broader institutionalized structures, and subsequently collapses the global with the local, is an appropriate trope—a didactic tool—for conceptualizing the internalized structure that guides Q'eqchi' action (Portes et al. 1999:220). First, transnational networks have contradictory poles with no centers (Kearney 1996:124; Roseberry 1989:216). Power reveals itself through interaction, rather than originating at one pole or central core and then dominating the periphery. Likewise, there is no center in the web of relations in which the Q'eqchi' perceive and practice; connections are constantly refigured and reified through practice, and subjects are in a constant state of positioning. Second, in transnational networks, communities are no longer bounded territories but rather webs of circuits that change, wane, and ebb through processes of migration, globalization, trade, politics, and tourism. Borders are proliferating and the community is "a site in which transnationally organized circuits of capital, labor, and communications intersect with one another and with local ways of life" (Rouse 1991:10).[13] The "Q'eqchi' community" I speak of is not bounded by spatial markers, but rather is fluid and transmutable across fields and through time and space.

Lastly, a transnational network is a congruence of present, past, and even, potentially, future relationships; it is manifest in practices and perceptions that are bolstered by cross-temporal and multi-spatial links (Hannerz 1996:34). Practice unfolds in time, allowing actors to anticipate and define the future, and governs the connections to the past and future that always occur within fields of power (Bourdieu 1990:81). In the Q'eqchi' imaginary, not only are Q'eqchi' people connected to the Garifuna in New York City and Livingston, but also to sixteenth-century Dominican friars, nineteenth-century German exporters, and twenty-first-century backpacking tourists. All of these relationships are conceived, explained, and maintained as part of a transnational network sustained by locals, migrants, tourists, foreigners, and transcendental owners. The network is an invented landscape of global and intimate connections that provides efficacy to social practices, perception, and morality in motion.[14]

Five

PRIVATE CONSUMPTION,
COMMUNITIES, AND KIN

Imagine a ravenous outsider who, after an initial bite of difference, salivates to consume more. This is not an image unique to Guatemala or to the Mayan people. It can be applied to many relationships, whether colonial, filial, cultural, or economic. Though Q'eqchi' people may direct the process through ritualized action, consumption is clearly associated with foreign paternalism. Like Tzuultaq'a, who ingest sweet copal smoke and indigenous bodies in exchange for security, foreign owners of fincas or hotels and restaurants consume local labor and foreign dollars while they also protect and pay their workers. Foreign treasure hunters and tourists are different. They are criminals, eating cultural wealth without permission and consuming without reciprocating. So too is Guatemala's government conceived as a criminal institution that consumes social and economic capital. Through military force, land appropriation, surveillance, tourism, debt-peonage, neo-liberal economics, corruption, and laws, the nation maintains a political economic system where practically all the land, power, and money remain in the hands of a sliver of the population.[1]

The Río Dulce area — an environmentally protected region — demonstrates how policies of the Guatemala government favor foreign investment and the wealthy elite to the detriment of local people and the environment. EXMIBAL (Empresa Exploraciones y Explotaciones Mineras de Izabal), the Canadian-owned company granted the concession to freely mine nickel throughout the Franja Transversal del Norte (FTN), is no exception. Supported by the government through policies and tax exemptions while destroying the local environment, EXMIBAL is another example of a cannibalizing criminal (see Mejía 1997).

Alberto once told me that when EXMIBAL arrived to build its nickel-mining plant in El Estor, the gringos (for the Q'eqchi', any pale-skinned foreigners) went to a big serpent in the hills to ask permission to mine the ore. The serpent denied their request. Since gringos will do anything to earn money, the foreign bosses gathered up Q'eqchi' people, took them to the hill where the snake lived, and threw them into a hole. With his great hunger satisfied, the serpent granted permission to the gringos to build their factory and dig deep into the earth.

EXMIBAL's actions are interpreted by the same moral logics that guide Q'eqchi' interaction with deities, finqueros, and other outsiders. Thus, the company bosses feed and pay homage to the mountain spirit. However, instead of paying with ideological reverence or candles, the gringos, ironically, pay the mountain spirit with local indigenous bodies. And, even though the company must adhere to moral codes, these foreign owners assist in the consumption and exploitation of local people, because even benevolent outsiders have the potential to harm. Therefore, Q'eqchi' people make the ultimate sacrifice when they are consumed by the hungry owner of the mountain, paying with their lives for the assumed "development" of the community.

Unlike locals, foreign owners can leave at will. EXMIBAL, in fact, did pack up, sever moral and economic ties to the El Estor community, and safely return to its faraway home. Similarly, tourists, travelers, and treasure hunters traverse the Q'eqchi' imaginary as criminals, never stopping long enough to create moral links or economic exchanges. Consuming monetary and cultural treasures, they are conceived as selfish and extremely disrespectful. Because they pass through the community only briefly before returning to their native homes, these criminal visitors are not expected to reify a moral relationship with the Q'eqchi' community and with their mountain spirits, nor are they easily punished for extreme displays of wealth. They are not even peripheral members of the community; they are malevolent outsiders who consume without reciprocating (see Chapter 9).

Ambivalence permeates Q'eqchi' understandings of foreigners—an insidious criminal and a benevolent provider can exist within a single foreign entity. All foreigners have some criminally orientated characteristics, as they can all assume positions of being hungry and expecting to be fed in the form of labor, food, knowledge, and reverence. But some foreign institutions reciprocate by providing. They forge a bidirectional exchange with people, community, and the land. As well as stealing riches and bodies, foreigners can create affinities with the Q'eqchi' by serving as providers, patrons, and partial and ritual kin. They are then categorized in the Q'eqchi' imaginary with other owning outsiders, such as finqueros and Tzuultaq'a. The foreigners who do not make social connections—tourists and treasure hunters—are expected to be completely selfish. Not related as kin or exchanger, these types of foreign criminals are not bound by a Q'eqchi' morality. They have no obligation to anyone but themselves, and they are only concerned with their foreign interests. EXMIBAL, on the other hand, ate up nickel, lands, and cultural knowledge, exploited labor, destroyed the environment, and collected debts, but they were equally expected to reciprocate by providing food, wages, houses, and security.

CONSUMPTION: THE HUNGRY Q'EQ

Consumption has various tangible and abstract meanings. It is a form of cultural cannibalism where the exertion of power symbolically eats difference. It is the commodification of social relations where people and objects are exchanged (hooks 1992:21–39). Consumption is knowledge, power, and pleasure gained through visual politics and sight: photography, voyeurism, surveillance, pornography, and lust (Barthes 1981:99–100; Foucault 1977:195–228; Mulvey 1989:14–26; Rose 1988:115–126). It ranges from tourists snapping photos and ethnographers envisioning culture to colonial powers erasing difference, displacing people, raping women, torturing bodies, and appropriating native cultures (Root 1996:1–25).

Consumption, however, is also about power and choice (Lash and Urry 1994:57–58; Strathern 1991:594–598). Power shifts back and forth between subjects through acts of consumption, respect, and exchange. As consumers feed on products, they forge relations with the producers. Whether the products are humans produced through biological reproduction, cash crops from agriculture, or cultures, communities, and ideas, consumption is possible only through active practices.[2] Q'eqchi' people are unable to direct or deter with global economics, free trade, and tourism—all contemporary economic and cultural forms of grazing—and they cannot prevent anthropologists from entering their communities to consume ethnographic subjects through text and image. Neither can they immediately alter the inequality that persists in Guatemala. But they can act-in-place and control consumption in such a way that they ensure abundant harvests, healthy hens, and stable communities. By feeding outsiders, Q'eqchi' symbolically labor and recreate communities and selves (Foster 1997:5; Strathern 1991:594–595). Foreign consumption is controlled and used for empowerment.

> **Juliana:** Q'eq? The thing that kills people? That animal kills people.

Hilary: Do they live around here?
Juliana: No, not around here.
Hilary: Where do they live?
Juliana: In fincas, in large fincas. Maybe they live in Tameja where we went, where they tap the rubber. I think they are there.

The mythic Q'eq[3] demonstrates the ambiguity between foreign owners who reciprocate and foreign criminals who endanger and perpetrate. I once recorded Felipe as he explained the mythical Q'eq. On this day, he brought me plantains and I offered him sweet bread and coffee.

> It is a black man that walks, that likes to roam during the night. Yes, but he looks like a dog. And he smokes a cigar. He begins to smoke. What he is going to rob is in the house, he will rob something there. He will come look for things to steal. They say that this little black man eats eggs. When you pass nearby him, your hair will stand straight up. Yes, your hair will stand straight up. (Audiotaped interview)

Martín also talks about his father's experiences with Q'eq:

> My father told me that when he lived in Alta Verapaz, he worked with a finquero, and this finquero owned some two or three Q'eq. He says that they are like dogs. They guard the coffee plantations so that robbers will not enter, so he tells me. Many Q'eq existed in Alta Verapaz. I am not sure if they still exist today, but people say they do. Sometimes at night when someone hears whistling from the bush, they say it is the Q'eq passing by. He is an animal who walks but fast, fast, fast! They say he is as fast as a car, but he is an animal. (Audiotaped interview)

Everyone knows of this half-man/half-animal, although there is some minimal disagreement as to which type of animal this being represents (dog or cow); its potential to harm; and whether or not these creatures wander throughout Livingston today. Patrocinia, who lived down the hill from me and who taught me how to make proper tortillas, says there is a Q'eq at the finca in nearby Crique Maya, where her husband is from. Most people explain that Q'eq looks like a dog because he is small and hairy. Covered from

head to toe in thick black hair, he demonstrates his humanity by walking on two feet. Other than his bipedalism, he is a bestial transgressor. His
hairy chest is plated with iron that resists bullets, his knees and elbows are
bent backwards, and he is always smoking a cigar.

Q'eq was born on the German-owned fincas of Alta Verapaz when a
man had sexual intercourse with a cow. Most people explain that this person was a *moreno* (sp. a black person),[4] and Germans did have East Indians
working on their plantations during the nineteenth century (King 1974:31).
According to Felipe, the father of Q'eq is not a black man, but a cowboy or
ranch hand (sp. *vaquero*). Q'eq are owned by and submissive to the German
finqueros, some of whom possess as many as five or six of these animals.
They are the watchmen of the finca, protecting the coffee and cattle from
theft. If a criminal is trying to steal a cow or some coffee plants from the
finca at night, the Q'eq grabs and carries the thief to the owner's home for
sentencing.

Yet, Q'eq are more than guardians. Owned by powerful land-consuming
foreigners, they themselves are imbued with extraordinary strength and a
ravenous hunger for consumption. At night, they leave the fincas and fly[5]
to local homes in search of food and material items to satiate their incredible hunger. Individuals usually hear Q'eq rather than see him, so people
tell me that it is Q'eq flying by when the wind whistles or when dogs begin
barking in the middle of the night. If he wants to enter a home, Q'eq will
not use the door but will enter through the break between the walls and
the roof typically found in *rancho* houses.[6] When Q'eq is passing by, it is
best to stay inside because you may fall ill if you see him.[7]

Patrocinia told me about the day her brother saw a Q'eq. As she talked
to me, she removed dry corn from the cob. She pretended to mimic her
brother's frightened voice in a high-pitched, airy tone.

> When he is walking, he looks like he is walking backwards,
> backwards, backwards, but he is coming near. Your hair stands
> straight up and you do not feel anything. You cannot walk
> nor run. It is like you want to scream but you cannot. When
> my older brother was in El Estor, he saw one. He said "who is
> that standing over there smoking a cigar? I am going to pass
> by but I will grab a rock just in case." My brother neared the
> figure but he became very frightened. He wanted to run away
> and scream but he was unable. He was mute and could not
> move because he was so frightened.

Like other foreign entities, Q'eq have the ability to scare, cause illness, interrupt sensory perception, and devour.[8] Q'eq will eat anything left out —tortillas, chicken and beans—but their favorite food by far is eggs, which they consume by the dozen.

A notion of uncontrolled sexuality is associated with Q'eq. Like other foreign representatives (especially the Garifuna and foreign tourists in Livingston), Q'eq are viewed by Q'eqchi' people as hyper-sexualized beings.[9] Their consumption of eggs, symbols of fertility and reproduction, reinforce this image. This ravenous sexualized consumption is not very different from the Spaniard's past theft of wealth and women. Although no one explicitly said that Q'eq will enter homes to have sexual liaisons with females inside, this was clearly alluded to by women's warnings. Lola and Patrocinia would tell me to close my windows at night, admonishing me that something could slip into my bed while I slept. Sex always plays a prominent role in colonization (Behar 1989:178–180; Corbey 1988:76; hooks 1992:61–77; Mitchell 1988; Said 1978:219) and the hungry Q'eq are pseudo-colonizers. Taking into account that they are themselves owned by German finqueros, Q'eq represent foreign interests. Q'eq are possessions that obediently follow the orders of their masters and acquire their power to cause fear from their invisible foreign owners.

During his nightly escapades, a Q'eq indeed scares people and consumes what he encounters, although he also steals edible and inedible items (often shoes), in order to bring this loot back to his foreign owner. In typical foreign fashion and contrary to Q'eqchi' concepts of morality and community, Q'eq takes what is not his without sanction or permission. Likewise, it is the consuming foreign owner—the German patron—who is enriched by his *china q'eq* (q. little black man). Q'eq himself is only a possession. Like a dutiful son, Q'eq protects foreign owners and his bovine parents, both of which are European imports symbolizing foreign commerce. Maintaining his political and sexual strength through consumption, Q'eq pays reverence to his owner by supplying him with the wealth stolen during the night.

Tracing the origin of Q'eq is not simple. Many scholars of Maya folklore assume that these beings became part of Mayan mythology as a result of the Africans brought over after the conquest (Bricker 1981:129–144; Cabarrús 1979:31). Although African slaves were indeed brought to the New World as early as the sixteenth century and the myth was strengthened with their arrival, the mythicohistorical figure of Q'eq, like Tzuultaq'a, may well have a pre-Columbian origin. God M is a Postclassic deity who was black. He most likely became Ek Chuah (also a black god), the contact-period deity from the Yucatan who held special significance for cacao growers (Sanchiz Ochoa 1993). Ek Chuah (*ek* means "black" and chuah means "star" in Yucatec Mayan), God M, and the black God L, from whom the former gods may have emerged, were merchant gods who were worshipped by traders and travelers (Taube 1992:88). The origin of Q'eq is likely with these deities, who were eventually conflated with the few black slaves used on foreign plantations. Iconographically, Q'eq is also linked to Tzuultaq'a. The black deities associated with commerce resemble the black Chac, the ancient Mayan rain god whose essence now reverberates in the revered Tzuultaq'a. And, similar to Q'eq, Chac figures have been represented smoking a cigar (Taube 1992:79). Both Q'eq and Tzuultaq'a partially represent pre-Columbian deities that through time have shifted and shared characteristics. Still associated with business, money, agriculture, travel, and foreign interests, neither Q'eq nor Tzuultaq'a is simply a colonial invention.

DOMESTICATING THE FOREIGN BEAST

It is possible to domesticate Q'eq. I heard of various means by which individuals can control this consuming being. One method involves covering the hairy animal with the traditional female woven skirt and tripping it with the string belt that is typically wrapped around the skirt. This form of ensnarement reveals the ability of cultural traditions to overcome foreign-endowed and immorally orientated action.

> When you shoot him nothing will enter. But many say that one controls it when it is in the house. And if it is a woman, let's say that when women use corte, if one throws it on top or the string that is wrapped around corte is placed on the road and there they will stay. These are the secrets to capture them. (Videotaped interview with Armando)

Armando also mentions that when the Q'eq is in the house, it is under control. What this emphasizes is how easily a criminal entity can slip into a moral member of the family, simply by being inside the domestic unit. In a similar vein, Javiér, a young, highly educated Q'eqchi' man who now owns the previously foreign-owned hotel on the river, describes how Q'eq can be beaten into submission and made kin.

If a china q'eq comes into your house, you can grab it and start beating it with a belt. You beat this animal until he says "papa." Then it is yours and you can keep it, but you have to take really good care of this animal. People make extra rooms for the *negrito* and they keep lots of eggs on hand for him to eat. (Videotaped interview)

In this familial context, Q'eq is a child who acts-in-place by respecting his newly found parents. Therefore, it is not unrelated that Q'eq is restrained through a form of physical punishment I saw used on young children, since the relationship between children and parents is also governed by moral logic. Parents are recipients of obligated respect, and they often complain that the children of today fail to properly revere their elders. Incidentally, parents also describe themselves as the owners of their children. From my perspective, the manner in which some children are physically used as labor confirms that they are metaphorically "owned" by their parents. However, children can reverse the situation when they alter the socio-political relations of owners and the owned. Children grow older, get married, or get educated, thus transforming the structure that once maintained them as the "owned" youth.

Individuals do have agency within the socio-moral structure. Javiér's father, for example, resisted outside ownership and fought and earned himself a store, some land, and a motorboat. His story is worth repeating.

Javiér's father came from Cobán in the mid-seventies. Like other migrants, he went first to a small aldea located up-river from Livingston where he met his wife. There he had a milpa and a small cayuco that he used to fish in the river. Javiér's oldest brother was born during this time. Eventually, a wealthy Ladino family from Guatemala City came and told Javiér's father that he had to get off his land, that they were the "real" owners (they could have had a valid nineteenth-century title or else they blackmailed some official in Guatemala City). Javiér says that these rich people offered little compensation for the land and they were threatening to kill the people of the aldea if they did not succumb to their wishes. Javiér says his father knew the community had some rights simply because they had lived on the land for such an extended period, but he was unable to organize any formal resistance to the capitalaños. While each family accepted the one hundred quetzals offered to them for their parcels of land and left without a complaint, Javiér's father refused to succumb. He decided that he first needed to reap his corn harvest, which was not yet ready, and also that the rich family from Guatemala City would have to pay him more than one hundred quetzals. After telling the outsiders the appropriate value of his corn harvest and land, he said that they would have to pay him in full for both the corn and land. Otherwise, he would reap his harvest and expect payment for his land thereafter. Because of his insistence, the wealthy capitalaños paid Javiér's father what he wanted. With this payment, Javiér's family moved into the town of Livingston where they were the first Q'eqchi' family residing in the town proper. They purchased land and a small store that is now one of the primary stores for Q'eqchi' people who live in the aldeas outside of town. Felipe, for example, sells his corn to Javiér's father, who then sells it to people who live in town. Javiér attended college in Puerto Barrios and now owns a popular tourist hotel with his European wife. He is well educated and well-off financially. It is not surprising, then, that he is the man who reverses ownership by beating the foreign Q'eq into submission.

CONSUMING KIN AND COMMUNITY

> Ah, when I told you that I wanted to go to school? Oh, yes,
> I want to go, but my mother won't allow me to attend. This
> is because I have to help my mother make tortillas, wash, and
> do everything around the house. (Videotaped interview with
> Matilde)

Girls, more so than boys, are *often* forbidden to attend school so that they can stay home and assist with domestic chores. Even though parents and children value education highly, they are in an economic position where they cannot afford to lose a laboring body. Even for children who do attend school in Livingston, after school and on days off they are dutiful to their parents. Boys help their fathers in the milpa or in carrying loads of firewood. Girls learn how to make *wa* (q. tortillas), wash clothes, and cook. From the time girls are big and strong enough to hold an infant, they help care for their younger siblings. It is not uncommon to see a little girl carrying and tending to a child only minimally smaller and younger than herself. While children are obligated to help with domestic chores, most parents complain that their children are lazy and disobedient and that they refuse to help when needed.

Since children are virtually "owned" by their parents, when a young couple wants to get married, the couple's parents must strike a deal. The boy's parents find an intermediary to help with the negotiation. If the family is Catholic, the boy, his family, and the intermediary, who is called *testiig* (a Q'eqchi' loan word from Spanish—*testigo* means "witness"), go to church to first ask God's permission. Then they head to the girl's home, where they proceed through a highly ritualized set of questions, answers, denials, and requests. This practice is known as *tz'aamank* (q. request) or *pedida* (sp.), and in most cases it occurs over three, if not four or five, separate occasions. On the first and second visit, if the households are Catholic, the boy's family typically brings a few centavos, which they leave on the girl's family altar as a symbolic offering. The boy does not come with his parents the first time.

Parents tell me that they always refuse initially, stating that their daughter is too young or that they still need her to help around the house. They often hand back the centavos in order to symbolically demonstrate the rejection of the offer. By the third or fourth visit, after the boy has talked to the girl's parents, the girl's parents relent or else the boy's family negotiates a deal satisfactory to both families. The girl does not participate in this formalized ritual. Instead, she hides in another room. Ultimately, it is up to the father whether he permits his daughter to marry or not.

Post-marital residence traditionally follows a patrilocal pattern—girls go to live with the boy's family until the couple are able to build a place of their own. However, there are exceptions to this. For example, Lola's daughter Herlinda initially remained with her mother rather than going to live with her mother-in-law. Herlinda is Evangélica, and for her tz'aamank the groom's family came to her house three times. Each time they offered a few items, mostly pots, pans, and some food. Once an agreement is reached, the boys' families typically give monetary bridewealth, but Herlinda's situation was different. Her mother Lola's tortilla business required at least two women on a daily basis in addition to Lola herself. These women would make tortillas and help Lola with the many customers who waited patiently for their hot tortillas for breakfast, lunch, and supper. I would even assist Lola when she had large pre-arranged orders or when she was short of help (even though my tortillas were sub-standard). Lola did not want to lose her daughter's assistance, so the families made an arrangement. Herlinda was marrying Manuel and Lenora's son, Bex, and Manuel agreed that he would not provide any bridewealth if the newlyweds would reside with the bride's family. This seemed to work out fine for everyone. Manuel's family had little money and they were pleased to include Herlinda's family as part of their extended kin group. Anyway, Lenora had an older daughter who could help her in their kitchen. Monetary bridewealth offers are typically used to buy a new *huipil* (q. blouse), corte, and shoes for the bride.

One family, who received three hundred quetzals from the groom's family, said that brides' families rarely have any money left after purchasing the new *traje* (sp. traditional indigenous clothing) for the bride-to-be.

Along with the mandatory civil ceremony conducted in the municipalidad, many couples also have a religious wedding at their church. Both these marriage rituals are called *sumlaac* (q. wedding). For Catholics, there is yet another ritual that symbolizes the unity of both the couple and their respective families—the *uk'iha* (q. drinking of the water; also referred to as sumlaac), which can occur before or after the civil and religious ceremonies. Uk'iha refers to both the actual drink, a mixture of cacao and water, and the ritual itself. The ritual is also called *la entrega* (sp. the delivery), because the families escort the bride to the groom's home. I was able to attend two uk'iha, both of which were similar in structure, form, and content. Both times, I went with Mariano who, because of his prominent position in the community, was the testiig for both weddings. Uk'iha functions as a social exchange where the two families and the community share food, beverage, prayer, and advice with the newlywed couple. The ritual symbolically and physically delivers the girl to the boy's family, an often traumatic and tearful experience for the young girl. Lastly, the ritual feeds Tzuultaq'a and God, and in return these deities bless the newlyweds' union.

Uk'iha is an all-day event. Early in the morning, the boy's family goes to the girl's home. Upon reaching the house, the boy and each of his relatives light candles and walk toward the house where they are greeted by the girl and her family, all of whom also hold burning candles. The couple leads. The bride's family allows the boy's family to enter the house first. Upon entering, all kneel and pray before placing their candles around the altar. The burning of copal pom below the altar, the candles, and prayers are to please God and Tzuultaq'a so that they bless the young couple.[10]

Benches are set up for the families and friends and a *petate* (sp. reed mat) lies in front of the altar for the newlyweds. The couple takes their place on the petate. On one occasion, at the uk'iha of Candelaria and Juan, the couple sat on a vegetable crate rather than the traditional petate. The boy's family brings a pot of *caldo* (sp. spicy chicken stew) and *poch* (q. tamales), which they place on the altar. Another pot of caldo is already in place, put there by the girl's family. The tamales are food-offerings to Tzuultaq'a so s/he approves and offers permission for the union of the young couple; the families exchange the pots of caldo. Everyone drinks the uk'iha from individual gourds (sp. *guacales*). The couple shares the same guacal.

The father of the bride stands up and offers his advice to the young newlyweds. This advice usually demonstrates appropriate moral action, or

action-in-place. Honor your parents. Love your wife. Do not forget your mother. Dress well. Wash your husband's clothes. Cook his food. Do not fight. Work hard. Take care of your husband. Provide for your wife. Have children. This advice (sp. *consejos*) reinforces moral codes and, specifically, gender roles. Others follow the father, including the mother, the grandparents, and the godparents of the girl. The intermediary who initially helped with the marriage negotiations may also speak.

Bread and cola are served by the women of the girl's family. An elder spreads pom smoke over all the participants and the food, thus blessing everyone and everything involved. The sharing of the uk'iha signifies and sanctifies the bond formed between the couple, the families, and the community. The two families reciprocate by feeding one another and opening up their homes to their newly extended families and the community. The boy's family leaves early to return to their home to prepare for the second half of the day—the delivery of the new bride—although the groom stays with his bride. They now form their own union. Women from the bride's family offer caldo (a batch other than the one on the altar left by the boy's family), tortillas, and poch to everyone.

First served are the bride and groom, who are handed the food by the *madrina* (sp. grandmother) of the girl. The elder woman symbolically breaks apart either a wa or a poch, offering half to the boy and half to the girl. Food is then served in a hierarchical order that simulates community prestige: first the grandparents, then the parents, the intermediary, and the rest. Children are served last. The father says *wa'eko* (q. let's eat) and everyone sips their caldo and picks apart the chicken, while constantly dipping the tortilla or tamalito in the spicy liquid.

After eating, the girl's family helps the bride get ready to go to the husband's home, where his family is now preparing for her arrival. These days can require an incredible amount of walking. I attended one uk'iha where the girl lived in town and the boy lived out in Plan Grande Queveche. By the time we were done with the morning ritual at the girl's home, it was intensely hot and the two-hour walk through the jungle was not looking overly appealing. One long rest period and a bottle of *aguardiente* (sp. firewater), was needed to keep energy and spirits up.

When the girl's family arrives at the boy's home, each family member lights their candle. The couple again leads the group. Mirroring the morning's ceremony, the couple and the girl's family enter first, followed by the groom's family. All kneel and pray before placing the candles around the altar. On the altar are one or two pots of caldo and poch wrapped up in banana leaves. Pom burns continuously. Whatever saint images the family has, or has borrowed, are also on the altar.

The newlywed couple sits down on the petate in front of the family altar, patiently awaiting the advice of their elders. Uk'iha is served first. The girl and boy are now served their caldo by the boy's grandmother, if she is present. If she is not present, any female elder hands the couple the caldo and halves the wa or poch for them to share. (On one occasion, Mariano's mother broke and offered the tortilla to the couple, as the boy's grandmother was absent.) By the time the sumlaac has moved to the boy's home, most people have not regained their appetite from the morning. Banana leaves are handed out for people to carry meat and tortillas home to share with their loved ones. The practice of carrying home these ritual leftovers

(q. *xeel*) allows those of the community who are not present to share in this social event.

In this ritual context, consumption is a means of acknowledging a new set of social relations. The community consumes while the couple shares their own guacal and tortilla. Bringing home the xeel allows all members of the community to symbolically affirm the wedding bond. Plus, while people are physically expressing the new social ties through eating, Tzuul-taq'a eats tamales and smoke from the altar. Community consumption is sanctioned only through the feeding of the quasi-foreign Tzuultaq'a and the burning of candles for God.

In the boy's home, the father of the groom usually begins with the consejos, although Mariano did go first on one occasion. Consejos last for hours, sometimes with one individual, like Mariano, speaking for over an hour. Throughout all this advice, the boy and girl sit patiently on their petate, looking neither around nor at each other, quietly listening to the elder's advice. At the end of the advice, which is often the same as that given by the girl's family in the morning, everyone drinks another round of cacao water and this is the end of the uk'iha. The girl now stays with the boy. Sanctioned by the community, she is his wife. Some elderly people say that the newlyweds wait three days before engaging in a sexual relationship, but I am told this is not adhered to by all.

No longer do the parents "own" their children. A new structure and a new set of social ties are created. The boy and girl, now a unit, distinguish themselves from their families. Throughout the uk'iha ritual they sit together on petates and are united as they lead the family processions. Symbolizing the new social and political arrangement thus created, they now have the authority to lead, to break away from their families and redefine themselves as part of a new one. Although the young couple lives with the groom's family, they have some sort of space of their own. Either a little house is constructed for them or an area is created that offers minimal privacy. However, because they live with the groom's family, they are not fully independent. The boy still must help the father and the young woman is required to help the mother-in-law with domestic chores, a responsibility about which all new brides complain. In addition to helping the mother-in-law with cooking and making tortillas, she is also required to cook, clean, and care for her new husband.

When married children go to live in other households, some sort of moral obligation still maintains parental concern for that child. For example, when Herlinda's husband Bex fell ill, it was Manuel who had to purchase the needed injection. Lola, his mother-in-law, was mildly apathetic to the situation. She did not see it as her responsibility, but as his father's. Behind the larger rancho where Lola, Alberto, and their other five children slept, I visited Bex in the tiny wooden structure where he and his wife had their bed. Covered with a shroud-like sheet, Bex was shaking, sweating, moaning, and convulsing. I was quite nervous as I found myself in an ethnographic point of conflict, wondering whether I should or should not get help. I did not. And neither did Lola nor Herlinda, who waited for Bex's father to arrive in town after work so he could purchase the prescription. In no way did Lola feel any sort of moral obligation to this young man. She, after all, was not his mother.

Mariano told me that a man essentially owns his children and his wife. His wife is his possession (sp. *le pertenece,* she belongs to him). Because of this, it seems that a man has a socially sanctioned right to kill his wife if she is caught having an affair. For instance, stories circulated about the man who shot his wife, her lover, and then himself with a double barrel 16-gauge shotgun, and about the man who sliced his wife's throat with a machete after finding her in bed with another man. Reinforcing the moral codes on adultery and the social acceptance of male violence, these narratives infer that women should consider themselves lucky if their men merely beat them. Domestic violence is common and accepted; yet this does not mean that Q'eqchi' women passively accept this situation. Herlinda told me that she would hit and throw things at Bex when he beat her. Domestic violence is also an acceptable and a commonly offered reason for a woman to leave her husband and return to her family. Women would always ask me if my man had beaten me and they seemed skeptical when I claimed he had not.

While I was doing my fieldwork, I would occasionally go out at night and walk around town as many local people (although few single Q'eqchi' women) do to escape the heat of their homes or to simply get out. This is known as *paseando.* While this translates as "walking," what it really means is "wandering around" or "hanging out." My favorite place to *pasear* was in front of a K'iche' store where the owner's wife, Rosaria, cooked vegetarian tacos to sell during the evening. I would buy a bottle of cola or seltzer and watch people, an activity quite common in Livingston. I always found curious the manner in which a Q'eqchi' family walked through town. Rarely was there any variety. The man is first. The eldest son follows his father with younger children of both sexes trailing behind. Last, and always so, is the woman, usually carrying a young infant on her back. Rarely did I see a Q'eqchi' husband and wife walking side-by-side, although it is more common with young unmarried couples. Other people in town—Ladinos, Garifuna, and tourists—stay together as a group and couples often walk side-by-side, if not hand-in-hand. A Q'eqchi' family, on the other hand, walks in a straight line that often extends for a block or more. This style of walking through town is symbolic, as the man leads and thus decides where they stop and with whom they talk. The woman, who can keep an eye on the children, lags far behind, where she can make sure that the children do not stray and that they follow the father's directions.

And it is a man who gives direction. Child punishment is the responsibility of the father. I do not know how common this is in Livingston, but I did see Alberto threaten his children with his belt, and I even saw him tie his disobedient child up to a pole. In this case, the punished child seemed more to enjoy it than feel castigated, while Lola turned a blind eye as her older son sneakily untied his younger sibling. Mothers often explain that it is the man's duty to punish, that they would prefer to wait until the father comes home before taking any action. Men are the ones with the belts that are used to enforce a patriarchal authority, similar to how an owner establishes his right when he beats Q'eq. Belts enforce a dominant position. But this is also the man's right because, like his ability to hit his wife without retribution, he firmly has the right to physically punish his children who disobey his commands. Thus, the family walks in a straight line. Fathers lead and mothers follow behind, shooing children back into line before the patriarch sees that they have strayed.

Even so, gender relations are not easily defined. Women, it seems, are in charge of the money. If people have titles or usufruct land rights, these documents are often in the wife's name. Women own the small livestock, such as chicken, hens, turkeys, and pigs. Women therefore have considerable power within the household and with their husbands. Many men allude to the strength of women. They fear this power, especially at certain times of the month, such as during menstruation or when the moon is full. Furthermore, in sacred realms, egalitarianism seems to reign. During rituals, both men and women often have equal roles and responsibilities. Tzuultaq'a (and nature in general) is dual-gendered and referred to as Our Father, Our Mother (q. *Qaawa' Qana'*). Gender equality in religion, economics, and agriculture demonstrates that men are far from dominant, even in a so-called machismo society. Although a man does consider his wife and his children as possessions, he is far from completely controlling his woman. Her body, her power to reproduce, and her own economic viability keep her quite active in defining herself and resisting. To be possessed, owned, or consumed does not mean that you are docile (Strathern 1988:332).

CORN AND CONSUMPTION

Si no hay maíz, no comemos—If there is no corn, we do not eat.
(Lola while making tortillas)

Social scientists often describe colonial and other unequal power relationships as the consuming colonizer and the consumed colonized. Whether displayed through pornographic voyeurism where women are eaten by invisible eyes or through commerce where "primitive" art is appropriated and commodified by hungry Western capitalists, a metaphor of consumption is at the heart of relationships of power. Q'eqchi' Mayan people and Guatemala are no exceptions. Westernized countries have not just been nibbling, but symbolically gorging themselves on this country's Mayan culture. Yet, Q'eqchi' people also consume physically and metaphorically, and ritual consumption acts to bind the community and to acknowledge social ties while sanctioning payment to outsiders (Sieber 1999:99).

Corn (q. *ixim*), maintains a prominent position at the heart of Mayan identity and practice. Even when economic and religious changes undermine subsistence agriculture, the milpa as a way of life, although redefined, is maintained through flux (Annis 1987:60–74; Re Cruz 1996:76–78; Rojas Lima 1988:73–76). In Livingston, while most men hold permanent and semi-permanent hourly-wage jobs, the majority of them still keep their milpa.[11] An average of one to three manzanas of corn are grown in the aldeas by men who live and work in Livingston. This figure is significantly lower than the amount of land required for complete subsistence (Wilson 1995:42–44), although there are two corn harvests per year in Livingston. In May, the harvest is known as the *milpa quemado* (sp. burned field) and in December the harvest is called *matambre* or *milpa de verano* (sp. summer field). Men grow corn to supplement their wages. Women grind the corn into tortillas until it is gone and then they buy more from the store. Every day of the week, women cook and prepare eight to ten pounds of corn for tortillas.

Only those men who live in the aldeas and do not work in town actually sell some of their milpa for minimal profit. In 1996, a *quintal* of corn (approximately one hundred pounds) sold for about seventy quetzals and in 2005 it sold for approximately one hundred quetzals, although the price fluctuated depending on the national market.[12] Men complain that work in the milpa is too tough, too risky, and that they barely have enough time to keep their fields clean of weeds and overgrowth.[13] Their sons must help after school and on weekends. Men also complain that it costs too much to hire additional help during harvest. In fact, men (and sometimes their children) often came to me during this time, asking to borrow money so they could hire individuals to help them pick corn.

Q'eqchi' men, being recent migrants, do not own the land where they grow milpa. In the aldeas, many people have community rights to their land, something they are in the process of making official through INTA (*Instituto Nacional de Transformación Agraria*—The National Institute for Agrarian Transformation). With help from the organization CONIC (Coordinadora Nacional Indígena y Campesina—National Indigenous and Peasant Coordinator), Q'eqchi' communities from the aldeas are petitioning INTA to grant communal title to the land. Bureaucracy keeps this process at a snail's pace. The government sees communal land as an impasse to modernization, instead glamorizing individual ownership (Hernández Castillo et al. 1998:136–145). And, to some, INTA is a criminal arm of the government, benefiting wealthy and foreign investors and not following through on the delivery of titles (Mejía 1997:85). Conflict between different claimants may also deter the process. The signing of the Peace Accords, with its indigenous rights platform, promises to help indigenous people gain titles to communal land, but most individuals are rightly skeptical.

Everyone looks forward to March and late October when the young corn (sp. *elote*, q. *kux*) is ready to be picked. Corn atole, sweet tamales, and corn-on-the-cob are abundant at this time of year. Some people think ritual is necessary during the early harvest. Manuel tells me that he places kux on his altar and burns pom and candles as offerings to God and Tzuultaq'a, asking permission for the recently cut young corn and the future harvest. However, Juliana says that ritual is unnecessary at this point in the harvest. She and her husband do not request permission from Tzuultaq'a to cut their young corn.

Catholics participate in numerous rituals involving the corn harvest. The ritual performed by both the "owner" (not in a legal but in a spiritual sense) of the milpa and his wife at the time of planting is referred to as *k'ajb'ak* (q. to pray, perform ritual). For a certain number of days before and after the sowing, the man and woman must adhere to dietary and behavioral restrictions. People claim that these restrictions are in place for either three, eight, fourteen, or twenty days before and after the day of planting. Only the couple that is doing the sowing has to follow the restrictions; other members of the family and laborers who assist in the planting are not required to do so. Sex is prohibited, as is the consumption of processed food. Tortillas, beans, and coffee are the main staples during this time, and white bread and cheese are strictly forbidden. If one eats this type of Ladino or outsider's food, worms and insects will come and ruin the harvest. This food taboo prevents infestation by actively demonstrating respect to the sacred corn, God, the Q'eqchi' community, and, more importantly, to Tzuultaq'a. On the day chosen to plant, the owner of the field, who is always the male, rises early to pray in his milpa. During his prayers, he mentions the Tzuultaq'a in the Livingston area and from Cobán (or as many as he knows or can remember), asking for their permission to plant his corn. Male kin and friends then gather at his house. The wife of the house serves them breakfast and her husband gives each man his share of seeds, which are blessed having remained on the altar throughout the night.

I attended a sowing ritual at Matilde's home, where we both videotaped the event. While the men were out in the field, Concepción (Matilde's mother), her two daughters, and the four wives of the men who had gone to Matilde's father's field prepared the afternoon meal. At noon, Matilde's mother offered three large poch to Tzuultaq'a while burning pom and candles. Pom, she told me, is Tzuultaq'a's favorite food. Part of paying respect to Tzuultaq'a is feeding because s/he needs to consume if people want permission to also produce and consume corn. Matilde's mother told me that they invite the *mu* (q. shadow or soul) of the mountain to come eat. Just as a woman nurtures her children and family, she feeds Tzuultaq'a. As a man reproduces with his own "seeds," he plants his corn throughout the milpa. Woman and man have equal responsibilities in this ritual act of cultural, social, economic, and biological reproduction.

When the men returned from the field, the women quickly served them. The women were unsure whether I should be served with the men, although I assured them that I would wait and eat with the females. I expected more ritual or prayer associated with this lunch, but none occurred; it was simply a well-deserved meal (although, of course, one ritual cannot serve as an archetype for all other k'ajb'ak). After eating, the men left. Not one "thank you" was offered by either the men or the owner of the milpa. Expressing gratitude in this way is not necessary; this sort of community involvement is obligatory and expected. Planting reaffirms community as one that is moral, respecting, and economic. Owners are respected, paid, and fed. Permission for sowing is granted after both the man and wife demonstrate their reverence by acting-in-place. They must maintain their food taboos and sexual restrictions if they expect Tzuultaq'a to grant them an abundant harvest.

Tzuultaq'a, like Q'eq, is always hungry. Consumption, whether in the form of pom, candles, poch, turkey blood, or eggs, reaffirms the power and authority of these figures, both of whom have ties to foreign interests. Sacrifice maintains the relationship between the individual, the community, and the greater powers. Consumption, however, is not something practiced by the Christian God. People would tell me that God is different because he does not have an appetite for consumption like Tzuultaq'a. This distinction, I suggest, occurs because God is not manifest as foreign. God has no ethnicity, and this is why Q'eqchi' are averse to describing him physically. While people conceive Tzuultaq'a as either Ladino, German, gringo, or ancient Mayan, they hesitate when it comes to describing the Judeo-Christian God. They respond that because he is enveloped in light they cannot see him, and they have no idea what his ethnicity would be (though God is always considered male). Externally manifest only as a bright light, God may represent the purest and most supreme power, because he is intangible. Further, although in its origin Catholicism may have been a foreign institution, today people do not perceive the Christian God as serving an outside interest. Tzuultaq'a is externally manifest as foreign. (Even when perceived as an ancient Mayan it can be argued that this deity is still understood as a partial outsider with a voracious appetite.) God—unethnicized, intangible, and non-categorized—is not hungry like Tzuultaq'a.

People who fail to feed Tzuultaq'a or ask permission from God are blamed for many societal problems in Livingston. The soil's poor fertility is a result of people disregarding their responsibility to the spiritual authorities. Q'eqchi' continuously complain about the inadequate harvests and the inability of the land to produce as it used to. They blame their neighbors who act-out-of-place.

> The Evangélicos? They do not ask permission for anything.
> (Videotaped interview with Juliana)

Sentiments like Juliana's are commonly expressed. Catholics complain that because the Evangélicos, Garifuna, and Ladinos fail to ask permission and feed Tzuultaq'a and God, Livingston yields scant harvests. While much of the poor soil fertility has to do with the karst base, thin soil layer, and salt air, Q'eqchi' people continue to blame a non-acknowledgement of the symbolic relationship between the mountain spirit, the community, and the individual that structures daily and historical practices. Outsiders do not participate in these economic and moral relationships where, if one wants to be fed, one must also feed. To be an active member of the community, one must pay respect and sacrifice. Feeding and consuming are practices that reproduce the structural integrity of the Q'eqchi' imaginary and the social community.

Six

PUBLICLY PERFORMING MORALITIES AND INTERNALIZING VISION

Mariano once told me a story about a gringo who planned to go to a local cave to remove the treasures inside. The gringo was an incapable and slow walker (Q'eqchi' people always complain about gringos' lack of physical endurance), so he and his two Q'eqchi' guides had to spend the night in the bush. During the evening, the gringo had a dream. He was inside a cave filled with chickens when he heard a voice that told him that only natives were permitted to see the cave and its contents. He was warned that he would be punished if he went any further. The foreigner reported the dream to the local guides. They told him that he must not enter the cave, that a snake would bite him if he did. He turned back in fear and went home.

The ability to see and be seen is integral to the maintenance of Q'eqchi' moral networks. Peripheral keepers of the community, such as Tzuultaq'a and ancestors, remain out of sight until they become visible when social mores are disrupted. Overseers, those who see but rarely are seen, maintain power through metaphoric sight as means of control, consumption, and knowledge. The treasure-hunting gringo that Mariano spoke of was an outsider interested only in robbing wealth from the mountain spirit's home. Because he was an immoral intruder, the mountain spirit came to him in a dream to warn him of his digressions. But since the gringo was only passing by and was not an actively engaged member of the Q'eqchi' community, Tzuultaq'a remained out of sight. The gringo heard only a voice.

XAJLEB' KEJ: THE DEER DANCE

The Q'eqchi' people of Livingston had never seen a traditional dance in Livingston proper, other than the Garifuna dances of Yancunu and Pororo. In 1991, there was a Deer Dance in Crique Chino, and there was going to be one in Crique Chino Barrio Nuevo in 1996, until the Catholic Church decided against it because of the extreme expense involved.[1] Costumes cost three hundred quetzals to rent and the entire Catholic community of Crique Chino Barrio Nuevo had to support the endeavor in the form of money, food, labor, and time. Because there was no unified Catholic community in Crique Chino Barrio Nuevo or in Livingston, a situation common to many Latin American locations, consensus was not possible.

Martín told me that the community rejected the idea of having a Deer Dance because of the opinion of one man, Agustin, one of the active members of the video project. According to Martín, Agustin represented an orthodox form of charismatic Catholicism that opposes traditional rituals, community ritual payment, and reverence to saints and natural deities. Agustin vocalized his opposition to spending excess money on ritual and he classified certain traditional practices as the work of the devil. Yet, in an apparent contradiction, Agustin also spoke of visits and appearances by mountain spirits and ritual payment to these deities of nature. (Agustin, as I discuss in more detail later in this chapter, does not actually represent a contradiction: his belief in mountain spirits is an internalized and potent form of Q'eqchi' morality that emerges from a history of reciprocity, inequality, and respect. His orthodoxy is merely external rhetoric.)

Nonetheless, in the mid-1990s, Crique Chino Barrio Nuevo entered an orthodox phase where it practically split from the Catholic church in Livingston, *Iglesia de Nuestra Rosario,* and it was during this time that the community rejected the offer to host the Deer Dance. I remember the day when the *padre* (sp. priest) came out to give Mass and he repudiated and admonished the congregation for having no saint images on the altar (an indication of the more orthodox form of Catholicism). He asked harshly, "You call this a church?" By the time I returned the following year to Crique Chino Barrio Nuevo, Agustin had been ostracized and the community was trying to mend the cleavage he had helped create. They then had saint images on their altar.

I was invited to videotape the Deer Dance in Crique Maya by a Guatemalan sociologist who was conducting research there. Located up the Río Dulce and down a side tributary, this community is populated by predominantly Catholic traditionalists and they gladly hosted the Deer Dance. After a ninety-minute boat ride, a one-hour walk through dense jungle led us to this small village. Because the ground was muddy from rain, people preferred to walk on top of the large oil pipeline that runs through this area all the way to Puerto Barrios.[2] The dance troop was traveling around the Río Dulce area from village to village; it was the same group that wanted to come to Crique Chino Barrio Nuevo but was not invited.

The Deer Dance is one of the few Mayan dances performed today that has pre-Columbian origins (Garcia Escobar 1989:12–14).[3] The *Popol Vuh,* the K'iche' creation story, depicts an important location under K'iche' reign as "Deer Dance Plaza" (Tedlock 1996:341). The dance was likely a hunting ritual originally, a form of imitative magic used to appease gods and control the outcome of the hunt. The tension between deer and hunter was probably emphasized in order to alter or transform the often powerless human in the face of the elusive deer. While the human versus nature context of the Deer Dance is still evident (Lumb 1989:12–13), there are now other elements that deepen the complexity.

When the Deer Dance was performed in Crique Maya, I had not yet formed the video project. I went alone, although I showed the subsequent footage to numerous people who had witnessed the dance elsewhere. The individuals who watched my footage, particularly Manuel, helped me interpret the meaning of the dance. The Deer Dance lasts all day, and I videotaped as much as possible before my batteries lost their power in the hot and humid weather.

There are twenty-three dancers in total: eight deer, eight conquistadors or kings (sp. *reyes*),[4] two jaguars (also called *tigres*, sp. tiger), two monkeys, a *dueño* (sp. owner), his wife, and his dog. All eight deer have large, multicolored and mirrored cloaks, a short shawl that covers their upper bodies, silver-painted antlers with tassels and mirrors, brown-painted wooden masks, and bandannas covering the dancers' hair. Underneath they wear ruffled pants of various colors, and mirrors. Their costumes are shiny and brilliant as they reflect the bright sun. There are two types of kings: the main kings have beards while the secondary or auxiliary kings have only a mustache. Both types of kings are pale skinned with blond hair. Most of them also have a tassel of blond or red hair coming out from the back of their masks. They wear long, colorful cloaks with three mirrors (compared with the deer's eight) and a shawl with one mirror. Their tri-cornered hats are mirrored, with resplendent feathers streaming from them. In his right hand, each king carries and continuously shakes a maraca covered by a bandanna that, in most cases, is red with white dots. Like the deer, kings wear pants of many colors that jingle as they move through the dance steps. Mirrors are on their hats, cloaks, pants, and arm sleeves.

The owner is quite distinctive. He wears a Mexican *mariachi* hat that is stuffed with feathers and plastered with mirrors. Rather than a cloak, he

wears a short jacket reminiscent of the Spanish-style *anguarina* jacket popular in the Guatemalan highlands (Altman and West 1992:39). His foreign origin is also evident in his ability to speak Spanish, something that differentiates him and reveals his dominant position within the community and the dance itself. The owner is the only dancer with dark hair and a beard. He carries a baton (or staff) and a gun. Always followed by his dog and then his wife, this man's central position is clear. His woman (played by a man) is light skinned and blonde. She wears a long dress and a short shawl, both mirrored and multicolored. Her round hat and gun are smaller than her male counterpart's. Manuel says the owners and the kings, while white, are not gringos, but Ladinos. The couple's dog, sporting a mask that resembles the *Peanuts* character Snoopy, wears a cloak and carries a bag, as

do his male and female owners. In fact, the male and female owners, and all the animals other than the deer, carry little bags. The jaguars, monkeys, dog, and the woman use their bags to collect the change they beg for during the day. Unlike the kings and deer, the wild animals and the woman enter into the audience area and jest and perform for spare change. While the monkeys and dog wear clothing, the jaguars have only their fur. Costumes and masks are extremely heavy; I estimate they weigh up to twelve pounds. Three men tirelessly play the marimba.

Kings and deer follow certain choreographed steps, which keep them more or less in the same spot. The owner, his wife, their dog, the monkeys, and the jaguars wander throughout the dancing area and the crowd. Reflecting their authority to intrude in the space of the others, the owner exhibits his power and the jaguars and monkeys demonstrate theirs. This, in fact, is the main point of the dance. The Q'eqchi' people who watched my videotape tell me that the dance signifies the fight between the jaguar owner of nature/jungle and the human owners of the land. In many ways, the performance represents opposing ideologies defining ownership.

> The jaguars represent, well, we say that they are the owners of the mountains. I can't really explain very well, but it is because the deer always come from the mountains and the jaguars are from the mountains. (Videotaped interview with Armando)

> The jaguar comes from the bush and deer are also from the bush. And the dog is from the house. And the man comes from the house. So, there are always two things from the bush and two things from the house. Because of this, they are in contrast. (Audiotaped interview with Manuel)

The man, woman, and dog oppose the jaguars and deer. Manuel tells me that the pale-skinned dueño is a hunter (sp. *cazador*) who believes he has the right to capture and kill the deer. Thus, he is constantly yelling for his dog to find the deer. In the earlier (morning) part of the dance, the owner whistles and urges his dog to go find the deer so he and his woman can shoot them. This angers the jaguars, since they symbolize Tzuultaq'a (among other entities) and consider the deer their property. They, after all, are the true lords of the jungle, not these foreign intruders.

The jaguars demonstrate their power in a set of dances in which they domesticate the deer. The marimba slows down to a chime-like, mesmerizing, high-pitched pace. The two jaguars position themselves in front of the deer, who are lined up in pairs, one behind the other. Waving their bandannas, the jaguars tame and control the deer and the deer bow down in recognition of the jaguars' authority. The deer rock back and forth, to and from the jaguars, each time bowing and lowering their heads in submission as they retreat, backing away from the kings of the jungle. This is my favorite part of the dance.

Next there is a confrontation between the jaguars and the white men. Rather than pairing off into four rows, the kings and owner create one line. The owner is in the middle with the four main kings to his left and the four secondary kings to his right. Because they form one frontal line of solidarity, the men appear more unified and powerful than the deer. Behind this line of men are the two monkeys and then behind them, the woman and the dog. As in the taming of the deer, the row of pale-faced people demonstrate their respect to the felines by quickly bowing before them. While the bowing is not as obedient or graceful as that of the deer, the owner and the kings do temporarily acknowledge the reign of the jaguars.

Eventually the jaguars kill the dog. This is the highlight of the dance, when the rulers of the jungle murder the dog, which represents foreignness, colonialism, and disrespect. Attacking the dominant symbolic order, the jaguars and monkeys reveal their power and disgust with the foreign owner by ridiculing him—kicking and tripping him, tugging at his clothes, and pulling up the skirt of his female companion. However, the foreign owner has a gun and a cane, and with these instruments of power, he one by one kills the jaguars and monkeys who guard his dead dog. He recovers his dog and resurrects him. Thus, in outward appearances, the foreign owner wins the battle and is left unscathed from his skirmish with the natural forces of the jungle. But, behind this public performance is a hidden transcript that reveals a deep distrust of colonial forces and white men and also plays upon conflicting ideas of ownership.

While this dance does not openly question the authority of dominant Ladino/foreign culture, because the owner "wins" the battle, this public transcript may be more a means of survival than a significant point about a regime of power. The dominant class, whether Ladino, Spanish, Creole, or German, can watch the Deer Dance without fear of an attack on the political structure that provides them with authority. Because the owner ultimately brings his dog back to life, outsiders witness their superiority.

> The power of the dominant thus ordinarily elicits—in the public transcript—a continuous stream of performances of deference, respect, reverence, admiration, esteem, and even adoration that serve to further convince ruling elites that their claims are in fact validated by the social evidence they see before their very eyes. (Scott 1990:93)

While the dominant class witnesses the dog bounce back to life, indigenous audiences concurrently watch the mockery made of the owner and his wife. They see the monkey pull up the woman's dress. They behold the murder of the dog and they watch foreign men kneel down before jaguars. They see a structural reversal performed by masked individuals. Since masks encourage "a direct challenge to the usual order of life" (Abrahams 1983:103), dancers are free to directly attack, transform, and invert the dominant structural order as they perform a reversal in status (Abrahams and Bauman 1978:195; Turner 1995 [1969]:172–177). The dancers also control the gazes of the audience, even going so far as to metaphorically reflect gazes by attaching mirrors to their costumes and masks. Thus, while moral codes maintain appropriate practice (action-in-place), disorder is possible through a performance of anti-structure (Turner 1995 [1969]). Since ritual is an arena where the control and meaning of signs are contested (Comaroff 1985:196), the Deer Dance brings to center stage many polysemic symbols as it acts as an arena for the reformulation and reinforcement of historical structures and hierarchical order (Turner 1995 [1969]:177).[5]

Manuel explains the Deer Dance to me by placing the human and natural owners in contradictory positions where they both vie for control of the land. While clearly a nature versus culture argument, this contest is more complex. Foreigners have always intruded on indigenous land. The Ladino owner fighting with the jaguars over the capture and killing of deer signifies more than a performance about hunting. Historically, Mayan people have watched hungry foreigners consume their land—land Q'eqchi' consider their own. By showing the "true" owners of the land fighting back, the dance displays opposing definitions of ownership, one about titles and words and the other defined in terms of ancestry, usage, action, and community.

Jaguars symbolize more than nature and Tzuultaq'a; they also typify the powerful ancient ancestors who lived deep in the jungles. Like the ancient Mayans who, according to contemporary Q'eqchi', lived completely nude, the jaguars—wearing only their fur—become their co-essences in this drama.[6] Jaguars also symbolize Q'eqchi' people of today who are fighting back, killing the white man's dog, pulling up the white woman's skirt, and making the outsider kneel before them. Deer too are multi-vocal composites, representing contemporary and ancestral Mayans.[7] Dogs, on the other hand, signify foreignness. Like Q'eq (who are often considered part-dog), dogs are owned by outsiders; they are guardians of the fincas and protectors of the foreign fortune. They are the co-essences of finqueros. If they are vulnerable, so too are their owners. When the jaguars kill the dog, they also smash the pretense that foreign owners are untouchable and almighty.

WAACAX DIAB': THE DEVIL BULL DANCE

Waacax Diab' (Devil Bull Dance) is another dance that plays with a maintenance and reversal in structure. I watched and videotaped Waacax Diab' being performed in 1997, when I returned to Livingston for two additional months of fieldwork. (Unfortunately, I had only returned two days prior to the performance and was unable to re-organize the video project members to come to videotape with me.)

The performance took place in Plan Grande Queveche during a *maya-haac,* a community ritual usually done before harvest season to assure a bountiful crop. Mayahaac, like other Q'eqchi' rituals, focuses on feeding and appeasing Tzuultaq'a. Agustin (who represented the orthodox form of Catholicism), told me about a mayahaac in his community when he lived near El Estor. Rats were eating the cornfields, and an elder informed the community that they needed to have a mayahaac. After Agustin and others fed and paid their respect to Tzuultaq'a by burning pom and candles on a local hill, the mountain spirit ordered the rats to leave their cornfields alone. Agustin says his community never had another problem with rodent infestations. (His admission that he once fed Tzuultaq'a in a community ritual, by the way, supports my assertion that even orthodox Catholics participate in economic and moral relationships with deities.) Manuel told me that after Agustin abandoned his position as community leader in Crique Chino Barrio Nuevo, the villagers had a *small* mayahaac outside the Catholic church in the presence of a priest. They dug a hole on church grounds that they filled with pom and candles to feed and appease the mountain spirit.

However, the mayahaac in Plan Grande Queveche was no minor or ordinary event. The rite was organized by a pan-Mayan cultural organization from El Estor, Movimiento Nacional de Resistencia Maya (sp. National Movement for Mayan Resistance). I had previously met the leader of this organization in El Estor. With microphones, K'iche' shaman priests, Chuj representatives, and local support from Livingston's Ladino mayor, it is more questionable than usual whether this was an "authentic" Q'eqchi' ritual. The Mayan movement had seized mayahaac as a pan-Mayan ritual where they replaced the local Tzuultaq'a with their pan-Mayan deity, Ahau. One attendee told me that Ahau was the K'iche' name for Tzuultaq'a.

I arrived Friday afternoon and stayed through Saturday afternoon. I watched and participated in the mayahaac ritual on Saturday morning, but I was unable to see another dance on Saturday evening, the *Baile de Kata-rina,*[8] where they actually set "bulls" on fire with firecrackers. However, I was able to see the dancing of the Waacax Diab' on Friday night, which initiated the beginning of the weekend-long tribute to Mayan culture.

Coming down a grassy road, the bull (sp. *toro,* q. *waacax*) led the dancers. The costume was formed from a triangular canvas structure, like a small pup tent with no bottom, carried over the torso and head of the dancer.

The canvas was painted with multicolored circles symbolizing the fur or hide. On the front apex of the small tent was a simply carved wooden bull's head with horns. Because the man was carrying such a bulky costume, the bull had the effect of charging, intruding, clumsily moving, and awkwardly bucking through the crowd. Following behind was a dog, a white man, a white woman, and a black man (or Q'eq). An older man with no mask carried a simple wooden drum that provided the rhythm for the dancers. Compared with the costumes of the Deer Dance I saw in Crique Maya, these dancers in Plan Grande were wearing rudimentary costumes that appeared, and quite possibly were, handmade. The man, dog, and Q'eq wore simple costumes—black with stripes of muted colors. Their masks were plainly painted and neither as colorful nor as intricate as the masks of the Deer Dance. Both the man and Q'eq carried ropes to restrain the bull and whip him into submission. The woman (again played by a man) was wearing a plain dress. The dancers' order—bull, dog, man, woman, Q'eq—was maintained throughout. People explained to me that the man and woman were the owners of the bull, dog, and Q'eq. As in the Deer Dance, the white man constantly yelled and whistled at his dog to catch the bull that had escaped the confines of the finca. When the dog found the bull, the white man whipped the animal, thus provoking it into charging at all four of its antagonizers.

Rather than the struggle for control over the sacred natural world represented by deer, the symbol of the bull represents neo-liberal economics, slave labor, debt-peonage, and potential resistance to foreign consumers and producers.[9] The bull is an object possessed and put to work. Armed with whips rather than guns, the owners are no longer fighting the natural powers of the land and nature, but instead are facing resistance from another type of possession, their cattle. Because cattle are domesticated animals that were originally imported from Europe, they are not representatives of nature, but rather symbols of foreign exploitation and ownership. Cattle are economic beasts of burden, toiling the fields, providing nourishment with their bodies, and producing through their semen. It is no coincidence that Marco Vinicio Mejía (1997) cites cattle as a primary component of Guatemala's destructive preferential treatment of foreign investment over domestic concerns and the environment. Mejía, in fact, demonstrates the intimate link between cattle, deforestation, and the foreign. Cattle were introduced into northern Izabal (subsequently destroying the landscape) only after the United States ceased importing cattle from the south coast of Guatemala because of high levels of pesticide residue (153).

Foreigners also own Q'eq, kin to cattle, which they use to protect their

fields and the precious beasts of burden. Q'eq searches for the lost and rebellious bull, but not of his own accord. Q'eq and the bull do their ill-famed
work for their foreign masters.[10] Likewise, the indigenous Q'eqchi' labor
for foreign interests in the fincas of Alta Verapaz and in the foreign-owned
hotels of Livingston.

Like the Deer Dance, Waacax Diab' has a public and hidden transcript.
Publicly, the owners carry whips as they demonstrate their control over
the cattle, the Q'eq, and the dog. However, this public display of political and social hierarchy has a hint of defiance that reverses the deeply ingrained sociopolitical structures, if only for a few minutes. To laugh at the
charging bull as he attacks his owner, to find humor in the murder of the
owner's possessions, to refuse to submit to authority—this is structure reformulated. The Q'eqchi' dancers are controlling their own consumption
and even reverting gazes back upon the dominant.

Some question whether this sort of symbolic mockery should be considered resistance, because, although they invert social and political structures,
these rituals do not directly or permanently alter them. Critical scholars
view contemporary studies of resistance as grounded in apolitical orientations, substantiated by thin ethnographic detail, and as rationalizing devices
turning the mundane into activism (Brown 1996:730; Ortner 1995:173–
193). Clearly, these Q'eqchi' performances and rituals do not create a revolutionary consciousness among the participants or the audience. Rather,
these rituals are "effective where they move people from one definition
of authority and power to another, where they find and exploit contradictions in colonial hegemony by re-encoding hegemonic culture into
some other structure" (Kelly and Kaplan 1990:135). By highlighting the
ambiguous facet of colonialism—that these supposed producing, owned
objects (whether bulls or land) are metaphors for other laboring subjects
who actively rather than passively define themselves—the public performance is a defiance of (and an adherence to) moral codes. Through reverse
mimicry—the controlling of gazes—Q'eqchi' people are active witnesses
to a re-encoding of their moral scripts, which usually position them as the
recipients of owners' authority (and sight) rather than active subjects who
react to and buck against their supposed submissive position. Simply by
watching, by viewing this re-encoding, Q'eqchi' people both defy and internalize the bull that charges at his owner, while maintaining the integrity
of these performances of morality.

Acts of defiance are endowed with moral logic. Fainting, for example,
is common during the Deer Dance, but people do not explain it as caused
by over-exertion or heat exhaustion from dancing in a heavy costume in

high heat. Rather, when dancers faint it is because they do not have enough respect.

> According to what they say, if, let's say, if someone is thinking about something else, if they aren't concentrating on what they are doing, they say they go insane. Then, what they do when this happens is at that moment the dancers, the deer, or whoever it is, the jaguar perhaps, comes and jumps three times over them in order to bring them back to normal. (Videotaped interview with Armando)

The dancers are struck down by the spirit of Tzuultaq'a and/or God for not concentrating or for allowing their thoughts to wander during the sacred dance. Irreverent people have been said to die after performing this ritual, and others are said to never be the same. Thus, while the structures are mocked, the dance is still governed by moral exchanges of active respect. In the same manner, to conclude Waacax Diab', the dancers lay down their masks in front of the large altar and proceed to pray to God and Tzuultaq'a. By showing reverence and respect, they ultimately provide these spiritual deities with unadulterated power. While these performances play with hierarchical relations, they also maintain these structures and concur with authorities, both inside and outside, both today and in the past.

IN-SIGHTFUL POWER

Orthodox Catholics and Evangélicos recapitulate an analytical rather than dialectical view of nature (Tedlock 1992:42), thus fearing dances such as Xajleb' Kej and Waacax Diab' because they are viewed as the devil's work or *del mundo* (sp. worldly). They decry these performances, alleging that they cost too much, are too dangerous, and require too much time and attention. Analytic, categorical thinking—where earthly (visual and tangible) hedonism opposes more abstract *obras del Dios* (sp. works of God)[11]—contradicts more dialogic and hybrid worldviews that envision good and evil fluidly within one entity.

Once I understood that orthodox Catholics and Evangélicos were differentiating and labeling various types of ritual as either worldly or Godly, I began to notice how the terms *costumbre* (sp. custom) and *tradición* (sp. tradition) parallel these distinctions. Conservative thinkers consider costumbre as nefarious "paganism." Yet most Q'eqchi' people, regardless of religious affiliation, also describe it as something you are born into, like faith. You cannot see it; it is not written down. Because you cannot copy it, you have to feel it or learn it from an elder.

> Customs come like faith. Tradition is something you can see but customs are something you cannot see. Traditions are public, in full view, visible. You can touch them. You cannot touch customs. Custom is a secret; it is like God's faith. Customs are born in the heart. (Audiotaped interview with Mariano)

Not being able to copy, touch, or see customs is what creates potency. For the Q'eqchi', if they cannot copy something, they cannot control it or mimic it, and if they cannot see it, they cannot own it. Private ritual, mask-covered faces, foreign-owned Q'eq, invisible colonial regimes, cave-dwelling Tzuultaq'a—all these images represent the omnipotent authority of the invisible, which is also intricately tied to the fear and power of costumbre. Customs represent something from long ago, something ancient, powerful, and communal, an essence that cannot be touched or viewed.[12] Likewise, because customs originated long ago, before Mayan people knew of God, orthodox thinkers consider these "pagan" practices *mundial,* or frivolous, hedonistic, and wasteful evil-ridden delights.

Mariano, a traditional Catholic, explained that costumbre is secret and invisible, even though it can be practiced in public. Dances, for example, are public displays often labeled as customs because they represent ancient Mayan practices supported by invisible and ancient realms of power. Yet these public customs also have double meanings, as they contradict the cultural hierarchy and re-encode the hegemonic structure. Thus, disguised behind masks and mocking authority, public customs are a threat to the established order. By ridiculing kings and killing dogs, public customs directly challenge the moral codes that position Q'eqchi' people as the producers and foreign owners as consuming authorities.

Public rituals are intended to be seen; they are visible and, therefore, capable of playing with sociopolitical structures. What cannot be seen is almighty, while what is visible—just by its being looked at—is dominated. This is why, I propose, Q'eqchi' traditional dances never have Q'eqchi' characters, because it would open the Q'eqchi' to exploitation and domination. Instead, we watch jaguars, bulls, and deer compete against foreigners. Thus, the anti-structure of public performances is possible only because the ritual is intended to be watched and because the dancers themselves are masked and made invisible. Through vision, customs become a means of resistance. While watching dancers who externally exhibit socially sanctioned reverence to authority, communities internalize the mockery and playful reversion.

It is for the same reasons that the private rituals discussed in Chapter 5, uk'iha and k'ajb'ak, reaffirm established norms of morality rather than contest them. Private ritual is a structure saturated with invisible potency that individuals hesitate to alter. There are no external manifestations, no masks, and no public transcripts. Private ritual is raw, uninhibited, and internalized power where the practitioners reveal their faces. Defaming this structured relation would be action-out-of-place.

I once attempted to make a list of practices labeled as "tradition" or "custom," but I was unable to arrive at a clear consensus. Most people consider public dances to be customs, although some say they are traditions because they are public. Mayahaac is almost unanimously labeled as custom and so is k'ajb'ak. The burning of candles and pom is considered both custom and tradition. Yet, what is interesting here is that Evangélicos and orthodox thinkers do not consider all forms of costumbre as the work of the devil. For example, a practice almost unanimously labeled as costumbre—the house-building ritual typically performed by Catholics as a means of asking permission from Tzuultaq'a to build—is also enacted by Protestants. Evangélicos do practice this ritual, though without candles, pom, or turkey blood (which is typically scattered in the four corners of the house). Rather, they invite a Protestant pastor to come and bless the future home. Without the more physical and visible sacrifices of traditional Catholics, the house-building ritual is still considered an obligation for Evangélicos before they move into a new home. Catholics and Protestants may not agree among themselves as to what is del mundo or del Dios, but both groups consider themselves in an intimate relationship with a greater authority—an owner of land, animals, and souls.

Evangélicos, too, subscribe to a moral imaginary that pays reverence to outsiders, even Tzuultaq'a, although the mountain spirit might be categorized as a criminal rather than a peripheral keeper of the community. For Evangélicos, Tzuultaq'a represents the devil, who sends out snakes to cause harm and demands that individuals participate in hedonistic and costly practices. Good and evil are no longer in the same body, but in separate entities, and this is a key difference between Protestants and Catholics (including more orthodox charismatic Catholics). While most Catholics imagine Tzuultaq'a as capable of good and evil, a dualism found throughout Mesoamerican indigenous religions (Gossen 1996:316), Protestants categorically divide good and evil into separate bodies. Protestants also separate good and evil into distinct practices: earthly, devil-laden customs, which gain power from invisible and internal sources; and traditions, which externally revere the Judeo-Christian God. Of course, the evangelical Christian God is also invisible, but this Supreme Being is made tangible through salvation and through one's personal relationship with his son, Jesus Christ. In this way, the power does not come from secret, invisible forces but from fortified and personal relations between savior and subject.

Protestants downplay the external, as indicated in their prohibition of earrings, makeup, dancing, saint images, and lust-inducing articles of clothing, and they suspect the internal power of ritual, which represents earthly vice. They distrust the internal because it is intangible (and out-of-sight) and also, I suggest, because it represents respect towards one's community. Instead, they attempt to redefine community into congregations consisting of *hermanos y hermanas* (sp. brothers and sisters). In this way, a community that is based on anything other than evangelical values is a threat to their newly established social and kin groups. It is no coincidence that the form of respect offered to fellow members of an evangelical congregation is the same form of respect that orientates oneself within a community and kin group (q. loq'inkil) rather than the type of respect paid to outsiders and ancestors (q. paab'ankil).

Not only am I suggesting that Evangélicos redefine their congregations as community and family, but I also propose that Protestantism itself is an external identity, that practitioners' internal perception is actually guided by an imagined script that enforces respect to external owners and internal "community" members, whether neighbors or church-going hermanas/os. First, even though Protestants oppose *obras del Dios* with *costumbres del mundo,* there is no general consensus as to how practices and ritual objects are appropriately categorized. Secondly, Protestants say they feel the mountains breathe, they believe the mountains live, and they discuss the mythical Q'eq that robs them at night. Further, Evangélicos explain that God is an invisible owner whom they must respect and from whom they must seek permission before building a house or planting corn, and they speak of expansive fincas deep inside local hills, such as Cerro San Gil. Therefore, while traditional, orthodox Catholics and Protestants seem different in external rhetoric and appearance, I propose that both groups adhere to similar culturally based, internalized structures that are formed and maintained through external respect to outsiders and internal respect to one's community. When viewed through action and perception rather than rhetoric or appearance, distinctions between Catholics and Protestants fade.

It is not that the qualities of internal and external are always in opposition to one another, or that they are even distinguishable. Only from an academic gaze are they separable, for in practice they merge into action. Inter-
nal/external, invisible/visible, insider/outsider, costumbre/tradición, and
Protestant/Catholic are not fixed dichotomies. They are in continuous flux,
and their contradictory meanings emerge from active relationships. Individuals and institutions can be both insider and outsider, practitioners of
action-in-place and action-out-of-place.

Mountain spirits provide examples of this hybrid identity. Externally
Tzuultaq'a typically appear foreign, but they can also appear as ancient
Mayans. Internally, it seems that they are insiders, but they also have the capacity to harm and injure those under their jurisdiction.[13] Sometimes they
are God; other times they are the devil. Likewise, on the outside, from an
objective perspective, Tzuultaq'a represent the payment of respect to foreigners. On the inside, however, this externally oriented respect is gathered
through community collaborations. Agustin's dream, in which three pale-
skinned female Tzuultaq'a appeared to demand food and respect (see Chapter 4), demonstrates how payment to outsiders is a means of forging community through communal redistribution. Agustin's friend interpreted the
dream as a message from Tzuultaq'a, from the women in the tall hills (sp.
de los grandes cerros). Agustin continued:

> We then went to look for seven more men, we went to chat
> with them and from there we said what we were going to
> do, how we were going to prepare, and all at once we said
> we were going to collaborate with fifteen quetzales from
> each one of us. And they said to me, "we will collaborate."
> There were some thirty-five people and all of us were going
> to give one pound of copal pom. (Videotaped interview with
> Agustin)

While respect is paid externally—to a foreigner/kin/owner—respect
is also spread within the community, actively reinforcing social relations.
Community, however, is not a stable, coherent entity either; it is in continuous flux as it is reinterpreted through practice and conceived through
translocal, religious, and interpersonal networks that are not necessarily
geographically linked (Castañeda 1996:40). Nonetheless, even if communities are imagined (Anderson 1983), shared feelings of internal membership
do exist; there is a specific form of respect offered to community members,
parishioners, and kin, as compared with outsiders and ancestors. And, although internal community membership is reinforced through interaction

with socially sanctioned and authoritative outsiders, it is still the internal members who are the agents practicing and perceiving their positions within the community and wider social, economic, and cosmological fields of action.[14] Members also can alter their affiliation. Being a member of a community is not a given essence, but a process that must be reinforced through action-in-place.

CAMERAS AND THE
ETHNOGRAPHIC GAZE

One of the dancers in the Deer Dance did not appreciate the gaze of my camera lens. He politely asked not to be filmed. I complied and immediately averted the watchful eye of the camera whenever he entered the frame. I understood how a camera can violate, how it carries invisible and intangible power through its ability to capture and consume others. It is an ethnographic irony, then, that through the collaborative video project I introduced two foreign forms of surveillance—the camera and the ethnographer's eye.

If consumption can be a trope for unequal power relations where subjects symbolically feed upon passive objects, then camera gazes are acts of consumption and means of solidifying power. Relationships are forged. However, it is imperative to understand that consumption is not just cultural cannibalism. Consumption can be controlled and used for empowerment. Visually, consumption is a political activity where certain hungry subjects have access to sight and others are blind, but viewed. Sight, though, can be guided and redirected. Reflection of gazes is a purpose of the mirrors on Deer Dance costumes. This is also, I assume, why the dancer did not want to be videotaped. He wanted to remain in a position of power, controlling his gazes upon others (he could see but not be seen), rather than be the one eaten by the eyes of cameras, anthropologists, and distant audiences.

This is exactly why it is so vitally important that readers and viewers of this book not only nibble and gaze upon Mayan culture and people, but that they also see through the practices, perceptions, and gazes of Q'eqchi' individuals. I aim to avert the academic/natural scientific gaze that during the Renaissance was proposed as the conventional perspective of science and knowledge, originating from a "single and unified point of view" (Henley 1998:43). Of course, this type of centralized objective perspective is integral in the production of photographic images, whether still or moving, and it may be the invisible and dominating potency of this technical and academic gaze that made the dancer request not to be videotaped.

Researchers who use methodologies involving cameras are extremely aware of how gazes have the potential to objectify and consume. This is why some researchers have begun to hand over gazing tools to their subjects, as I did through the video project.[15] By teaching the Q'eqchi' people video technology and by giving them the authority to create their own self-images, Proyecto Ajwacsiinel and other indigenous video projects reverse traditional forms of academic gazing. Instead of the audience looking upon passive or mute objects, viewers engage in a dialogue with people, sometimes looking at the Q'eqchi' of Livingston as a whole, or as individuals, but most often hearing from them and seeing through their eyes as they share their imaginations of the world.

Of course, the reader and viewer also see through my academically trained eyes. At the same time that the audience is gazing at ethnographic others, and the Q'eqchi' are looking upon themselves and outsiders, ethnographers are also gaining knowledge through sight, which is part of the Cartesian foundation of anthropology (Stoller 1989:39). Anthropologists have traditionally used visual conventions to produce ethnographic realism, claiming to produce total images of culture (Stoller 1989:49). Some have begun to include indigenous narratives in order to disperse some of the authority of ravenous, academic eyes. However, with the inclusion of subjects' gazes and words, there is always the potential for indigenous narratives to become politically correct subtexts within ethnographers' academic strategies (MacDougall 1992:29), thus once again imprisoning Fourth World members in the panopticon of the First World (Lavie and Swedenburg 1996:62).

In this research, I do avert my own academic eyes, not only emphasizing participation along with observation, but also placing myself in the position of being watched. I reveal the uncertainty of my own personal and academic gazes, and I do not whitewash Q'eqchi' culture in a veneer of traditionalism or modernity. Although there is a level of consumption through the natural tendency to gain authority through gazing upon others, the Q'eqchi' subjects in this research direct their own consumption, as they do in ritual. They produce the images for the reader/viewer to ingest. Though my perspectives are behind many of the images you gaze upon and I am the one writing the texts that confer subsequent meaning to Q'eqchi' narratives, I nonetheless endeavor to produce a work that matches the network of subjects that are internalized and embodied in Q'eqchi' practice and perception. A myriad of subjects and movement create a third eye (Rony 1996) to disperse objectifying gazes so that neither I nor the camera (nor readers) are the invisible overseers.

We can do this because civilizing missions are not exhaustive. Slippage and ambivalence blur lines between colonizer and colonized, and mimicry can become mockery. Reverse mimicry, where the imitator and imitated merge into a murky space, re-transforms colonial symbolic structures by exploiting the contradictions inherent in subordinate and dominant relations (Bhabha 1984:129–131; Taussig 1993:20–25). Reverse mimicry is the act of defiance, the reformulation (and reproduction) of cultural models. Reverse mimicry provides dances (and ethnographic methods) the ability to maintain moral logics and to defy power structures by adhering to cultural codes. Embodying the politics of sight, dances and methods criticize, question, and attack the dominant order that they also publicly applaud.

VISUAL DIGRESSIONS

> Lola told me that I had to be careful. Because I threw my candles in the pit, I was praying to the devil. She said that I should not eat any apples because they may be poisonous, that I may fall in the street, or that I may be bitten by a snake. I am very susceptible now because I was messing around with VERY DANGEROUS stuff. (Hilary's field notes)

Lola laughed but scolded me for attending the mayahaac in Plan Grande Queveche. After I told her that I participated by having a shaman pray for me and by throwing candles in the great pit of fire, she became even more agitated. Her fear entered my body and haunted my thoughts as I carefully walked down the grassy slope from my house. A few days after Lola's admonition, Patrocinia told me that my neighbor found an eight-foot snake in her bed. I wondered if my outsiderness provided protection from the wrath of the mountain spirit who was upset with me. Perhaps I was irreverent with my theoretical assessment, my internal lack of concentration during mayahaac, my video camera, or a number of the more external anthropological and foreign tools I used and perhaps with which I was disrespectful. Perhaps I consumed too much without giving. Perchance, gringas are not supposed to gaze within internal worlds where communities control the consumption of foreigners. Maybe that snake was intended for me.

Seven   ANACHRONISTIC
MEDIATORS AND
SENSORY SELVES
Exploring Time and Space

But, once more, my human gaze never posits more than one facet of the object
—MAURICE MERLEAU-PONTY, *The Visible and the Invisible*

The act of exchange is registered on the senses that seal it as a social relation. In turn, the senses are synchronized and crossed with each other and with the Other, *so that senses and subjects can witness and be witnessed.*
—C. NADIA SEREMETAKIS, *"The Memory of the Senses"*

The Q'eqchi' interpret social relations through an imaginary guided by visual metaphors, although perception is not exclusively based upon sight (Howes 1991:167). Intricately wrapped up with concepts of collective and self identities are nonvisual senses that, like the nuances of fieldwork, are typically de-emphasized in academic research and ethnographic products. The Q'eqchi' use all their senses—tactility, sight, hearing, olfaction, gustation, and temporalizing and spatializing processes—in the phenomenological maintenance of their cosmological and socioeconomic worlds. They pay respect to Tzuultaq'a through the offering of sweet-smelling pom smoke. They recognize Q'eq whistling through the sky during his nightly escapades when he hopes to satiate his ravenous appetite. They reproduce social relations through eating and feeding, hear ancestors knocking at night, and appease mountain spirits with loud firecrackers and melodic songs. Virtual owners are bolstered by their invisibility and by their ability to control space and overcome time. Action-out-of-place leads to sensory distortion. Illness causes muteness and cameras can turn people into senseless objects.

It was the Enlightenment ideal of ocular processes as representing truthful objectification and reason (seeing is believing) that distanced vision from the "lower," less informative, senses. Sight became synonymous with a centralized and dominating perspective. Visual gazes were marked as indices of purity and understanding *par excellence,* and processes of *being* were ocularly transformed into static *beings* (Merleau-Ponty 1968:3–7; Spanos 2000:9). Nonvisual senses were erased from processes of knowledge gathering and dissemination.

Yet perception is not only rooted in the mind and supported by visual metaphors. Perception is also a bodily process of social mediation. Our bodies are not mere receptacles of our intellect; they are "lived" (Merleau-Ponty 2002 [1945]) connections, spanning and dissolving differences of subject and object. However, the phenomenological dismantling of this constructed dichotomy and the ocular-centric Enlightenment paradigm demands a methodology that reintroduces all the senses into academic discussions (Stoller 1997). This chapter introduces a methodology that represents Q'eqchi' individuals, bodies, and selves as relational and mediating processes emerging from the "reverberations" of sensory lives (Stoller 1989:63).

ALL SAINTS' DAY

Todos Santos, or All Saints' Day, is an extremely important day for Catholic Q'eqchi' in Livingston and Catholics the world over. Every 1 November, Q'eqchi' Mayans prepare an elaborate feast not for Tzuultaq'a or God, but for their ancestors, *los difuntos* (sp. the deceased). In Crique Chino Barrio Nuevo, the entire community participated in preparing the feast for the dead and the living. I arrived early to help decorate the little rancho-style church. We hung orange, yellow, and blue crepe paper from the rafters and constructed a gate of palm fronds through which all had to pass.

We set up a simple altar, covered by a red and white checkered plastic tablecloth. On top, a young girl placed some colorful green and yellow leaves from a tree next to the church, a statue of the Virgin Mary, two candles, and an image of Christ. All morning long, women remained out of sight behind the church, cooking large pots of chicken caldo. Everyone brought something. Whether laden with vegetables, poch, a few pounds of chicken, or tortillas, no one showed up empty-handed. Some thirty pounds of chicken were cooked and at least two hundred poch were kept warm in big metal vats covered by banana leaves.

I had been in the field only one and a half months and had not yet found the courage to pull out my video camera. Nor had I yet organized the video project. I was still in a transitional period where I was getting people accustomed to me and my ethnographic methods. While the women prepared food, I went around snapping photos of them and of the large pots of caldo and poch with my 35mm still camera. I distinctly remember how uncomfortable I felt during the morning, how much I felt like an outsider. I had not attended the preliminary meeting the week before, so I did not have a particular task other than to take photos and hang crepe paper. I reflected upon my awkwardness in my field notes.

> Every woman but me brought dishes of poch, chicken, or cooking pots, water, and other needed ingredients. This made me feel weird and I wish I had not listened to Don Manuel when he told me to only bring my camera. . . . If this was happening in the States, I would have been right in the middle, working, giving and taking instructions. At least I would be doing something. Instead, there I sat and stood on the sidelines, every once and a while trying to help by holding a pot, moving the poch, or working the fire a bit. Basically, my only role was to watch and occasionally take a picture.

Around noon, a nun arrived with a small church choir comprising Garifuna and Ladina women. Women were serving up portions of caldo into bowls as an elderly woman lit pom and swung the incense holder over the food that had been allotted into portions, covering it with thick, sweet-smelling smoke. Another woman placed a bowl of caldo, a few poch, a glass of lemonade, and a bag of salt on the altar, all of which were covered by the pom smoke still being spread inside and outside the thatched-roof church by the elder woman. The nun blessed the food and we all sat down to eat. Here too, I felt extremely out of place, because I was invited to eat at the table with the nun and the choir. While we had chairs to sit on and a table on which our caldo, poch, and glasses of lemonade had been set, all others crouched on their legs or on the few logs set up around the church. I wished that I was with the others rather than at the table clearly designated for outsiders, even though I knew the invitation to sit at the table was a sign of respect. A priest came out to give Mass shortly after we had finished eating. After Mass and communion, he blessed the caldo, the poch, the lemonade, and the salt that had been left on the altar for the ancestors. The nun stayed throughout the evening until midnight, when it was assured that the ancestors had arrived. Kin sang religious songs as they awaited the return of the difuntos, although no one knows exactly when they arrive, because they are invisible.

The community of Plan Grande Queveche makes an enormous festival for this day. On their church altar, along with local fruits and caldo, they have *boj* (q. fermented alcohol made from pineapple and sugar cane). Other Q'eqchi' make household offerings. Patrocinia, for example, practiced this ritual in her own household where her family placed atole, bananas, oranges, caldo, and tortillas on their small altar. They awoke at five o'clock in the morning and waited until midnight for their ancestors. What everyone, whether household or community, is awaiting is the return of their ancestors' mu.

Mu is somewhat similar to the Christian soul. It is with an individual through life and at death, tenuously linked to the living body and easily lost through an illness like *susto* (q. *kaan,* meaning "fright"). At death, an individual's mu goes to live with God.[1] However, once a year it returns to earth; as it was explained to me, the mu takes a vacation from the sky. In return for coming to visit their loved ones, the mu demand gifts in the form of food. People are immoral if they fail to feed their ancestors.

> They will be very sad. They will say "Oh, you did not give us anything. We came but you gave us nothing." There are times they can be dangerous. They may throw something at you or they will pull your hair while you are sleeping. They are mad because there is nothing, because you did not give them anything. (Audiotaped interview with Patrocinia)

As with other invisible deities, Patrocinia says you cannot see the mu of your ancestors, although occasionally you can hear them knocking or whistling. Understood (and literally translated) as a person's shadow, the mu are bodiless selves that represent the once bodied individual. It is interesting, however, that the Q'eqchi' seem to conceive of their internal selves as a multiplicity of flexible, context-orientated entities. No consistent linguistic terminology is used to describe their inner essences. The abstract components that make up the internal self vary from person to person. The following is a list of these concepts, including the various Q'eqchi' terms and diverse definitions I have heard for each one.

> • *Aamn*—referred to as the heart, also referred to as a translation for *alma* (sp. soul) and spirit. Some people say that this is the part of the internal body that goes to God at death.

• *Ch'ol*—often referred to as heart, the physical beating organ.
Also used to describe a type of spirit residing in the body,
a force that wanes and ebbs. Ch'ol is the spirit carried by
women during the full moon. Ch'ol is also referred to as soul.
• *Mu*—translated as shadow. The body has two shadows. One
is the true shadow made when the body stands in front of a
source of light and the other is one that becomes the shadow
after death. Mu can also enter a house and scare its occupants
at night. A severe fright can shake a mu loose. If this happens,
the person has to find it and bring it back or else he/she will
fall ill with susto.
• *Muhel*—the spirit that comes back strictly to scare. This
spirit can come in a dream or through noises during the
night. Muhel seems to be the same as mu except it is the evil
side of the shadow, the one that haunts. Muhel is more spirit
than shadow, although the root clearly comes from the word
for shadow, mu.
• *Musiq'ej*—the spirit that goes to live with God. When someone dies, the Q'eqchi' say *xelc musik,* their spirit left. Musiq'ej
also means breath.

Ch'ol and aamn seem to be interchangeable, both being heart and soul
simultaneously. They are physical components of the body, but also considered spirits and forces that reside within and outside the human body. Mu
parallels muhel, although muhel is more often described as the shadow that
frightens living people and shakes loose their mu. However, even good-
intentioned mu can frighten away shadows from living people, which is
why children are not allowed to play near the altar during Todos Santos.
With difuntos coming back to visit, children may become frightened and
one of the muhel may grab the child's insecure mu. Because a young child's
mu is easily dislodged, youth are more susceptible to susto caused by the
coming of the muhel.

It appears that mu are less threatening than muhel. Perhaps mu who
are not given gifts of food or respect become muhel who cause fear until
satisfied. Or maybe mu, because it is a shadow, is more tangible than the
muhel, which is clearly a spirit. Because spirits are invisible and shadows
are possibly seen, the invisible muhel may be more powerful and dangerous. Recall that it is the shadow of Tzuultaq'a that is invited to eat during
the sowing ritual and that this revered guest is referred to as both *xmu li
tzuul* and *xmuhel li tzuul,* the hill's mu and the hill's muhel, respectively.
With this in mind, one sees the interchangeability of mu and muhel, and

again, the slippage between good and evil. Of course, this multiplicity is not unexpected, because spiritual selves emerge from the same dynamic network that forges perception of more tangible social and ethnic identities. Self and collective identities and institutions are not composed of fixed essences; they are relations that are dependent on exchange and context for meaning.[2]

DEATH AND TRANSCENDENTAL OWNERSHIP

When a Q'eqchi' person dies, the entire community assists with the preparation of the body, the organization of the burial, and also with the family's necessary expenses. Depending on the sex of the deceased, an elder man or woman is asked to help prepare the body. Young children, pregnant women, and women with small children are not allowed to assist with preparing the cadaver. If the person's godparents are still alive, they will be called. The elder assistant bathes the body and combs the hair, dresses the deceased in clean clothes, and places a white handkerchief over the face. The clothes that are chosen are often the best the individual owns; a woman is dressed in her favorite *poot* (sp. *huipil,* embroidered cotton blouse) and *uk'* (sp. *corte,* traditional skirt) and a man is dressed in a suit, if he owns one. A candle is often placed in the right hand of the deceased.[3]

Intimate belongings are buried with the deceased, either spread throughout the coffin or gathered in a cloth bundle placed on top of the body or behind the head. In a woman's coffin, her family may place one or two of her poot, an equivalent number of uk', her comb (usually of wood or bone) and barrette, and some guacal bowls and cups from her kitchen. If she smoked, some cigars (sp. *puros*) would go into the coffin; if she was a weaver, they would put in her thread. A man would have one or two suits, a hat, and perhaps his boots placed in the coffin. People traditionally buried their deceased in petates (sp. reed mats), but coffins are now normal practice. The body is placed in the coffin and kept inside the home throughout the wake. After the all-night wake, the family prepares a large pot of caldo and tamales that they serve to the mourners.

Martín told me the body is buried quickly, usually just after twenty-four hours have lapsed since the time of death. Burials occur at approximately one o'clock in the afternoon, as fears exist that if the body is buried in the morning another individual will fall ill and die in the same manner as the deceased. The entire community carries the coffin to the cemetery. If possible, the funeral procession stops at corners and crossroads where it is said the mu will eventually find the proper direction to God. Close family members often stay at home during the burial. Elders scold the young who want to go to the cemetery to see their loved ones for one last time. At the burial, those in attendance throw fistfuls of dirt onto the grave as the community symbolically shares in the internment.

The nine-day vigil that follows the burial is known as the *veladora*. Because the mu remains in the house for three days before it makes its final ascent to God, a glass of water is set out to appease the restless shadow, in case it is thirsty. After three days, an elderly man or woman catches the mu in a piece of pottery. While burning copal pom, the elder takes the mu to the cemetery where he or she tells the shadow to stay there, not to show its face to the family, and not to come back to scare the children. The mu is told that the entire family will be reunited in heaven. At the end of the nine days, people gather at the mourning family's home to pray. A cross is placed at the burial site. Some families now have a Mass in their homes at this time and again on the fortieth night after death, although Mariano told me that the ninth- and fortieth-night Masses are Ladino inventions. Before, people simply buried the deceased and went to the cemetery on the third day to burn copal pom and help carry the spirit upwards to God.

Most Q'eqchi' people die intestate, although it is currently becoming more common to write a will. A family cannot use any belongings left by the deceased other than land, which is inherited by the sons. Beds, petates, hammocks, and clothes are destroyed and often burned. If beds of the deceased are slept in or their clothes worn, two things can occur. The ancestors' mu can come back at night to announce their dissatisfaction with the behavior of their living relatives, or the material items themselves, imbued with a spirit of self, can haunt (sp. *espantan*) or scare the people wearing or using them. A woman would never wear her deceased mother's huipil because, although the mother is dead, her spirit still resides within the owned item.

> Even if the huipil is very pretty, you cannot just leave it alone. You cannot wear it either. No, because they would say that it is my mother's, that I cannot wear it. I would be sorry if I did. It would hurt me. This would bother my mother. This is what we think. (Audiotaped interview with Mariano)

Ana, a Q'eqchi' woman who does not wear huipils and who claims she does not remember how to make tortillas, told me a story about her aunt's death. Her family could not fit all the clothes in the coffin and they had to keep some of the aunt's clothing behind. Ana's mother decided that she would wait one year and then she would wear her sister's huipils. Shortly after she made this decision, Ana's mother began having dreams about her sister—that she knocked on the door, opened it, and entered the house. Ana's mother interpreted the dream as an indication that her deceased sister was angry with her because she planned on wearing her clothes. Ana's mother went to the cemetery where her sister was buried. She burned candles and told her sister not to worry, that she would not wear her clothes and that she would destroy them. She never heard again from her deceased sister.

> According to what my father told me one time, I don't remember how many years ago it was now, he was there at a dance in El Estor. Someone [a dancer] was thinking about bad things and then he began to mistreat the costume. It was really hot, so he spoke bad about the costume. This messed him up. A little bit after he removed all his clothes and ran around naked, running off to somewhere. (Videotaped interview with Armando)

Certain objects are fetishes that carry the spirits of their owners. Land, corn, and hens, for example, carry the spirit of Tzuultaq'a. Saint images possess the mu of God. Houses, clothes, dance costumes and masks, machetes, barrettes, and hammocks are endowed with another type of spirit that also must be respected. By disrespecting costumes, dancers can lose their minds, being attacked by the spirit of the clothes, which leads to insanity, illness, or death. Carlson and Eachus (1977:52–62) refer to this type of malevolent spirit in objects as *swi:nqul*. Although I did not hear this exact term—the Q'eqchi' people of Livingston instead refer to the spirit of clothes and houses as mu—I did hear about what occurred when and if an individual disrespected objects that were endowed with the spirit. *Chirlinkil* is the Q'eqchi' term used to describe the mistreatment of a deceased individual's clothing. *Chir* comes from *chirix*, which means "behind" or "after." The root comes from *ilok* (q. to see), which is also the root of the term Carlsen and Eachus (1977) found represented the spirit of certain possessions. I roughly translate chirlinkil as "after seeing." Others translated it for me as "after death," or when someone is "playing" (sp. *jugando*) with deceased peoples' clothing. I consider this powerful essence beyond the realm of sight as the "spirit of ownership."

Ownership is a relationship that imbues material items with the spirit of the individual owner. Just as Q'eq carries the spirit of his foreign owner and the land carries the spirit of Tzuultaq'a, huipils and corte carry the spirit of the woman who once wore them. Like the spirit of the thing given (Mauss 1954 [1950]:10–13), which possesses elements of the gift-giver, these material objects are injected with the spirit of the owner. If disrespectful family members ignore this mediated social exchange, they are vulnerable to the spirit, an invisible power that emerges from within the intimate relation between owner and owned. Possessions, therefore, are active subjects that mediate the dynamic linkages between life and death, time and space, and self and other. They are manifestations of selves.

Family members burn their loved one's material items as a demonstration of respect for the ancestors and their clothes, and as evidence of the transcendent nature of ownership.[4] Ownership, like sacredness and paying respect, is about doing; it is about clearing land, planting milpa, and wearing traje. Likewise, ownership and community are maintained after death through action, whether in-place or out-of-place. This action may be through feeding (or failing to feed) the ancestors during Todos Santos, or it may be the practice of burning a deceased person's clothing. Ownership/outsiderness/authority is actively maintained through reciprocity, respecting, consuming, and vision. In this way, anyone can be tentatively categorized as an owner if they appear as an outsider, are in a position of power, or are in control or possession. When people came to my rented home, I was envisioned as the dueña who had to give permission to enter and sit and who had to subsequently serve sweetened coffee to visitors. Men who rent milpas are called dueños during the sowing ritual because they are the individuals working the land and thus responsible for paying respect to Tzuultaq'a. Ownership, according to the Q'eqchi' Maya, does not necessarily entail owning, but acting-as-keeper. Thus, in situations where morality is actively practiced and maintained, when reciprocity enforces payment or respect, renters, parents, and ethnographers too are considered owners.

Echaniic is the Q'eqchi' term for "to own," but it can be translated more appropriately as "to make oneself the owner." It stems from the word *ech'alal,* which means "relative" or "kin." *Echkab'al* means "neighbors." Linguistically, ownership stems from acting within a community or among kin; ownership is a social relationship that binds one to a social network, whether a local community, a kin group, or a translocal order.[5] I argue that this concept of ownership as based upon action is at odds with more Westernized notions of ownership, and it is this conflict that is performed in the dances discussed in Chapter 6. While a Westernized understanding of ownership (i.e., individualistic, capitalistic) is based on words, recognition, titles, laws, and legal rights to the capital and income produced therein (Christman 1994:19), ownership among Q'eqchi' Mayans involves active use.[6] However, these conflicting ideas of ownership are not only practiced in myths and performances, but are also encountered every day. Consider how many Q'eqchi' people are forced to go through a sea of bureaucratic red tape (usually unsuccessfully) in order to legally obtain a piece of land, one which has been actively maintained by them for decades.

Although land and articles of clothing carry the spirit of the owner, there are differences between these possessions. Land, usually lineally defined through inheritance or communally used, has one spiritual owner and multiple users. Likewise, because it is never technically owned by people, but by deities, land is transferable at death, although it usually stays in the family. Clothing, on the other hand, has only one user, as Q'eqchi' women rarely if ever allow other women to wear their huipils. This simply does not happen.[7] Women are the sole owners of their huipils and at death their mu resides within this object. Carrying the spirit of their owner, huipils are animate objects that tell life stories and have embedded value (Kopytoff 1988 [1986]:64–91; Stallybrass 1999:30). They are articulations embodied with memories of the senses (Seremetakis 1994:225). As active subjects, these fetishes of self cannot be worn by others when death separates the deceased from visible landscapes.

When people die, their mu resides in a timeless locale and, because mu also resides within their personalties, these owned objects, too, become timeless selves. Yet, this atemporalism of ancestors' possessions contradicts the characteristic understanding of huipils and corte as anything but timeless, for, in fact, they continuously change and symbolically and physically evolve (Hendrickson 1995:177–180). Corte, for example, is typically worn until it is torn up, at which time it becomes a rag for the kitchen. Traje is never thrown out, but recycled and used until it finally disintegrates. During the life of its owner, cloth is embedded with vitality and morality. At death, clothing maintains itself as an active symbolic mediator, though it no longer only brokers relations between owners and action-in-place, but, like spiritual selves and ancestors, between timeless invisible death and time-endowed life.

Subsequently, in an act that shows reverence, acknowledges social relations, and ceases the power and viability of the clothing, people burn their kin's material possessions after death. Burning is one of the most common Mayan practices that demonstrate respect. Whether burning candles, sugar, liquor, or copal, to burn is to revere and bless. So, when a mother's huipil is burned rather than worn, the daughter is demonstrating the utmost reverence to her mother as she symbolically blesses her mother's soul. By burning, a daughter acts-in-place, acknowledging and maintaining the web of relations that gives her invisible mother power, creates selves, and constructs ideas of ownership, community, morality, time, and space.[8]

Death is cross-culturally understood as a cessation or rearrangement of time (Humphreys 1981:261–279). However, for Q'eqchi' people, death itself is not the cessation of time but a process that brings ancestors to an interstitial location where time stands still. Yet, spiritual selves, although residing in a realm of timelessness, are not timeless themselves. Time never stops for active subjects. There is no such thing as pure, still silence.[9] Land, bodies, spirits, and clothing remain in motion within external and internal structuring exchanges. When Q'eqchi' people die, their mu goes to a place that is out of sight and atemporal, although the ancestors themselves do not stop acting, nor do they go silent.

This active ancestral involvement is unlike Andrew Strathern's analysis of death in Melanesia, where he finds that exchange is abruptly stopped and subsequently rearranged (1981:220–221). Yes, there is repositioning, but death does little to the Q'eqchi' structural conception of "community," since it is continuously supported and defined by active ancestors. Rather than redefining social relations, death reinforces them, but because relatives are now invisible, they are more powerful and dangerous, and they demand the same type of respect offered to spiritual owners/outsiders (q. paab'ankil). Death perpetuates the community structure of invisible ancestors and quasi-outsiders as well as visible relatives and neighbors, although the content of the taxonomy shifts and power is repositioned.

Verging on foreignness, ancestors become virtual owners. Controlling history, heritage, and costumbres, ancestors are transcendental owners of the Q'eqchi' community. They are the symbolic intermediaries between history and contemporary social relations. Representing the complex relationships that construct and maintain cultural imaginaries, ancestors (and their remaining personal items) exist as external mediators of the community. They reside within a space of death, a colonized area full of ambiguity and conflict, and a mirror to the social relations that make up communities (Taussig 1987:3–36, 374). However, as it is constructed from social and historical relations, this timeless (and spaceless) realm is more than a conjunction between the ancestors and their living descendents. Global economies meet local subsistence practices, Germans encounter Q'eqchi' coffee pickers, Spaniards relate to caciques, and saints brush up against mountain spirits. This is a cosmological and transnational hyperspace (Kearney 1996:118) where histories, peoples, cultures, and communities collide and coalesce.

MAPS AND HISTORY: EXPLORATIONS INTO TIME AND SPACE

The lived present holds a past and a future within its thickness. (Merleau-Ponty 2002 [1945]:321)

Every person that entered my house on the hill had to pass in front of a large map of Guatemala that hung in my front room. We had instructional video classes in this room and we often used the map as a didactic tool for focusing and zooming. Even when we were not using it for video exercises, the project participants, and many other guests to my house, spent much time perusing this visual representation of their country.

I would often ask people if they could locate Livingston on the map, a task that I initially thought would be simple because of the town's prominent position at the mouth of the Río Dulce. Few located the town. I would point out Livingston and the river before I would ask my second question. Can you find where you came from? To do so, people had to follow the river west to Lago Izabal and then to the western corner of El Estor, but no visitor (except Armando) was ever able to locate his or her homes in Alta Verapaz or in western Izabal. Q'eqchi' people cannot read maps. Before I continue exploring this fact, I want to clarify that I asked numerous non-Q'eqchi' people the same questions. I learned that few people in Livingston had acquired the skill of reading maps. This was important, because I felt myself leaning towards ethnocentrism. However, I was quickly reminded that map reading is learned, not an innate ability to transfer landscapes to two-dimensional drawings. Although I do not remember learning how to read a map, I surely acquired this skill. Even so, teachers in Livingston tell me that all children learn how to read maps in primaria, and I often saw children coloring maps of Guatemala and Central America as homework. Why are these skills not easily acquired and applied?

Physical presence is how Q'eqchi' people understand, gain knowledge, desire, and feel pleasure. If one likes something, one says *nacuulaj chicuu* (q. it arrives at the face). When one understands something, one says *tau ru* (q. it is in front of the face). When something is needed, one says *taraj ru* (q. it is wanted in front of the face). It seems that tangibility—being in front of the face—creates comprehension. In contrast, when something is not tangible or intellectually graspable, then the dimensions of time and space begin to blur.

I thus hypothesize that Q'eqchi' people have difficulty reading maps because they are representations of land that are spatially flattened and missing time. Land is meaningful because it is full of time cycles and human practices. Rainy seasons, burning seasons, sowing, weeding, clearing, dry seasons, harvesting time, moon cycles, tides, suns, and stars all represent the movement of time as dictated by land. For Q'eqchi' and many other Mayan people, time and space is a whole, a coalesced idea that is manifested in the land (León-Portilla 1988:85–86). Time and space are not separate entities, as exemplified in the vocabulary used for both time and space. *Najt* (q.), for example, means "distant in length" and "far away in time."

When Q'eqchi' people talk about how distant a place is, they will never tell you "four kilometers" or "half a mile," as is expected and often desired by foreign anthropologists. As hard as I tried, I was unable to get answers in terms of quantitative length units, but rather heard responses like "a few hours," "a few minutes," and the typical response, "not too long" (all of which were usually inaccurate in my terms). Time and space are inseparable in the Q'eqchi' imaginary. Because time and space are interwoven, history is not conceptualized as another time but as another place as well.[10] While I, as a representative Westerner, perceive history as a reflection of a past timeframe rather than a distinct land, I argue that Q'eqchi' people perceive recent history spatially. Likewise, when land is synchronically represented as maps on pieces of paper, the images have no meaning. Without time, maps are ahistorical pretty pictures with no iconic or indexical value.

Perceptions of history emerge from the relationship of time and space with land and individual, such that the Q'eqchi' often conceive of the past as what was produced by the land. When they speak of their homes in Cobán, they tell me that they miss the produce, such as beans and tomatoes, rather than the family they left behind. This was quite common when I asked people to talk about their homes in Alta Verapaz. Immediately, they would begin to tell me about the land, the produce, and the refreshing cold climate. They would pine over the quality tomatoes and insect-free beans. For them, recent history is land endowed with the power of another time.

But, there is more than one type of past. There are two grammatical categories for the past in Q'eqchi'. The most recent past (*xin-*) is kept within personal memory, something that has occurred within the past few days, weeks, or maybe even months or years. The second past tense (*kin-*) is reserved for history that occurred long ago, but when people's ancestors still lived. This is the time of *abuelos* (sp. grandparents), when people who were living are now dead and when today's living, except for centenarians, were not yet born. Most people extend the application of this still-tangible past tense to approximately one hundred years ago. There is, however, a timeless and spaceless realm that goes beyond these grammatical categories. Mariano called it *yeomeb,* and explained it as a third past tense for things *muy, muy antiguo* (sp. very, very old). But, it is less a tense than a concept.[11] This is the time of myth, Jesus, Adam and Eve, and long-dead ancestors such as the ancient Maya. This is when time and space cease to exist. This is when timelessness becomes power. Mariano says that this is the time that you cannot see or touch.

So, when I asked Q'eqchi' people how many years ago did the Mayan people build their temples, they would first respond with a vague answer such as "a very long time ago." After some academic urging, most people responded "one hundred years ago." Almost unanimously, "one hundred years" represents an extremely distant time, a temporality when the oldest deceased family members that are remembered were actually born. History, thus, is understood in an extremely physical sense, in a way that goes back through a lineage only a few generations, and before this tangible time is the invisible and incomprehensible period of myth. Since Q'eqchi' Maya cannot imagine the mythical realm—it is completely intangible—when they are obliged to quantify this period (for an ethnographer's queries) they offer a unit up to where their tangibility (and kin) ends—at one hundred years. Mediating the foreign and familiar, ancestors are the interlocutors between the distant past and very recent, the intangible and the in-your-face. Before ancestral time, history becomes an unimaginable and intangible space where time and vision cease, a mythical dead-space.

History and ancestors are intrinsically linked in the Q'eqchi' imaginary. Ancestors are responsible for carrying the knowledge of costumbres, of maintaining a Mayan way of life,[12] but they are also on the verge of becoming timeless, foreign, and completely unknowable. Both history and ancestors traverse the Q'eqchi' imaginary, mediating between powerful beings who control time from within their bodies—like the ancient Maya—and contemporary individuals who sense time and space through the tangible land. However, the tangibility necessary for historic meaning applies to practically all forms of knowledge, which is why the Q'eqchi' language has no verb for an essentialized being (such as *ser* in Spanish), but only for being at a certain location or time (q. *waank,* sp. *estar*). Meaning, in all its senses, emerges from active connections that are fortified and made tangible through temporal and spatial mediation and reproduced through practice and perception. Significance comes from motion.

PURO MAYAN: TIMEFUL, INVISIBLE, AND UN-ESSENTIAL

Matilde: The Ch'olwiinq scare people too.
Hilary: They scare too?
Matilde: It can occur at night . . . at midnight.
Hilary: At midnight, the Ch'olwiinq come here?
Matilde: Aha.
Hilary: And what do they do?
Matilde: They rob everything. Perhaps there is treasure in the house. They carry everything they find outside. Then they carry everything away, everything, everything.
Hilary: The Ch'olwiinq?
Matilde: Aha.
Hilary: I thought that they didn't come here. This is the Ch'olwiinq or the Q'eq?
Matilde: The Ch'olwiinq.
Hilary: And what do they look like? Are they people?
Matilde: Aha.
Hilary: Where do they come from?
Matilde: From the mountains.
Hilary: They come from the mountains? And they come here to steal things from people?
Matilde: Aha.
Hilary: From the Q'eqchi' and all?
Matilde: Everyone.
Hilary: Everyone. And they pass by at midnight?
Matilde: Aha.
Hilary: Have they come to your house?
Matilde: No, only outside.
Hilary: Outside?
Matilde: Because we were sleeping, the door was closed. They make a lot of noise outside during the night.
Hilary: You heard it?
Matilde: Aha.
Hilary: You heard it? What type of noise do they make?

HILARY AND MATILDE

Matilde: Some other kind.
Hilary: You heard it?
Matilde: They were talking outside.
Hilary: They were talking? In what? They speak Q'eqchi'?
Matilde: No.
Hilary: What do they speak?
Matilde: I think English.

Ch'olwiinq are mythical beings that mediate between the far past and today, between intangibility and physicality, and between time and space. The Q'eqchi' word *wiinq* means "man" and *ch'ol* comes from the Ch'ol Mayan people, although it also means "heart." Ch'olwiinq has traditionally been translated as "men of Ch'ol." Others have translated it as "wild men" (Wilson 1995:83–84). But because the internal components of the Q'eqchi' body are interchangeable, Ch'olwiinq could also be understood as "spirit men" or "men of essence."

Ch'olwiinq are very wise and powerful people who live deep in the jungle where they cannot be seen. They never die. They are extremely old, although they do not age like human beings. They have abundant gold and they have capabilities unknown to the average person, such as the power of telepathy and levitation. Ch'olwiinq speak numerous languages and they are pale skinned. They can move stones simply by whistling. In many ways, but by far not all, the Ch'olwiinq symbolize the ancient "pure" Maya.

Felipe told me that there are two types of Ch'olwiinq, some that are good and others, like the one described by Matilde, that are mean. He says that both types speak Maya, the term Q'eqchi' people use to refer to the Mopan Mayan language of Belize. Some around Livingston, he says, only speak Q'eqchi'. Felipe says there is an old Ch'olwiinq in San Antonio, Belize who speaks Q'eqchi', Maya, Spanish, German, and English. Ch'olwiinq eat raw meat and they do not have salt. While they usually go unseen, it is possible to see Ch'olwiinq either by appointment or by accident. If they are met unexpectedly in the bush, similar to a sudden appearance of an ancestor or Tzuultaq'a, a Ch'olwiinq causes susto. When Ch'olwiinq are in the bush, they are completely nude, occasionally using large tropical leaves to cover their private parts. This is when they exist unseen. However, when someone has an appointment to see one, the Ch'olwiinq dress in fine clothing for the meeting. An appropriate and appreciated gift for the guest to bring would be a bag of salt. Felipe told me that the Ch'olwiinq in San Antonio, Belize, is an ancestor (sp. *antepasado*) and is adorned with medallions of gold. He has a home in town although he passes his time in the hills. People go to him for advice about things like work, love, and, particularly, the milpa. This old Ch'olwiinq does not need a chair because he levitates, and if you are lucky he may give you a piece of gold.

Q'eqchi' people understand that they are the descendents of the ancient Maya, but unless they have had contact with the Mayan revitalization movement more prevalent in the highlands, they see little continuity between the ancient Maya and themselves. According to the Q'eqchi' in Livingston, the ancient Maya were powerful and wise people who did not cook their food. They were noble and valiant, and when they needed something all they had to do was ask for it and it would appear. This is how they made their magnificent temples and pyramids, simply by thinking and moving stones by telekinesis. Because there were no watches, they told time by the sun, which showed them when to sow and reap their harvests. Ancient Mayans were very rich and they buried their gold and other wealth in the ground because banks did not exist at that time. They lived for over one hundred years. The ancient Maya were pure, *puro Maya*.

> They were always very powerful and they had incredible things. When they wanted to go hunting, all they had to do was call and whistle and the animals would appear. The animals would appear and they would catch them, but us, . . . we are in the last phase. We do not have anything. We do not have courage. We are very weak, very poor, and we do not do anything. But they had courage. The Mayas had strength. (Audiotaped interview with Alberto)

Alberto represents the common attitude among Q'eqchi' people on the topic of their ancient ancestors, the Maya, and his reference to the phases (or stages) of Mayan history echoes statements I often heard in Livingston. The first stage was when the Maya were most powerful, when all they had to do was whistle, and a machete would start chopping a field. The second phase was when they still had power, but at this stage it was physical power and brute strength. Then the conquistadors came. Mayan kings heard that the Spanish were coming so they hid all their treasures in the hills. The Maya were no longer rich, but poor and colonized. This began the third, final, and current phase.[13]

When I ask people what happened to the ancient Maya, many say that they escaped to Belize. Similarly, Felipe told me that the Guatemalan government used airplanes to gather the Ch'olwiinq in order to relocate them to Belize. The relocation of Ch'olwiinq with airplanes may symbolize the forced movement of Mayans during the sixteenth century into *reducciones*, or the more recent military practice of placing Mayans into development poles and model villages for surveillance and "protection" against the guerrillas (Manz 1988:105). Regardless of the symbolism, Ch'olwiinq clearly represent ancient Mayan people who had extreme power and wealth. The necessary offerings of salt indicate how these beings typify the ancient Maya, as salt was an important trade item for the pre-Columbian Maya, and there was a large salt mine near Cobán that was exploited until the twentieth century (Andrews 1983:98–101). These ancient Mayan traders, however, were not practitioners of a pristine, unadulterated Mayan culture. Salt was a trade item that connected Alta Verapaz to foreign areas as early as the late Formative period.[14] Ancient Mayan people were involved in a broad, regional economy, and salt and other products mediated relations and trade between foreign powers.

Ch'olwiinq are no exception. While they clearly represent ancient Mayan people, they also symbolize outsiders and foreign interests. They speak English, German, and Spanish. Lola tells me that Ch'olwiinq look like Q'eqchi' people (sp. *paisanos*), but that they have a boss from the "outside" (sp. *un jefe de afuera*). Therefore, like Q'eq and Tzuultaq'a, Ch'olwiinq represent and gain power from outsiders. And like foreign others, Ch'olwiinq reside within atemporal worlds, where they neither age nor need watches to tell time. Ch'olwiinq, who seem so essentially Mayan, are far from *puro Maya*. Like ancestors and Tzuultaq'a, Ch'olwiinq mediate the articulations of the Q'eqchi' imaginary, traversing the contemporary and ancient, local and global, foreign and familiar. As arbitrators—actually, the embodiment of the exchanges themselves—they control time both symbolically and physically. With this ability to capture time, they control and capture power.

Likewise, costumbre is associated with temporal and spatial differences. Indeed, Mayan costumbres are practiced today, like uk'iha, the Deer Dance, and the practice of tying a turkey feather to an infant's hair to protect against ojo. However, when most people discuss costumbre, they use the past tense that represents the intangible and invisible time before grandparents were born. Or they tell me that costumbre is practiced in Cobán (another space), but not in Livingston.

Costumbre symbolizes and taps into an ancient time and a sacred other space where and when ancestors practiced rituals; it is powerful because it is imbued with invisible and timeless power from afar, the same potency inscribed upon ambiguous and mediating figures like Tzuultaq'a, Q'eq, Ch'olwiinq, and ancestors. The practice of costumbre likewise is a means of mediating the dynamic network in which Q'eqchi' people act and perceive. Costumbre links the past with present, all the while it actively pays familiar foreigners with pom, food, candles, and respect. It is ironic, therefore, that costumbre and the Ch'olwiinq represent the last unadulterated vestiges of the Mayan civilization (for ethnographers, tourists, Mayan people, etc.), because they are far from puro Maya. Or maybe they are puro Maya. Perhaps what is needed is to rearrange our understanding of puro Maya, and of essentialism.

Ethnographers, tourists, and Mayan people themselves are among those accused of essentializing the Mayan people and their culture, creating lists of cultural traits that are extractable from the dynamic fields of action from which they emerge (Robert Redfield's work is a prime example of this). Essentialism, however, need not always be a malevolent reification; it can be the benevolent objectification of multiple and aestheticized identifications (Werbner 1997:226–229). Collective agents do not automatically adhere to essentialist discourse. The Q'eqchi' Maya, although practicing shared dispositions, are not reifying but rather performing and defining themselves as dynamically created individuals and communities.

Mayan costumbre and the Ch'olwiinq, therefore, are not merely abstract linkages to the past—they are also contemporary forms of mediation that express Q'eqchi' people as collective units and as individual people practicing cultural models that connect them to the past, present, and future. The Q'eqchi' perform costumbre and narrate myths which embody the social relations that form ideas about who they are and who they are not. Costumbre and myth are practices and perceptions of the world that link internal and external identities, connect the foreign with the familiar, and reveal how Q'eqchi' people actively recreate this montage of positional and hybrid identities. Most concepts of personhood reinforce a theoretical concept of self within the confines of the skin-bound individual or as an essentialized, inner subject in opposition to collective, social identities (Battaglia 1995:5; Kondo 1990:34). Yet selves (and illnesses) need not be bound to human bodies (Comaroff 1985:8). Identities spill out of bodies into the social (Douglas 1982 [1970]:xiii). Selves do not stop at porous skin or community boundaries, but reach far beyond through time and space. There is not one Q'eqchi' Maya, but rather multiple, active agents who similarly perceive and identify within social and historical webs where people, mythical entities, and cloth fetishes are given meaning through social exchanges and where the control of time creates power.

MORE TEMPORAL EXPLORATIONS: ILLNESS AS SOCIAL AND SENSORY MEDIATOR

Ilabil (q.) or *ojo* (sp.) is the illness known in English as "the evil eye." Children are vulnerable to ojo when they are near pregnant women, drunk men, angry people or foreigners, and during a full moon. Even someone who is neither drunk, nor foreign, nor pregnant can give a young child ojo if that person is physically hot, such as when he or she comes in from a long walk. I inadvertently gave Lola's infant ojo, something for which I felt terribly guilty, although Lola assured me it was no big deal (sp. *es nada*). Foreigners, she told me, have *sangre fuerte* (sp. strong blood), and this is why they can easily give ojo to little children.

When individuals have "strong" or "hot" blood, it does not necessarily mean that they are bad people. Rather, it simply means that their blood does not harmonize with that of the surrounding society and that they emit too much heat and conflict. According to Carol Hendrickson, "people believed to be 'hot' or to have *sangre fuerte* . . . are considered powerful, domineering, rigid, and able to do harm; they exert themselves in the world and, in doing so, ignore proper social relations and appropriate social boundaries" (1995:99). Social deviants with hot and strong blood can kill chicks, ducks, pigs, and puppies, and they can ruin food. Atole, for example, will separate if a hot-blooded person looks at it while it is being stirred. Also milk, baby formulas, and cake mixes will separate when looked upon by hot-blooded people. Men generally have stronger blood then women, but during full moons and during their menstrual cycles women have incredibly strong and hot blood (Orellana 1987:34–36).

Infants are protected from ojo by wearing little red bracelets or caps or by wearing a feather in their hair. At night, caps and shawls are used to cover infants in order to prevent them from contracting ojo from the powerful moon.[15] Mariano told me that strong-blooded people will not give ojo if they touch a baby or cuddle chicks. Gazes carry visual power, and looking without physically touching is too strong a force, to which babies, chicks, and atole are susceptible. Q'eqchi' are not the only ones who believe this. When I saw Blanca, my East Asian neighbor, cooking atole, she quickly handed me the spoon and told me to stir. By only looking at and not stirring the cooking atole, she said I would make it separate and I would ruin the delicious hot corn drink.

While infants get ojo, older children and adults are susceptible to another, similar form of illness. Susto is acquired in a number of ways, but most often from sensing (seeing or hearing) one of the quasi-foreign spiritual beings such as Q'eq, Ch'olwiinq, Tzuultaq'a, or an ancestor. People also get susto from a severe scare or an extremely disturbing and emotional experience. People come down with susto at riverbanks or wells where Tzuultaq'a may be upset by the intrusion and grab the trespasser's mu. Unlike ojo, where the victim does not have to see the individual who gives the illness, recipients of susto must sense the being or the act that causes their fright.

Commonly exhibited symptoms of susto are restlessness, muteness, insomnia, loss of appetite, heart palpitations, nightmares, depression, inability to breathe, fear, fever, paralysis, and swelling. Although it is often characterized as a folk illness, which tends to diminish its import and physicality, there are documented cases of susto causing an individual's death (Rubel et al. 1985:108). Many of the symptoms of susto involve the severance of the senses from action and the inability to properly perceive within time and space. Susto, caused by witnessing invisible entities or social deviance, strikes by attacking an individual's ability to sense.

Susto is actually a form of soul loss, when the mu is dislodged and separated from the body. In order to heal the individual, the mu must be located and appeased. I was also told that you must go to a curer, an *aj ilonel,* who would bring you to either a crossroads or a riverbank, where the curer can often capture and retrieve a person's mu. However, Alberto told me that if a husband contracts susto after finding his wife in bed with another man—a major social transgression—he must drink her menstrual fluids to be cured. While this might seem far-fetched and disgusting, Alberto says this is the only means of regaining control of an unfaithful wife. By consuming her blood, which is strengthened during menstruation, a man absorbs her power into his body and cures the illness that would otherwise kill him.

I acquired susto after a dog attacked me from behind and bit the back of my thigh. My skin was not broken, but I had a bruised imprint of teeth to remind me that it could have been more serious. While I was certainly startled, I did not think much of it after I had returned home to change my torn shorts. But, the following evening I was walking from my house when I heard a dog growl. My heart skipped a beat. I stopped dead in my tracks. I had never in my life been afraid of dogs, but suddenly I was filled with terror. To have a fear of dogs in a Guatemalan town like Livingston, where vicious dogs rule the back streets, is a problem. Within the next few days, two more dogs tried to attack me and I became terrified to leave the house. I could physically sense my fear. I felt nervous, agitated, restless, and weak. Lola informed me that I had susto and that I had to burn the hair of the dog that bit me in order to cure myself. She told me I need not go to a curer, but that I could do it myself.

Blanca's little boy found the dog that bit my thigh and asked the owner for some of its fur. Then, with copal pom, charcoal, and garlic braids, I burned the dog hair in an old milk can underneath my bed. When sleeping, a person is most susceptible to susto, so the bed is the most important place to protect. While in bed, people can dream of dead ancestors or hear them knocking on the door and rummaging through their things. I took the episode quite seriously. I let the smoke fill my bedroom and my entire house before I walked around the exterior with the burning embers. I prayed and asked for help in finding my mu and ridding myself of this fear. My heart only fluttered once upon hearing a dog bark the following evening. I was no longer afraid. I had been cured.

I was somewhat of an exception, perhaps due to my proximity to the local community, because foreigners are more likely to cause illness (which I also did) than to be recipients of it. Foreigners' ability to bring about illnesses corresponds with their invasive place in the Q'eqchi' imaginary, although it may also be a result of the historic and tangible link between outsiders and deadly epidemics among the Maya populations of Guatemala (Carey 2001: 115–135). Another local example of an illness-causing foreigner is the individual who, to the dismay of the Q'eqchi' community, purchased the land containing the *pozo* (sp. well), a gorgeous, deep watering hole outside of town. This gringa or gringo—locals vary the gender when telling the story—is very mean (sp. *muy brava*). Armed with a gun, machete, guardian, or dog, the gringa/o fervently protects the land, and will shoot anybody who enters the property. (Among the versions featuring a male protagonist, I often heard that the individual is an American soldier who has an arsenal of guns and money cached nearby.) Q'eqchi' people used to go to the well to retrieve water, wash clothes, and bathe, but they are no longer allowed. Locals are upset because they believe that people do not own water. Water belongs to God or Tzuultaq'a, not to the gringa/o who is *muy mala,* a very bad person.

> They say that he sold it to some gringos . . . We used to go there to bring water, to wash in the little spring. But, now that they sold it this is prohibited. This is the problem we have with those who come from elsewhere. Instead of helping the poor, they remove things for someone, somewhere else—and well, the water isn't costing them anything. They aren't maintaining it, God gave it to us . . . the water is for everyone. . . . This gringo is fencing the entire place in. It is prohibited for anyone to enter. (Videotaped interview with Armando)

One day a little boy wanted to go swimming at the pozo. The gringa/o appeared and grabbed the little boy. The boy escaped the foreigner's grip but was chased off the property. He was terrified by the foreigner and by these immoral actions, and he soon fell ill with a severe, but curable, case of susto.

Susto is always a form of mediation (Rubel et al. 1985:9). It reproduces ideas of appropriate action and cosmological positions, and it illuminates the connections between Q'eqchi' people and a host of anachronistic and invisible outsiders. Susto is caused by the sight of a social transgressor or of someone who is not involved in the reproduction of moral relations. Because the wicked gringa/o forbade people to bathe and wash clothes in the watering hole, s/he was not only interrupting established social patterns, but denying Q'eqchi' people access to a locale they felt they had the right to visit. It was not his/her place to regulate access since wells are controlled by Tzuultaq'a, and it is ultimately the mountain spirits' decision whether to give permission. But people told me they could no longer enter the pozo without receiving permission—which everyone appears too terrified to do—from the foreign owner, who has never actually been seen, yet who remains an almighty social deviant. Further, the male/female duality of the foreign owner, and references in the stories to the ability to cause susto at sources of water, the incredible arsenal of guns and wealth, and the inappropriate regulation of access, suggest that Q'eqchi' people may have begun to imagine this person as a composite entity of foreignness, like Tzuultaq'a, although the evil qualities seem to outweigh the benevolent ones. This conflict also demonstrates the disharmony between conceptions of ownership as legally bound (and physically fenced in, as is the well) and a more active, communal, and transcendental understanding of possession and use.

Disharmony and conflict also created illness for Mariano. He became ill with what he called *desaparación* (sp., disappearance, as in the disappearance of his mu). He was unable to eat or sleep and he was sleepwalking through town. He went to a Ladina curer, who told him that he had given away too much to a certain person who was not appreciating his kindness. Indeed, Mariano was constantly giving gifts, lending money, and offering hospitality, food, and a place to sleep to a young Q'eqchi' man. With all this giving, one would expect something in return, but Mariano's young friend never offered him any gratitude; he just continued to take from Mariano. Eventually Mariano fell ill, and with the help of the curer he realized that it was this nonreciprocal relationship that was causing his illness.

Accumulation of wealth, or at least the sumptuary display of it, is also considered nonreciprocal action-out-of-place. Breaking moral codes that emphasize collaboration and reciprocity and breaching the egalitarian structure of community can lead to envy, allegations of witchcraft, and illness.

> We don't know how to advance ourselves, and see, among
> the Q'eqchi' people there is much, well, if someone is ad-
> vancing, there is a lot of jealousy. This is what happens, there
> are a lot of divisions among us Q'eqchi' . . . Yes, if someone
> is advancing or progressing, we don't want them to succeed.
> (Videotaped interview with Agustin)

Matilde told me about the time her father and mother were *embrujado*
(sp. hexed, cursed) by a woman in El Estor who was envious of the small
plot of land that Matilde's father owned in the area. Matilde's parents were
losing weight unexplainably. They traveled to Puerto Barrios to visit a
Ladina curer, who told Matilde's father, Venancio, that he had frogs in his
belly. She placed live frogs on his stomach for multiple hours per day for
two weeks to rid him of the hex. Sorcery of this type is not common, but
you do hear of it on occasion. Envy and longing for other people's possessions is a social transgression and is considered a vice and a wrongdoing.
Equally, excessive displays of wealth and success are also considered action-
out-of-place, as it disturbs the reciprocal and collaborative framework of
the Q'eqchi' community. Coincidentally, Mariano told me that shamans
cure sickness by feeding blood to the *duenos del monte* (sp. the owners of
the jungle, or Tzuultaq'a). Feeding and consumption are always part of the
process of curing, balancing the exchange, and regaining control.

Q'eqchi' people are also susceptible to susto when they attempt to make
a profit from the discovery of ancient silver coins. I heard numerous stories
about treasures that *espantan* (sp. scare) and make noises during the night.
In fact, there were said to be treasures on the hill where I lived, and people
asked me if I ever heard them at night. Coins, in this case, are like clothes,
anachronistic mediators that embody an internalized (and externalized)
network and traverse the three phases of Mayan history. Relevant here is
that the German company Ferropazco was once located in the area where
I lived. While Q'eqchi' people explain that the caches of gold and silver
were buried by their ancient Mayan ancestors, it is more likely that these
haunted coins were from the German export company. So, not only does
the accumulation of coins violate appropriate modesty in regards to displays of wealth, but it again exemplifies the conflation of foreigner and
ancient Mayan, the blurring of self and other.

People fall ill when they ignore moral obligations of reciprocal exchange and respect, or when they witness a social transgression (Hendrickson 1995:99–102; Orellana 1987:30). This is why illness is caused when

timeless mediators become visible and when powerful people who control time look upon others without physically touching them. Social deviance is revealed through the senses. And, since time is a powerful asset when separated from the physical landscape, the myriad of peripheral keepers also bolster their positions of authority and respect by controlling space, vision, and the perception of time.[16]

Mariano told me about a young man who encountered a messenger of Tzuultaq'a in the bush. He found himself—in a blink of an eye—in the mountain spirit's cavernous home.

> He saw snakes hanging from the ceiling like ropes, all in a row. The old man was sitting on top of the pens full of animals. The young man thought he was only there a few seconds because he closed his eyes and then was back at the same place where the messenger had found him earlier. He walked home and told the people what he had seen and they told him that he was gone for three days, but he didn't believe them because he thought he was in the cave for only a few minutes. (Audiotaped interview)

Others narrated similar tales about visitors who believed they were in caves of Tzuultaq'a for merely minutes, but upon returning home would learn that they in fact had been gone for days. Tzuultaq'a, it seems, controls time by making his home a landless invisible locus where individuals enter and lose track of time. Ch'olwiinq also control time and relations through age-lessness and by reading the sun, while ancient Mayans controlled time by using telekinesis to clear a field or build a pyramid.[17]

We can move this further, to the meta-realm of postmodernity and globalization, where powerful (at times illness-causing) entities control time. Common technologies such as email, cellular phones, and fax machines sever land from time (Lash and Urry 1994:242). Microwaves dismantle cooking times and fertilizers decrease growing seasons. Airplanes are time machines, transporting fashion-laden travelers who carry trends from the United States to Guatemala before the styles would normally make it into stores (Hendrickson 1995:71). Tourists (and ethnographers) snap photographs that freeze, flatten, and desensitize. In this context, temporal and spatial processes are means of dealing with the social disruptions of postmodernism. Specific modes of production and sociality produce particular concepts of time and space. Space and time are created and appropriated, rather than accepted, as means of defining history and social disorder (Harvey 1989:202). Sensory deprivation and illness are means of understanding and restoring social order.

By attacking senses and the ability to perceive, illness maintains moral obligations. Failing to feed ancestors, wearing clothes of dead people, forgetting to ask Tzuultaq'a for permission to plant, digging up ancient coins in the ground, running into a crazy gringa, witnessing a social transgression, having an emotional experience, encountering a Q'eq at night, and seeing Ch'olwiinq in the jungle all can cause susto. Illness reifies who is an outsider and who has power, and it mediates exchanges of respect and consumption, between historical networks and contemporary linkages. Illness is a process, like death, that mirrors social action, attacks the senses, and reproduces morality through practice and perception.

CAMERAS AS MEDIATORS OF TIME AND SPACE

Community is mirrored within and supported by an external web of relations where ancestors reside and where histories, economies, moralities, and social practices converge. Tzuultaq'a, Q'eq, ancestors, foreigners, and Ch'olwiinq are symbolic brokers of this space; they are interpositional beings between time and space and interlocutors between people and their fields of action. They arbitrate between the living present and the timeless past from their third timespace (Lavie and Swedenburg 1996). But this is not only a space of death; it is also a transnational hyperspace where distinctions of time and space explode. Q'eq negotiate between German finca owners, African slaves, and Q'eqchi' workers. Tzuultaq'a fall between Mayan deities, Ladinos, Christian Gods, and tourists. Ch'olwiinq are interstitial beings who represent Ancient Mayan pyramid builders and contemporary Mayan milpa agriculturists. Arbitrating the local and the global, anachronistic mediators are partial outsiders who require respect and constant reverence. By controlling time, these brokers control the relations that form community.

But Tzuultaq'a, Q'eq, Ch'olwiinq, and ancestors are more than mediators of social relations. These beings are the social and historic links that construct cognitive moralities and meaning. Embodied within these figures are relations of inequality, religious conversion, active costumbre, and colonial mimicry. These beings, as they emerge from complex webs of relations, are themselves icons of these exchanges. And as this timeless circuit of mythic historical connections mirrors contemporary social bonds,

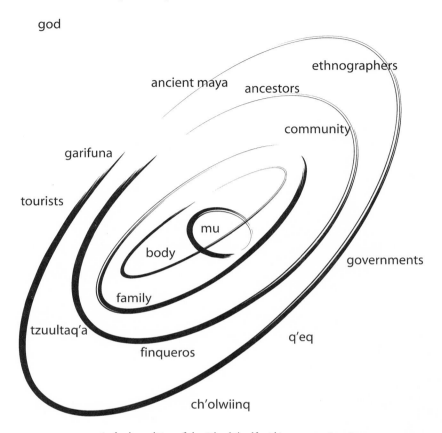

god

ancient maya

ethnographers

ancestors

garifuna

community

tourists

mu

body

governments

family

tzuultaq'a

q'eq

finqueros

ch'olwiinq

FIGURE 7.1.   *Author's rendition of the Q'eqchi' self within a greater imaginary*

Proyecto Ajwacsiinel and the meaning given to cameras and images also emerge from this imagined network of relations.

It is not coincidental that the one person able to read the map in my house was by far the most accomplished and skilled videographer. It is not that the others were incapable, but it seems that Armando had an ability that far exceeded the others. Perhaps this is because his visual representations of culture matched my Westernized perception of how to frame subjects, handle cameras, and create aesthetic and informative images. Possibly, it is Armando's ability to separate time from space, as is shown in his ability to read maps, that aids him in using the camera. Perhaps this is necessary for a Westernized aesthetic—the ability to categorize time and space separately, to make them into beings rather than processes of be-ing.

Still photography is clearly the surveillance of space rather than time

(Barry 1995:43). Because of their timelessness and their domination of space, still images have been ruthlessly criticized as "flat death" (Barthes 1981:92). Cameras are considered colonial agents and producers of passive, motionless objects for the pleasure of active, hungry, consuming, viewer/voyeurs (Hartmann et al. 1999; Mitchell 1988; Mulvey 1989:14–26; Pinney 1992:28–32; Root 1996:8–12). In this vein, photographic processes are considered tools of the modern era's classificatory natural sciences, creating extractable facts and satiating the contemporary need to know through visual imperialism (Foucault 1980:146–148; Jay 1988; MacDougall 1998:64–66; Pinney 1992:75–82; Poignant 1992:42; Rorty 1980:38–40).

On the other hand, moving film "breathes life into the record" (Collier 1995 [1975]:249). By adding the flow of time to desensitized photographic objects, video and moving film have the potential to overcome the inherent political inequalities in snapping shutters and freezing others for consumption. Unlike maps, where space is severed from time, video spatially and temporally mimics lived experience. Not that photographs do not carry the potential to provoke. They certainly do. Even Barthes recognized their ability to come out and prick you with their subjective "punctum" (1981). Emotions are evoked. However, with temporal and spatial codes somewhat more intact, video has a greater capability of creating sensory-enriched stories of people practicing and perceiving within their dimensional fields of action (Collier 1995 [1975]:251). Therefore, video should be an appropriate medium for the display of how Q'eqchi' people reproduce their cultural imaginary through time and space. But, is it?

My answer to this question is ambivalent, because I feel that video has offered us—the Q'eqchi' people, myself, and the readers of this text—the ability to go beyond traditional academic gazing. This, of course, is one of my goals in this book—to show how culture, the people who embody culture, and practices and perceptions are movements within dynamic structures, rather than products. This work is also a representation of processes, which is why it is vital that I visually depict the Q'eqchi' people in motion. Triptychs suggest the vitality, temporality, and movement of interviews, landscapes, practices, and lives. Multiple simultaneous frames from a solid course of time clearly do not match the actual temporal flow, but they do infer the importance of representing time along with space, in order to fully recreate the practices and fields of motion that reproduce cultural structures.

However, I have yet to answer the question above. Is video an appropriate medium? How did the project participants merge time and space in video expression? If the Q'eqchi' people of Livingston have trouble reading maps because they represent space removed from time, then perhaps video cameras are tools that capture time but eliminate space. This would then lead to the same difficulty working with video that Q'eqchi' people encountered reading maps.

Q'eqchi' people do not clearly distinguish between time and space in the everyday. However, we have seen how time and space can be severed, such as when Ch'olwiinq remain ageless and Tzuultaq'a steal time from social deviants and trespassers. However, where are these ageless entities? Some are located in the *monte* (sp. the bush), which is a general term for anywhere beyond the outer extremities of town; in other words, the untamed jungle. Ancestors traverse the skies with God, and Tzuultaq'a live in deep, unknown recesses of the earth. Q'eq reside on fincas, but they also fly through the sky at great speeds. So, when entities become timeless, they also become spaceless. Therein lies the inability of Q'eqchi' people to read maps. Without time, space has no meaning.

Video cameras rely on temporal manifestations of action, at least by my Westernized visual codes, though the space they represent is flattened. Yet both temporal and spatial components of film/video are envisioned only after being squeezed through a small (in our case, black-and-white) viewfinder. Even though the particular processes of action are viewed through this viewfinder, they are severed from the fields that give them meaning. In this way, video cameras, too, create images extractable from the whole processes and networks from which they emerge. Not only is space flattened and washed out; it also loses its sense of value when it is extracted from the surrounding landscape. Could this be what happens when Q'eqchi' people pick up a video camera? Is this why, for example, the participants of Proyecto Ajwaacsiinel had such trouble focusing? Q'eqchi' people attach meaning to time through its connection with not just space, but the processes of space—such as movement of moons, agriculture cycles, death, rain—rather than categorical, constructed spaces, such as hours and minutes. Did the participants have difficulty understanding the spatiality of life through a small, black-and-white viewfinder, because they are accustomed to comprehending the reverberations of life through all their senses and through the physicality of time and space? Perhaps.

Yet there is Armando, who upon first picking up a camera was able to focus, zoom, hold the camera still, and create full frames of action. What makes him different from the others? He was the most educated in the project (he had finished high school), and he had been in the military. Perhaps the difficulty the participants encountered not only involved artificially confining temporal and spatial manifestations of life, but also stemmed from their inexperience with learning new (and completely foreign) technologies, which Armando had had to do while in school and in the army. Also, although our lessons were informal, perhaps the participants were not accustomed to learning in a class setting for a specific amount of time. Did we (the camera and I) objectify fluid time to a specific structure (Spanos 2000:13–34)? Should I have handed them cameras and taken them out to their milpas instead of my living room?

I did not envision the video camera as a neutral tool that would allow subjects to express themselves in unique cultural means, although I was open to this possibility. I did, however, conceive of the camera as a means to see through Q'eqchi' eyes (Worth and Adair 1972). Even so, I did not expect to recreate a Q'eqchi' reality, because cameras are foreign technologies, videotape is not life, and there is no thoroughly unified Q'eqchi' way of envisioning the world that consistently preempts individual interpretation. And even though photographic and filmic images do emerge from networks of meaning and power,[18] they are not the same as living and acting subjects. As much as I believe in the power of video and imagery to evoke emotions and sensory reactions, cameras may indeed produce sensory-deprived images. While at a theoretical level, a videographic image is an active subject that exists within complex webs of meaning, in practice it may be devoid of life.

Clearly, images of all forms have the potential to embody phenomena and evoke deep sensory responses. They can be spaces of dislocation that produce visceral reactions. The production of their meaning is not merely a visual or an intellectual act; it is a complex bodily process (Marks 2000). Yet I am not completely convinced that this is how the Q'eqchi' perceived the imagery produced through the project. Can it be the way that space and time are so integral to knowledge, understanding, and history? Does this somehow negate the tangibility and bodily reading of imagery for the Q'eqchi'? If sensory perception is as cultural and historical as it is biological (or even more so), then the sensory reading of imagery will obviously differ in various cultural contexts. If our bodies are, as Phenomenology argues, sensible and sentient entities of perception (Merleau-Ponty 1968:150), then the Q'eqchi' might not conceptualize imagery as something tangible, or real, or knowledge-laden, or evoking. However, as Vivian Sobchack explains, film is not only a visual object (1992:21). Images are phenomena that reach deep into sensory bodies in ways that gazes do not. Thus, perhaps it is I who am not capable, because of my own sensory limitations of knowledge gathering, to fully grasp and comprehend exactly how the Q'eqchi' people perceive imagery.

What is consequential for the Q'eqchi' is that these video images are not tangible, that they cannot really get in front of their faces, which means that they cannot fully comprehend them. Images may embody some level of the abstract or out-of-sight that they are unable consciously to grasp, or that they fear. Consider how Q'eqchi' people imagine history only as far back as the generation of their grandparents' birth, or how knowledge occurs when it is brought in front of a face. When knowledge is hidden and separated from time and space, it is a powerful resource that must be feared and respected, like the internal potency of costumbre. Thus, only divinely trained shamans can cure social disruptions and serious illness by seeing into and traveling through intangible realms of time and space. It is no coincidence that the word for curer, *aj ilonel,* stems from the verb *ilok,* "to see." Aj ilonel have the ability to help others by envisioning and traversing the usually invisible worlds of timeless social mediators. Even the *ilob'aal* (quartz crystals) they use to divine, provide insight, and reach these intangible worlds, are translated as "view" or "something that provides vision." Sight, for the Q'eqchi', is a primary metaphor of knowing and accessing not only tangible, visible worlds, but even more so the whole realm beyond seeing. This, then, may explain why some Q'eqchi' people perceive cameras and the images they produce ambiguously, as something that can destroy and create life.

In this way, the project participants were acutely aware of the theoretical components of the camera—its ability to desensitize and freeze (similar to how susto causes muteness and paralysis) and its simultaneous ability to aesthetically recreate realities—because they put this theory into practice. They physically experienced the Cartesian perspective of the master eye that turns temporal processes of gaining knowledge into reified images to be conquered. The camera was a powerful quasi-foreign entity, like Tzuul-taq'a, that captured time and life processes and severed the senses from action, but that also had the capability to reproduce, nurture, and provide. In this way, cameras are appropriate tools for the Q'eqchi' people in Livingston, maybe not for the production of Westernized images, but most definitely for the recreation of how Q'eqchi' people position themselves through the processes and places of their imagined and videographic worlds. The Q'eqchi' practiced and perceived through their embodied Q'eqchi' imaginaries and in true phenomenological fashion dismantled the distinctions between mind and body and subject and object. Bodies, after all, are not for an "I think," but rather are groupings of "lived-through meanings." (Merleau Ponty 2002 [1945]:177). And sight is only one of the sensual processes that embody these meanings and allow us to step into realms beyond seeing.

Eight   # DÍA DE GUADALUPE
Identity Politics

DÍA DE GUADALUPE: 12 DECEMBER

Town has become more and more crowded. Relatives from Belize, Guatemala, and the United States have come to celebrate the opening of Livingston's fiesta season that lasts through New Year's Day.[1] Morning Mass ends to the sound of pulsing drums and rhythmic blowing of the traditional local instrument, the conch shell. Young children wearing indigenous dress dance frantically in front of the altar, up and down the aisle, screaming, laughing, and bouncing with the beat. Two Q'eqchi' families, one of which I know, remain standing within the pews as they curiously watch the explosion of body movement in the aisle. The musicians and children move out to the street, where dozens of people have gathered, waiting. The music stops temporarily while the group organizes. Older dancers arrive.

Soon, the drumming and blowing again commence and the dancers circle around the street, grabbing their skirts, twisting, bobbing, and speeding up with the blowing of the large conch shell and the shaking of maracas. By the time the group gets to the middle of town, hundreds of participants and onlookers walk the teeming dancers through town, to the muelle, and then to the gymnasium. Inside the gym are freshly painted walls covered with large Orange Crush logos and a stage with microphones and loudspeakers. A sign hanging above the stage announces that the Guadalupe Brotherhood, established on 31 October 1994, has organized the festival. Below the sign hangs a brightly colored towel with the image of Guadalupe. The Virgin is pregnant; she stands within a coronal sun, and wears a deep-blue dress with a star-speckled, caped hood.

Dancers and onlookers roam around, find seats, and wait while the energy rises. When the drumming begins, the dancers, now numbering in the hundreds, circle around and around, picking up velocity and intensity

each time the man on stage blasts the conch shell. Dancing, jumping, shaking, and spinning to the beat of the shell and accompanying drums — this is the Pororo dance, so named after the noise the dancers make while gyrating to the music.[2] PO-RO-RO . . . PO-RO-RO . . . PO-RO-RO. Winding itself through the streets from church to gymnasium, this is one of the biggest fiestas in Livingston. Hundreds enter the gym to watch the spectacle that continues for three days. The two Q'eqchi' families I saw in the church are now at home, preparing their afternoon meals.

The dancing is indeed wild: constant swirling motion, frenetic energy, contained entropy, raw emotion. Inside the gymnasium many more join and the dancers speed up and became more alive within the enlarged space.

Dancers are twirling and lifting their skirts, revealing their legs and shorts and flirting with the crowd and each other. The music is captivating and the constant drumbeat makes me want to join the dance, although I remain an engaged overseer, pointing my video camera and tapping my feet.

The dancers are mainly young women, although a few young boys and men do participate. Most of the male dancers wear ordinary street clothes, while the majority of women wear traditional Maya huipil and corte. Many women exchange the huipil for a T-shirt that is bound at the waist by a thick red scarf, and others add a straw hat, the kind one might win at a North American country fair. Quite a few of the women are made up like cherubs, with red cheeks, outlined eyes, and puffy, painted lips. Many have braids in their hair tied together at the ends with a ribbon, as Mayan women do in the highlands. Little boys have beards and moustaches etched on their faces with eyebrow pencils.

With all this veneration and imagery of indigenous dress, this may appear to be a typical, albeit unparalleled, indigenous Mayan celebration, but it is not—there are no Q'eqchi' dancers or spectators in this gymnasium. Only Garifuna and a few Ladinas dance the Pororo. Q'eqchi' people refuse to enter, either because of the entrance fee or, more likely, because they do not want to watch their neighbors dance around in corte. Q'eqchi' people in Livingston, while understanding Guadalupe as an indigenous figure, say that here Día de Guadalupe is for the Garifuna.

In the sixteenth century, Guadalupe appeared on the hill of Tepeyac, before the indigenous man Juan Diego. The Franciscan Bishop Juan de Zumárraga, after a series of miracles, came to believe that the Indian had in fact seen the Virgin, and he sanctioned the construction of a chapel for the Virgin of Guadalupe.[3] Only a few individuals in Livingston know the story of Guadalupe's sixteenth-century appearance. Mariano knew the narrative, which he (not surprisingly) told me occurred one hundred years ago rather than the more accurate five hundred years, only a decade or so after the "conquest" of the Aztecs. A number of people, indigenous and non-indigenous, point out that this is a day that celebrates women, particularly indigenous women. Garifuna, Ladino, and Q'eqchi' people tell me that Guadalupe is the indigenous Virgin and that this day celebrates the indigenous people of Mexico and Guatemala. Patrocinia points out the Virgin's pale-brown skin as an indication of her Indianness. Alberto tells me that this day celebrates the ancient Maya, *los puros Indios*. Yet, if this day is believed by all to celebrate *indigenismo* in some form, then why do Q'eqchi' people not participate? Why do they not even enter the gymnasium? Why is this a day for the Garifuna?

The twist is that for extra cash, Q'eqchi' women can and do rent their huipils and corte to Garifuna girls for the festival (the going rate was ten quetzals for the three-day period). Garifuna women can choose to rent the traditional Mayan dress or they can wear a more generic "indigenous" dress that is often made by their mothers and kept from year to year. Some female Garifuna get into business by renting these Pororo skirts to other Garifuna, hanging them out on the street to notify passersby of their intentions. This more generic skirt is usually a red corte made of lesser-quality, thinner material and cut much shorter at the knee than a typical Q'eqchi' corte, which is generally cut closer to the ankle. Q'eqchi' women consider these red cortes to be ugly and the T-shirt and wide red bands

to be even more offensive, almost polluting, to their beautiful indigenous corte.

> My sister rents her cortes on Día de Guadalupe for ten quet-
> zals. She only does it when someone asks her. The morenas
> do not often borrow the huipils because they wear T-shirts
> instead. I do not like that. They are ugly and I do not like that
> ugly band they wear around the waist. I never rent my corte
> to nobody. One time I rented it to a morena for a school
> project but she never paid me. (Audiotaped interview with
> Patrocinia)

> It isn't the same as we do it. They use them and then take
> them off after a little while, and they also carry them around
> in their hand out in the street. It is not like what we do.
> (Videotaped interview with Juliana)

Q'eqchi' women and men dislike the way the Garifuna women dance; they
find it offensive and disrespectful when the Garifuna women spin and grab
their skirts, revealing their legs, underwear, elastane pants, and short-shorts
below. *Chirlinkil*, the Q'eqchi' term used to describe the disrespectful act of
wearing a deceased woman's clothing, is also used by people discussing the
aggressive grabbing practiced by the Garifuna women while dancing the
Pororo. Q'eqchi' women would never grab their corte like that; the only
time they would be so rough with their clothing is when they are washing
it at the pila.

> I do not dance because you need a lot of guts. It is real tough
> out there and you have to be really strong. The women will
> pull your hair, hit you, and push you. They will throw you
> out if you cannot keep up. . . . I do not want to go watch
> them wear our clothes. I do not like it and I will not go.
> (Audiotaped interview with Patrocinia)

If Q'eqchi' women so adamantly dislike the Pororo dance, then why do
they continue renting their traje to the dancers? Why does apathy lie alongside aversion? This question is even more complex when you consider the
intimate relationship Q'eqchi' women have with their traje, which is endowed with essences of their personhood. Many answers to these questions
exist. First, although they do not necessarily distinguish between them—
rather envisioning themselves through more boundless forms of practice—

JULIANA

Q'eqchi' people do have internal and external identities. Because internal selves are invisible, potent symbols of community and ethnicity—linkages that embody what it is to be Q'eqchi' Mayan—then women are free to rent their external symbols of Mayanness. Second, Q'eqchi' people are constructed out of foreign and familiar relationships, and the figures they revere are often outsiders. Thus, it is neither strange nor unusual for people to pay reverence to an outsider, as Guadalupe is to the Garifuna. Third, the Garifuna are part-Indian, so they revere the Virgin as an expression of their own indigenousness. Fourth, Q'eqchi' people understand Día de Guadalupe in (misconstrued) accordance with all other Garifuna rituals and practices, which they see as wasteful, irreverent, and immoral.

Relations between the Garifuna and the Q'eqchi' are strained. In church, they sit apart from one another. Soccer rivalries exist. Schools are practically segregated for younger children. Even on Todos Santos, when the entire town goes to the cemetery, they remain separated. Only during the Easter procession do both Q'eqchi' and Garifuna get involved equally (except that Jesus is always a Garifuna). Therefore, unlike most research on Mayan people, where scholars indicate significant oppositional difference between Mayans and Ladinos, I find there to be active mutual disdain between the Garifuna and Q'eqchi' people. Whereas elsewhere Ladino people are the symbolic oppressors of and opposites to Mayan people, in Livingston the metaphorical antitheses are most certainly the Garifuna people.[4] Perhaps because they know them and their history, Q'eqchi' people find Ladino people more kind, more familiar, and less threatening than the Garifuna.

Demonstrating how flexible and inaccurate this Ladino/Indian oppositional positioning is in Livingston, it is the Garifuna who consider the Ladinos as their colonizers and oppressors (see the introductory image of Ash Wednesday in Chapter 1). A Ladino/Mayan opposition is not a truth; it is a situational construction that emerges from historical, social, cultural, and economic exchanges (Smith 1990a:72–92). In Livingston, the friction occurs between the Ladinos and the Garifuna, and between the Garifuna and the Q'eqchi'. The Garifuna and Q'eqchi' categorize each other with stereotypes and rarely interact socially. Garifuna label the Q'eqchi' as dirty, smelly, and stupid, but hard workers when properly instructed — typical Ladino stereotypes of the *Indio* (Adams 1990:147–152). Meanwhile, Q'eqchi' people consider the Garifuna aggressive, mean, dishonest, immoral, promiscuous, lazy, and criminally inclined. Obviously, the Garifuna and the Q'eqchi' are reifying images of one another that are timeworn but far from accurate in experience.

Since they consider the Garifuna tradition of Pororo a waste of time, Q'eqchi' tend to work during the festival. Either by renting clothes, selling street food, or tending milpas in the outlying aldeas, Q'eqchi' people view this as an opportunity to be productive in some manner. While the Q'eqchi' do not understand why the Garifuna spend their time and money venerating the indigenous Guadalupe, at the same time it makes perfect sense to them. The Q'eqchi' venerate foreigners: Tzuultaq'a, for example, can be Ladino, German, or gringo. Why then should not the Garifuna adore Guadalupe? That she is indigenous rather than Garifuna is not the problem. The issue is that the Q'eqchi' believe the Garifuna do not receive anything in return for their reverence. Indeed, Q'eqchi' people do not see this festival as reverent at all. Q'eqchi' ritual is based on ideas of active and productive exchange, reciprocity, respect, feeding, and consuming. By feeding deities, ancestors, and one another, Q'eqchi' people assure good crops, health, and strong communities. Because the Garifuna do not appear to receive anything for all their dancing, Q'eqchi' consider Día de Guadalupe unproductive, disrespectful, and wasteful, as they view all Garifuna ritual. Mariano complained about this issue:

> In Livingston, no one has respect. No one believes. No one has faith. People do things but they do not ask permission or show respect. People sow their fields without asking for help. The morenos are the worst offenders. They have respect for nothing.
>
> When the morenos have a dream where they see their deceased mother, they plan a Mass or they make a *dugu* [a ritual involving sacrifice]. There, they will have lots of food but they do not eat it, they just throw it out. They throw it out for their dead. They make two big pots, one for them to throw out, one for them to eat. They just throw it out to the sea. [I ask if the Q'eqchi' do not do a similar thing for All Saints' Day when they leave food out for their dead ancestors?] Oh yeah, sure, but they throw it out, we gather it all up in the end. (Audiotaped interview with Mariano)

Whether it was his failing eyesight, his store's empty shelves, or his aching back, Mariano often found something to gripe about. But his protesting about the Garifuna is something I hear from many people. It is not uncommon for outsiders (including tourists) also to consider the Garifuna ritual of *dugu* as wasteful, although the food is actually redistributed rather than thrown away. Donors bring unused food to the poor and needy of the community, or they feed ancestors by depositing sacrificial food in a hole by the sea (Jenkins 1998:162). Some of the distortion, therefore, may be a result of a Garifuna reverence of ancestors that are associated with the beach and water, rather than with the land. Because the Garifuna, too, reinforce ideas of community by feeding ancestors that demand respect and active reverence, quite similarly to the logics and semiotics of Q'eqchi' ritual. But for the Q'eqchi', rather than exchange, Garifuna rituals are seen as fruitless displays of wealth thrown to the sea. The Q'eqchi' imagine Garifuna ritual as irreverent and unproductive and their devotion to an indigenous Virgin as meaningless.

Because they interbred with Arawak Indians while on San Vincente, the Garifuna are indeed part-Indian. Individuals involved in Garifuna cultural movements emphasize this facet of their identity, particularly since they witness the social and political capital amassed in the pan-Mayan cultural movement. Some celebrate this part of their heritage during Pororo, while others commemorate that the Garifuna were almost, but not quite, slaves. In this latter case, Pororo venerates their freedom from and continued avoidance of the bondage of slavery to which they were destined before the shipwreck near San Vicente. Once again, it is the young, educated Garifuna, those who are trying to organize their culture in the same manner as Mayan people, who emphasize this explanation of the Pororo dance. Most other Garifuna merely explain that the dance venerates Guadalupe, the indigenous Virgin. They say they do it for the fun of it, *solo por gusto;* they enjoy wearing the clothes of their indigenous neighbors.

Does this wearing of traje verge on cultural consumption? Q'eqchi' clothing and identity is appropriated to such an extent that it extends far beyond this particular fiesta in December. In fact, indigenous traje—the red corte and thick sash—has become a symbol of Garifuna. During the festival of San Isidro in May, older women wear gingham-printed cotton dresses, while younger girls don the Pororo costumes as a means of demonstrating their Garifuna identity. Mayan traje is utilized and usurped by Garifuna people as a way to celebrate their own unique identity as Garifuna people, which, like Q'eqchi' identity, is an amalgamation of connections.[5]

Q'eqchi' people imagine and identify themselves in ways that are not always externally marked. Traje, though the most visually communicative, is not the only means of claiming a Mayan identity. They identify collectively by perceiving through shared imaginaries where invisible and internal selves oversee, mediate, and give shared meaning to ancestral and social realms. Thus, Q'eqchi' women who do not wear traje can still assert their indigenous identity through private affirmation, even if this type of internal identification is scorned by some members of the Mayan cultural movement and their own community (Otzoy 1996:154). *Vestido*-clad Q'eqchi' women in Livingston are labeled indigenous by themselves and others, in contrast to female Q'eqchi' in Alta Verapaz who after discarding their traje are no longer considered indigenous (Wilson 1995:24). Ana, who worked in an American-owned restaurant and could not remember how to make tortillas (although she ate them), wore vestido. When she worked, she wore shorts and a T-shirt. Although she appeared Ladina on the outside, she proclaimed she was still paisana on the inside.

Remember that Livingston is situated in the sweltering lowland tropics, where traje is burdensome, bulky, and stifling hot. Women often refer to the sticky climate to explain why they choose vestido over traje. Also, since the peace accords of 1996, which officially identified the Garifuna as indigenous peoples of Guatemala, Livingston is where Mayan cultural activists come to meet the Garifuna, but not the Q'eqchi' Maya. Unless they hear about it through the Catholic Church or read about it in the hard-to-come-by *Prensa Libre* newspaper, few Q'eqchi' know about the cultural revitalization movement's emphasis on costumbre, language, and dress.[6] Even the mayahaac held in Plan Grande Queveche in 1997, which was sponsored by a Mayan organization in El Estor, received very little if any publicity in town. The previous year, it was I who had heard about the mayahaac in Tameja and suggested to the video project that we go as a group. Without my suggestion and transportation, the people in Crique Chino Barrio Nuevo would neither have known about nor attended the gathering that focused on Q'eqchi' culture, language, and indigenous rights.

Thus, Q'eqchi' women in Livingston do not necessarily draw upon traje as means to express an indigenous self. A stifling climate, exclusion from the Mayan movement, and a multicultural environment where so-called disrespectful neighbors rent one's traditional dress, have all contributed to a more private ethnic identity. The Q'eqchi' conceptualize internal and external manifestations of identity, and visibility assists in distinguishing one identity from the other. They can rent their external markers of identity because the inalienable indicator is internal, multiple, and in the consciousness (Anderson 1983).[7] Unvoiced, unethnicized, and invisible, to be *indígena* is to have the history, interpersonal relationships, behavioral and ideological norms, language, and moral commitment inside (De Vos and Romanucci-Ross 1995:366). Built upon centuries of dealings and rapport, a shared imaginary, action-in-place, and a framework of exchanges draw Q'eqchi' people into one communal relation.

But this collective identity is not homogenous, nor so simply binary. Q'eqchi' people conceive of themselves as a composite, a montage, one could say. Multiple, internal, external, and embedded in motion, Q'eqchi' identity is not a single entity; it is fluidly self and other, foreign and familiar. Foreignness, however, is not a mirror image of self nor an oppositional object to Q'eqchi' identities (Lacan 1977:1–7)[8]; it is an intricate subject embedded in processes of identification. Foreignness coalesces into an identity that is constructed with layers or strands rather than one objective self (Narayan 1993:673). Like the Catholic Trinity—one substance with three manifestations—Q'eqchi' Mayan people understand themselves as a variety of co-essences (Gossen 1996:533; Watanabe 1992:85–87).

This is also why Tzuultaq'a is not easily understood as a symbol of either redistribution or exploitation (Goldin and Rosenbaum 1993:120). Because binary oppositions do not come close to portraying its essence accurately, Tzuultaq'a is conceived as essentially ambivalent and hybrid. Considered at once Ladino, gringo, and ancient Mayan, Tzuultaq'a is also a deity, a male, a female, a patron, an owner, and a mayordomo. Even when securely understood as a deity, Q'eqchi' people waver between calling the being God, Tzuultaq'a, or Ahau, as espoused by the Mayan Movement. People even disagree upon the linguistic breakdown of Tzuultaq'a, some proposing it means "mountain-valley" while others understand it as "up-down." Tzuultaq'a, like Ch'olwiinq, ancestors, and the Virgin of Guadalupe, are not single entities but polysemic be-ings that are formed by historic, social, and economic relations. Similarly, Q'eqchi' identity is far from a unified entity, but rather a "radical empire of mingled unities" (Neruda 1970:46).

SOMOS RAMAS: WE ARE BRANCHES

The Q'eqchi' of Livingston often discussed the German men who arrived without women. They needed to find female companions to fulfill their domestic needs, so they *juntaron* (sp. got together, literally "got near") with Q'eqchi' women. Consequently, Q'eqchi' people speak about the pale-skinned indigenous people who live in Cobán, which, you may recall, was the pulse of the German export industry in the nineteenth century. One day, Alberto spoke about a white man in La Tinta who demonstrated his indigenousness by knowing no Spanish:

> One day we went to a municipio called La Tinta. We went with my uncle. I was 15 years old. OK? We went to buy a few things. All of a sudden a man was there. Where did he come from? He came from Semuy, the little aldea of Semuy. But I tell you, he was German! But he did not know how to speak Spanish. "Really?," I asked him. Yes. He wore the same type of hat that we did and he had on rubber boots. But pure German, with really pretty eyes and white, white hair. Do you see? So things were crossed! (Audiotaped interview with Alberto)

When I wore my huipil and corte on the street, a handful of people asked Lola, whom I usually was with, if I was a relative from Cobán. I could not believe it—people thought I was Q'eqchi'! With my blonde hair, I am ac-

LOLA, HILARY, SAIDA, AND SULMA

customed to sticking out in Guatemala, but among the Q'eqchi' I felt like and was perceived as less of an outsider. In Livingston, many young children have pale skin and light, even blonde, hair. Lola's little boy had hair so blonde that they called him *mi hijo,* my son, because he resembled me more than his biological mother and father.

Q'eqchi' people in Livingston consider themselves a mix of Indian, German, and Spanish. Even those who call themselves *puro Maya* acknowledge that the Q'eqchi' are not really "pure" because they have Spanish and German blood coursing through their veins. People describe themselves as *mesclado* (sp. mixed up), as *una cruz* (sp. cross-between), and as *ramas* (sp. branches).

Branches suggest the centrality of physical home space in the identities of displaced people, an ideological focus that often leads social scientists to see ethnic identity as an essential ordering of self (Malkki 1992:24–31). In Guatemala, this material essentialization is theoretically supported by research that sees the ancient Maya as the symbolic root of a contemporary Q'eqchi' identity without acknowledging that, while this may be the root, many other subjects have "pollinated" the tree. Likewise, Mayan identity is often considered as emerging from an intimate connection with the land, which is unquestionably viewed as sacred. Branches—descending from ancestral roots—reify this objectifying notion of place-based knowledge, where temporal processes are intrinsically linked to observable locations (Spanos 2000:19).

However, while suggesting a material connection with the landscape, branches also imply a multiplicity of connections. Branches are relations saturated with and forged through inequality, power, morality, and difference. Branches symbolize hybrid identities that emerge from contemporary and past political and cultural systems. Branches also represent the ambiguity in identities that are subjectively defined and objectively reified. They grow, change, and fall off while the tree maintains its integrity. Q'eqchi' identities are passages and structures that are modified, altered, and sustained. They represent durable and flexible links to pre-Columbian beliefs and exchanges, to colonial inequalities, to capitalism, and to contemporary tourists, ethnic relations, and identity politics.

By endorsing a tenuous connection between ancient Mayan ideology and contemporary practice, I could be accused of essentializing a Mayan identity. I affirm that the ancient Maya are manifested in contemporary Q'eqchi' social processes. By ignoring this presence and focusing only on the nineteenth and twentieth centuries, I could as easily be accused of essentializing capitalism and neo-colonialism. Why, though, I would like to ask, are many contemporary scholars suspicious of collective identity? Does collective naming automatically distort and obscure cultural distinctions? Werbner (1997) claims that there are two forms of essentialism, one that perniciously silences through reification and another that objectifies for positive politics. These latter forms of collective identification are rhetorical performances that reflect changing hybridity through the construction of moral and aesthetic communities (Werbner 1997:228–230). In this way, massed identities are not the result of objectifying temporal processes into reified structures and identities through a dominant ocular metaphor of knowledge. Rather, collective identities emerge from dispersing gazes through networks of action in time and space, thus reflecting reverberations of difference.

Q'eqchi' identities—whether about self or strangers—are endowed with a lack of fixity; they are in constant states of repositioning. This is why, without a hint of contradiction, Q'eqchi' people can present themselves as *puro Indio,* while they proudly speak of their German blood. Likewise, Q'eqchi' individuals speak of Tzuultaq'a as a white English-speaker, and concurrently as an ancient Mayan man or woman. Verging on magical realism, Ch'olwiinq eat raw food, wear no clothing, are wise and powerful, and can move stones simply by thinking, while they are also fluent in English, German, Spanish, and Q'eqchi'. In this "third timespace" of hybridity (Lavie and Swedenburg 1996), traje intimately represent selves on one hand and fetishes to be bartered on the other. Indigenous clothing is only one active process of all the historical and contemporary exchanges involved in composing oneself as a branch, as Q'eqchi' Mayan.

Readers should also understand that indigenous dress in Livingston has no particular affiliation with the local space. Huipils, in this case, do not represent where a woman was born or from what municipio she "stems" (Hendrickson 1995:51–55). While some older women wear huipils from their original homes, most Q'eqchi' women have the option to choose from a plethora of designs, styles, fabrics, and colors, regardless of what municipio or town these particular forms represent. Without a uniform dress code for Q'eqchi' women, Livingston is a conglomeration of diverse peoples, both inside and out.

This is not to say that traje carries no importance to representing oneself as Q'eqchi'. Men particularly complain when young women switch to vestido, but it seems that these men are more concerned about the accompanying change in behavior, such as when a Q'eqchi' woman works in a hotel and is seen talking to a tourist. They explain their criticism by saying that when you see these women on the street, you do not know if they speak Q'eqchi'—i.e., you do not know whether the woman is Q'eqchi' or not. They emphasize that language is intertwined with clothing and that the appropriate behavior associated with vestido is the ability to read, write, and speak Spanish. Alberto told me that if his young daughter wanted to wear vestido, this would be okay because she knows how to read and write in Spanish. Women who speak only Q'eqchi' should not wear vestido because people will speak to them in Spanish and they will have to remain *muda* (sp. mute). It is no coincidence that this type of action-out-of-place, like the type punishable by susto, as well distorts the ability to properly sense and perceive.

In Livingston, language is more a primary manifestation of Q'eqchi' identity than is dress. When people speak of themselves as *paisanos,* they are clearly affiliating themselves with those who speak Q'eqchi'. However, the Q'eqchi' language is also less visible than traje, and perhaps that much more powerful as a cohesive medium of identification. According to my Q'eqchi' teacher, Juan, even the Academy of Mayan Languages of Guatemala, which has standardized a Mayan alphabet (Nelson 1991:6–7), emphasizes oral over written use of the Q'eqchi' language. Juan is a schoolteacher who attended a course on the new alphabet in Alta Verapaz, but he tells me that there was no need for him to learn to write the alphabet as long as he can speak it. Here, too, internal knowledge surpasses external text.

While Mayan men need not bear the visual markers of an indigenous identity, Mayan women still bear this responsibility as defined by communities, the nation-state, academics, and Mayan political and cultural revitalization movements (Hendrickson 1996:131–134; Smith 1995:723–728). In Livingston, Q'eqchi' identity can be expressed through coherent external ... oundary enforcers like dress. However, Q'eqchi' identity is ... nternalized, and multiple. Even when physical markers such ... ped from female bodies, the genders are still bound by cul- ... define Q'eqchi' identification with particular practices of ... ange.

... ke the Q'eqchi' themselves, is both foreign and local. She ... thing they are not and simultaneously everything they are. ... her respect through ritual even though, according to the ... rs her adorers nothing in return. She is difference on dis- ... ference is not simply binary. Difference is contradictory, ambivalent, and complex. Difference, formed through webs of relationships, is neither oppositional nor straightforward. Difference, like identity, is internal, external, similar, separate, foreign, and familiar.

MONTAGE IDENTITIES

People innovate as they identify themselves and others, although this process is not necessarily a conscious agency that acts without regard to histories, relations, or events. Identification is a process of strategizing in which individuals seek to create their own places of knowledge within power relationships constructed through the meeting of history and event (Sahlins 1985:xiv). Identification is the creation of the "proper" (de Certeau 1984:36).

Most theories of ethnic identity emphasize allegiance or a sense of belonging (De Vos and Romanucci-Ross 1995:360–371; Royce 1982:24–33).

Affiliation, however, ranges from one that is socially constructed, to the psychosocial, and to a primordial human need to identify with others (Comaroff 1996). There are elements of identity, however, that most researchers now agree upon. At least two parties are necessary, because identities must be defined against each other (Wilmsen 1996:4); ethnic identity comes from power (Royce 1982:55–57); and ethnicity is found in one's consciousness (Anderson 1983:4). For some this latter point is key. If ethnicity is only a state of mind, John Comaroff argues that the makeup of ethnicity can never truly be reached, defined, or analyzed without addressing the historical networks from which it is created. He writes that "there cannot be a theory of ethnicity or nationality per se, only a theory of history capable of elucidating the empowered production of difference and identity" (1996:166). For Comaroff, identities are not things but relations, and through everyday practices and encounters they take on the appearance of the natural and essential. But they are not. To get at the heart of identity, social scientists must study how the essentialist belief was constructed. They must analyze where naturalized ways of thinking arise and how things become objectified and "primordial."

Q'eqchi' identities are processes of identification (Hall 1989:15) that originate in equations of power (Comaroff 1996:166). These structural formulas are often statements of inequality and difference, such as are expressed in the historical relationships the Q'eqchi' people have had with the Spaniards, the Church, the State, Ladinos, Germans, and the United States. Inequality and difference, however, like consumption, does not imply that there is an active subject and an acted-upon object. In no way would I argue that colonial history or the State have more agency than the Q'eqchi' themselves in the construction of their identity. The Q'eqchi' are not passively responding to hegemonic forces.

Agency and identity emerge positionally through connections in transnational, intimate, and social webs. And because identities are continuously reshaped, it is the linkages that are the objects. The histories, individuals, and identities these connections help construct, on the other hand, are the subjects—the positional identities that mediate the objectified network (Holland et al. 1998:127–128)—although this does not mean that they cannot be reified as objects. History and individual are equally active in the formation of agency, and people do not exist in a continuous state of subjectivity or objectivity. Agency fluctuates back and forth along an equation of power (Strathern 1988:273), and objectification is only relative and arises, like identity, only through relationships. Meaning (and power) flows between the subjects of the relationship and is not permanently secured at one axis or another.

This way of theorizing about the creation of subjects and objects is not only applicable to lived social identities. Photographic and video-graphic images are as well created by similar semiotics (Ruby 2000:201). Images are subjects and objects, continuously being repositioned within webs of meaning, action, and perception (Sobchack 1992:23). They, too, are more than visible objects. As sensous bodies, they are groupings of "lived-through meanings" that are perceived, sensed, and expressed through embodied histories (Merleau-Ponty 2002 [1945]:177).

Nonetheless, I will not deny that video cameras put forth cultural images that, although created and interpreted through subjective lenses and biases, do objectively represent culture and people from "a mild realist position" (Winston 1998:66). Nevertheless, although they appear to preserve completely, the "wholeness" of imagery—like the cohesiveness of ethnicity—originates from its ability to exclude and annihilate (MacDougall 1998:132). Thus, images can be consumed and surveyed as reified beings as they can also—as subjective processes of be-ing—reach out and grab, shock, resist, and move people to act and sense (Barthes 1981:40–59). Images are positional identities that are defined as phenomena through motion and are dependent on a web of active subjects: camera people, ethnographic and videographic subjects, audiences, and cameras create the network of transmissible meaning. Like branches/identities, they are a "complex interplay between visuality, apparatus, institutions, discourse, bodies, and figurality" (Mitchell 1994:16).

Diversity and becoming (or be-ing) rather than being-oriented positions in identity theories constitute the doubleness of cultural identities today (Escobar 1997:218). I suggest that we take a step beyond even this quasi-binary model. If symbolic representations become identities within global, regional, local, and personal networks, then there is neither need nor justification for the maintenance of an oppositional stance of identity and difference. Clearly, at least two parties are needed to have identity, but where, I ask, are lived identities created in such a sterile environment? When are images and objects provided meaning only through viewer and subjects? Where are selves and collective identities distinguishable as subject or object and psychological or sociological (Kondo 1990:33–43)? In practice, we do not encounter self and other, nor do we imagine ourselves as categorically internal or external. Others and selves, like moralities, identities, and photographic images, are as complex as the multiple historical and contemporary relationships from which they emerge and that provide them with positional meaning.

Likewise, researchers of Mayan identities are beginning to challenge the institutional binary oppositions (i.e., Indian/Ladino, Colonizer/Colonized, Continuity/Change, Pre-Capitalist/Capitalist, and Migrant/Non-Migrant) that have traditionally guided academic representations of the Maya.[9] Even so, as researchers have begun to realize the multiplicity and globalized nature of Mayan identities,[10] a place-based identity still reigns in Mayan studies. Granted this phenomenon is supported by practice—Mayan people often envision themselves as intrinsically linked to a location called home, hence the use of terms such as San Pedrano (someone from San Pedro), Capitalano (from the Capital), Cobanero (from Cobán), and so forth. Yet, there is also a Western construct that frames and tends to replicate this sort of place-based interpretation of identity in academics, and, perhaps, in lived identities themselves (Hervik and Kahn 2006).

In Livingston, Q'eqchi' people are fairly recent migrants from Alta Verapaz and they do not have a definitive place-based identity associated with Livingston. Rather, as I have already discussed, their identity is more multiple and fluid through time and space. However, their non-place-based identities are more a response to lived identities being flexible, partial, and fluid within translocal networks, than strictly a reaction to a migratory status. It is possible that after generations have lived in Livingston, then the Q'eqchi' there too will accumulate a perception of an intrinsic link to Livingston. But for now, their identity reflects the translocal network that positions them as subjects in relation to multiple kinds of others. Even so, when identities are actually strung through transnational networks (Hannerz 1996; Kearney 1996; Rouse 1991) this does not necessarily indicate that they are conceived of as processes rather than products. Even as translocal points of articulation, I argue they are still conceived spatially—as things that are grasped, practiced, and forgotten—rather than as temporal processes of be-ing. However, though often misrecognized by practitioners, readers, and viewers, objectivity is only relative as it arises through relationships.

Stable, objectifying dichotomies clearly fall short in explaining Q'eqchi' Mayan identities in Livingston, Guatemala. Q'eqchi' Mayan identities here are formulated through relationships among members of the community and with various types of outsiders. Outsiders are Garifuna, Germans, and gringos; they are local and nationally foreign. Some are owners, givers, and some are only takers; they are ancestors, ritual kin, deities, and governments. Q'eqchi' Mayan people utilize these metaphoric and materially viable outsiders in their construction and maintenance of self, community, and ethnicity. Identities are not bound by ideas of a nation-state, nor are they wrapped around dualities. Identity, like difference, is neither oppositional nor straightforward, but rather contradictory, ambivalent, and formed through relationships among peoples, histories, ideologies, and power. Identities emerge as montages and composites of time and space.

It is our Westernized fascination with categorical surveillance-as-knowledge that clears the way for clear-cut, objective identities. However, in practice, self/other, internal/external, and Mayan/Ladino are not valid categories. Yet, we continue to label and distinguish, even as we persist in using hyphens and slashes to mark the obvious non-fixity of our subjects. Unfortunately, what we are reifying through academic use of hyphens and slashes are distinctions that do not exist in practice, as hyphens actually represent active processes that resist institutionalization (Lavie and Swedenburg 1996:168). However, when we expose hyphens as active conjunctions rather than divisors, we find "selfother," "internalexternal," "foreignfamiliar," which, although not suitable for a Westernized emphasis on bounded sites of knowledge, may be more appropriate means of representation in practice.

Likewise, the internalized structures and external social girders that create cultural scripts, which in turn guide practice and perception, are not so rigidly divisive. It is more for didactic purposes that we discuss internal and external structures for, in fact, these frameworks are meshed through dynamic dialogue into forms of practice. Although they are useful for academic clarification, for the practitioner and the perceiver, these categories are meaningless. Instead, when we investigate the fields of action and dig under forms of practice, we encounter subjects and objects that are fluidly linked to others and constantly repositioned in dynamic webs of action, connections that are "internalizedexternalized" and embedded in the practice and perception of "selvesothers" and "foreignfamiliar," among numerous other processes of identity.

Nine

CRIME, GLOBALIZATION,
AND ETHNIC RELATIONS IN
LIVINGSTON AND BEYOND

One day while I was in Livingston a young Garifuna man committed suicide. He was a popular youth and the funeral was too emotional to be translated into ethnographic text. My field notes simply read "so much wailing, crying, agony, fainting." The town mourned this tragedy. The next day I went to Crique Chino Barrio Nuevo, where a number of Q'eqchi' people told me that the young man had raped a woman and that the police had been after him. To avoid going to jail, he killed himself. None of this was true. For a moment I was angry and repulsed. After experiencing the deep emotional pain at the funeral the day before, I then saw how Q'eqchi' people coldly wrote this young man off as just another criminal, *un ladrón*. The manner in which they explained this incident demonstrated their cultural construction of crime, which in this case resulted in an utterly arbitrary explanation and assignment of blame. This sharp juxtaposition and my own repulsion spurred me to investigate just how these cultural beliefs surface.

FEAR, FOREIGNERS, AND FRIVOLITY

For the Q'eqchi', once a criminal always a criminal. Perhaps because justice is so rarely experienced in Guatemala, rehabilitation is not an option. Criminality is viewed as an essential feature that cannot be changed. According to the Q'eqchi', many of the Garifuna were stricken with an *enfermedad* (sp. sickness) that prevented them from working. Matilde, for example, says that the Garifuna "are not made for work" (sp. *el moreno no es de trabajo*). With no available cure, Q'eqchi' people would tell me that the morenos' only option is to steal.

> Violence comes with misery when there is no work. When there is work, there is no more violence. I believe the

morenos once worked with the company. Yes, there was a company with whom the morenos worked hard. (Audiotaped interview with Alberto)

Alberto was talking about the United Fruit Company and the Garifuna did indeed once live in a boom town. However, in the 1940s, Livingston hit hard times, and in the 1960s immigration to the United States began. Garifuna relocation to Los Angeles and New York has had an incredible impact on Livingston, and on the Q'eqchi' perception of their neighbors. Every Garifuna person I know has at least one relative, be it a sister, a mother, or an uncle, currently working in the United States. While earning dollars up north, these immigrants send money to their relatives in Livingston. Replacing one foreign enterprise with another, Western Union has become the supplier of much of Livingston's economy.

Those Garifuna who remain at home find themselves in a position where jobs are scarce. They may obtain work in the tourist industry, as motorboat drivers or assistants, tour guides, bartenders, servers, hotel procurers, or street musicians. However, they are in competition with the Q'eqchi' who are willing to work for lower wages. Business owners, who are primarily Ladino, Asian, North American, and European (with a growing number of Garifuna and K'iche' Maya), prefer to hire Q'eqchi' people because they work for little and complain less. This race-based inequality in hiring is evident at many restaurants and hotels that cater to tourists and it heightens the friction between Q'eqchi' and Garifuna. The Garifuna already blame their persistent need for immigration on the Q'eqchi', who supposedly occupied much of their land beginning in the 1950s. Although this may well be ethnic propaganda, the Garifuna and others (Gonzalez 1988:110) see this as shutting the door on any chance for a return to agriculture after the export boom went bust. Nonetheless, today they must again compete with the Q'eqchi' for land and jobs.

Garifuna who find work outside tourism are civil servants, educators, health professionals, carpenters, electricians, secretaries, and town employees. Some Garifuna are employed in fishing, although East Asians dominate this industry. An increasing number of Garifuna people have bought their own businesses with money earned in the United States: discos, bars, restaurants, clothing or video stores, cable service, and hotels. Livingston also has a handful of visible and aggressive hustlers who get tourist money up front in exchange for jungle tours, hotels, boat rides, fish, or bags of marijuana and crack cocaine. With no intention of fulfilling their end of the bargain, these petty thieves take the foreign money, lay low for a few days, and wait for the duped tourists to leave town in disgust.

Remittance checks from the United States uphold the view that the Garifuna do not want to work but prefer to sit around and wait for the next installment. Q'eqchi' say that when their money runs out, the Garifuna steal from their favorite marks—the tourists. Therefore, the Q'eqchi' understand foreign people and money as intricately involved in the illness that makes the Garifuna steal, take drugs, and rape. Gossip always circulated when Q'eqchi' women saw me talking to Garifuna men. Lola, Patrocinia, and Herlinda would bluntly ask me if I was "with" them, or if we were making babies. When I denied these accusations, they would persist, joking about the sexual relations I had with every man with whom I was seen with on the street. Q'eqchi' people explained to me that drugs made the morenos sexual, lazy, and deviant. They refer to the process of getting high as *fumando sus puros* (sp. smoking their cigars) which make them *waxiru* (q. crazy) and lustful. Alberto explains:

> I saw some gringas. I do not know where, on the beach, on the beach at Cayo San Jose. One of them was, you know, together with someone . . . I saw this, I saw it with my own eyes. I saw her first and she did not have anything, no children, nothing. But when I saw her the next time, she had children, but little black ones. Can you believe it? From a gringa came little black ones! So things go now . . . You know, it is the same with German blood as it is now mixed, as I told you. (Audiotaped interview with Alberto)

In various meanings of the word, foreigners have always come to "screw" the Q'eqchi' Mayans. After the Spaniards it was the Germans, and now tourists represent sexual outsiders. With their torn denims and uncombed dreadlocks, young backpacking tourists are considered dirty and disease-ridden. Tourists are believed to carry AIDS, and AIDS is indeed a serious problem in Livingston (Kane 1998:119–127). This elucidates why young Q'eqchi' women who work in the hotels are considered deviant—not because they do not wear huipils, but because they interact closely with polluted tourists. Tourists are believed to be aberrant to the extent that they eat dogs. Whenever Lola saw me wearing a bandanna on my head (which I would wear in my house and rarely on the street), she would instruct me to take it off because I looked like one of those dirty gringas who sell shells and play drums on the street. I heard stories of tourists running around naked on the beach, and tales about female tourists who had sex with multiple men each day. Juan, my Q'eqchi' teacher, told me that he was practically raped by a German woman, who then had sex with two Garifuna men the same day. The few white women in town who have biracial children are used as evidence of how gringa tourists get "hot" while in Livingston and "do it" with Garifuna men.

To the Q'eqchi', foreign influences have not only made sex more visually apparent, but they have tainted and shown disrespect for the sex act. Mariano told me that in the past when a Q'eqchi' man and woman had sex they would stay in bed for three days afterward. Because sex is such a hot activity, he explained, the couple would have to keep themselves warm and covered so as not to injure themselves. Covering their heads with handkerchiefs and their bodies with blankets, they would eat hot foods like caldo loaded with chile. If someone came to the house to see the man, the visitor would be told that the couple was ill and would be instructed to return on another day. Mariano complained that today people have sex wherever they want—in the water, on the beach, in a boat. Ultimately blaming the Garifuna and the tourists, Mariano explained that this is why people now walk around with bad backs, because they had sex in cold spots and did not cover their bodies to keep warm.

Furthermore, tourists do not buy things from the Q'eqchi' except for an occasional tamale or piece of yucca on the street. There is rarely exchange of money. Tourists give only bad things such as ojo, AIDS, and susto, and they take things like photographs without permission. Unlike foreign owners, who give housing and education in return for labor and respect, tourists do not reciprocate with the Q'eqchi' community. Tourists are categorized with treasure hunters who steal cultural wealth without permission. Tourists are also severed from kin and community; they are solitary figures stripped from their familial context. Through this difference, they become labeled as immoral and illness-ridden perpetrators of action-out-of-place.

Numerous criminal outsiders are found in the Q'eqchi' imaginary. Lola told me about three gringos who came to her finca in Senahú when she was a child. This foreign group carried big scales that hung from the rafters. They entered Lola's finca and weighed each child. Then they left. They returned without notifying the patron and rounded up the small children. Lola was spared because she was too big, already being twelve years old. These gringos (who Lola says may have been Germans) loaded the children into crates and then onto large trucks. She saw them pass in front of her home before they went to El Estor to do the same thing. The day the gringos were headed to her husband's finca, the big earthquake of 4 February 1976 struck Guatemala. His finca was thus spared even though the patron, as a true provider and protector of his mozos, had prepared a defense against these uninvited outsiders.

While many Q'eqchi' talk about the Germans with admiration and respect, there is an obvious fear of the foreign. While simultaneously providing, protecting, and feeding, foreign owners can appropriate, enslave, beat, and scare their Q'eqchi' workers and subjects. Q'eqchi' people, however, seem to be more afraid of non-owning foreigners such as treasure hunters and tourists. So extreme is this fear that some Q'eqchi' people ask me if the disease-carrying North American travelers eat children. This suspicion creates the social backdrop for the prevailing Q'eqchi' fear of child-snatching gringos. I heard numerous rumors about groups of gringos who were wandering through Livingston in search of children to bring back to the United States. People would warn me to be careful when I went into the aldeas, because the Q'eqchi' there were not used to seeing white people and they would think I was there to steal children. The radio from Puerto Barrios perpetuated this fear by reporting on child-napping rumors. During *Semana Santa* (sp. Holy week), there was a warning on the radio that parents should watch their children because there were four gringos in Livingston stealing babies. One evening soon thereafter Lola could not find her youngest son, the one they call *mi hijo*. I remember her teary, fearful eyes when she told me that he was missing. We spent hours combing the streets looking for him, until her husband walked out to Crique Chino to find the boy asleep in their house in the aldea.

In 1994, this cultural disquietude made headlines in the United States when Pokomchí Mayans beat and raped an Alaskan environmentalist accused of child stealing in Alta Verapaz.[1] The U.S. media represented this tragic incident as being caused by irrational and ignorant rumors; but we should understand that these indigenous fears originated from a long history of foreign intervention, rape, murder, and economic control. Why should not Pokomchí (and Q'eqchi') people assume that North American tourists, as cultural and economic ambassadors, come to Guatemala with the same evil intentions? Tragically, although the North American victim had only good intentions, she did not identify with the evil lurking within the structures of colonialism, global consumption, and third world poverty that allows the Q'eqchi' people to imagine all tourists as infected with AIDS and sleeping with the Garifuna.[2]

Q'eqchi' people fear and simultaneously desire not only foreign people but also foreign things. Foreign silver coins are convertible into capital, although they also have the capability to haunt. Western clothes—symbols of modernization, wealth, and advancement—are held responsible for debasing and sexualizing the individuals wearing them. This is why Lola protested when I wore my bandanna and why Q'eqchi' men complain when their nieces or daughters wear vestido rather than traje. Older people blame tourists for introducing new ideas like make-up, shorts, and nail polish to Q'eqchi' youth.

But what about the Garifuna? Where do they fit in this Q'eqchi' imaginary? They tend to pay their nationalistic allegiance to the Garifuna communities that reside along the coasts of Honduras, Guatemala, and Belize, not to mention New York and Los Angeles. When they travel through the interior of Guatemala, they say they are often treated as tourists or hassled as outsiders. Nonetheless, the Garifuna are proud to be Guatemalan. Q'eqchi' people, however, while not viewing them as foreigners, do not see them as truly Guatemalan. As a result of migration, they conceive of the Garifuna as pseudo-North Americans, even though the Garifuna conflict with the traditional image of the United States gringo—white, wealthy, and living in a guarded mansion. Like foreign tourists, Garifuna also bring the items and currency that Q'eqchi' people crave but fear because of a metaphoric and dangerous timelessness. Western Union supplies a symbolic currency that lends itself to a construction of fear.

On the other hand, the Q'eqchi' and Garifuna have similar histories and positions within a political web of power. Garifuna are not foreign owners who require respect because of historical relationships of inequality. Like the Q'eqchi', they have been victims of colonialism, capitalism, Catholicism, and various other forms of foreign intrusion. Furthermore, the Garifuna fear and dislike Ladinos even more than do the Q'eqchi' Maya. This particular oppositional ethnic disdain is picked up by Mayan cultural organizations that come to Livingston to discuss issues with the Garifuna people. The Garifuna of Livingston respond to this shared oppression because many of them blame the Ladinos for their lot.

Because the Guatemalan peace accords state that the Garifuna have rights to an indigenous identity and culture, many Mayan organizations, for example Fundación Rigoberta Menchú, have come to Livingston to meet with the Garifuna community and plan the implementation of the peace accords. Ironic in this cultural organizing, though, is that most of the Mayan revitalization groups that come to town are unaware that more than five hundred Q'eqchi' individuals live there and that thousands more live in the aldeas. Project directors were shocked when I mentioned that I was an anthropologist studying the Q'eqchi' culture in Livingston. Making an inappropriate assumption about links between ethnicity and place, Mayan organizations ultimately label the Garifuna as more indigenous than the Q'eqchi'.

Is this an additional form of cultural appropriation, like the adaptation of traje for Día del Guadalupe? Some Q'eqchi' people seem to feel it is. The Mayan revitalization movement does provide more for the Garifuna people than it does for the Q'eqchi' in Livingston, at least overtly. Only occasionally through the Catholic Church do Mayan organizations come to speak to the Q'eqchi' catechists-in-training. Q'eqchi' people and others, including an American priest, told me that the Garifuna are jealous of the Mayan people because the latter have books, teachers, and bibles in their own languages. Likewise, Garifuna people also want to wear Q'eqchi' traje on Día del Guadalupe. In this way, the Garifuna people are seen as coveting, taking, and appropriating. In addition to their criminal orientation, the Garifuna are perceived as cultural pirates.

Q'eqchi' people arrive in Livingston with ideologies constructed through historical and contemporary relationships of power with outsiders. Because they have had significant experience dealing with foreigners and Ladinos, my role as foreign anthropologist was easily understood. First I was feared, and then fright was mixed with respect. Because the Garifuna are not foreigners providing sustenance or requiring payment, but rather black, semi-indigenous people who venerate an Indian Virgin, they are not so easily comprehended.

Q'eqchi' understanding of crime is further reinforced by what the Q'eqchi' see as two disparate communities. They see their own community maintained through local exchange, while they envision the Garifuna community as stretched and hidden through transnational networks. They do not see how their own community is in reality similarly reproduced through local and global networks. Q'eqchi' people see Garifuna individuals who value foreign currency rather than intimate exchange between land, individuals, and owners. In their eyes, the Garifuna community values foreign goods and selfish behavior. And, because many of them live in the United States and only come to Livingston for holidays, they are perceived as passersby. Like tourists, the Garifuna are considered disrespectful, immoral, and natural transgressors who serve foreign rather than local interests.

Patrocinia told me that the morenos are mean at the *pila* (sp. public washing area) where she goes to get water. I asked her why and she replied ". . . God knows, because they are morenos maybe. If you go to get ahead in the line, they will hit you. They are bad." Numerous other people would tell me that the Garifuna *no tienen respeto* (sp. they do not have any respect).

They do not respect God, the Q'eqchi', or the tourists whom they rob and rape. Although Q'eqchi' people tell me that the worst offenders are the Garifuna, they do not spare anyone in their descriptions of lack of respect. This defining characteristic is also used to differentiate among themselves, particularly with regard to religion. Young and old Q'eqchi' individuals tell me that their ancestors used to respect each other, the land, and God. Everyone tends to criticize the general lack of morality in Livingston, and elderly people in particular complain that the youth do not respect God anymore. Crime, let alone poor crop yields, bad weather, rodents, insect infestations, illness, and death are all results of this decaying moral fabric.

However, if everyone is at fault, why are the Garifuna labeled as the worst offenders? Why are they perceived as any more disrespectful than the next? Is it simply a matter of racism? Q'eqchi' people tell me that the Garifuna used to work the land and grow cassava, yucca, plantains, and bananas; but they are no longer agriculturists, and Q'eqchi' say that today their neighbors only hustle tourists and wait for checks from Western Union. Since the Garifuna are no longer connected to the land but to the United States, Q'eqchi' people accurately understand Garifuna economy as a circulation of foreign currency. Whether wired money or individual tourists, what the Garifuna value, according to the Q'eqchi', is foreign and self-serving.

The Garifuna fall between historical categories and, therefore, because the Garifuna are black people, the Q'eqchi' use the mythical solitary Q'eq as a reference point as they define their new neighbors. A bestial black man who travels alone at night and dances by himself under the eyes of his white owners, Q'eq, like a tourist, is a solitary figure. Like unaccompanied tourists, it opposes a moralized corporate community. Physically displaying his societal opposition in his backward elbows and knees, and in his ability to traverse through the sky, Q'eq represents the foreign, mischievous, sexual, and deviant. Symbolizing the unknown and the adversity, Q'eq is bad weather, poor crops, and blight. Owned by German finqueros, themselves metaphorical criminals of land and labor, Q'eq's sole purpose is to scare, steal, secure the finca, and eat eggs. Consuming symbols of reproduction, acting as a lone henchman, and propelled by foreign interests, the Q'eq is the epitome of disrespect and nonproductivity. Impure and crossing boundaries, the Garifuna are thus transformed into threatening monsters (Rony 1996:161).

When asked whether the Garifuna and the Q'eq are the same, the Q'eqchi' tell me that they are different but similar. Although Q'eqchi refer to the morenos as Q'eq, because of their skin color, they also say that

Garifuna people cannot transform themselves into animals, so they are not really Q'eq. However, because the Garifuna and Q'eq are both perceived as cigar-smoking, black criminals, Q'eqchi' people reply that they may be related. Although clearly differentiating between the Garifuna and Q'eq, I argue that the Q'eqchi' apply a manifestation of this mythico-historical figure to their understanding of their black neighbors. This is why the Q'eqchi' create such shocking and distorted images. This is why they tell me their Garifuna neighbors are rapists, drug addicts, and criminals, and why they are supposedly violent, mean, and inconsiderate, and kill dogs just for fun. They are monstrous because they are the same but dramatically different, impure and dangerous, acting-out-of-place, and threatening cultural imaginaries.

On the other hand, in 1997 it was reported that at least 500 million dollars was sent annually to Guatemalan households from relatives working in the United States (Campos and Marshall 1997:12), and this annual figure has more recently been estimated at more than 2.5 billion dollars (International Organization for Migration 2004). And, contradicting the cultural construction made by the Q'eqchi', the Garifuna in Livingston use their remittances to buy food, build houses, purchase medicine, educate children, finance businesses, pay debts, and, like increasing numbers of indigenous people globally, maintain an active traditional culture. Secured in Livingston, the New York and Los Angeles Garifuna have a place they call home. Through wired money, they keep up their future. When relatives from the United States come each year to participate in Garifuna ritual, most know that someday they will return for good. However misunderstood by the Q'eqchi', the Garifuna, too, maintain their community through reciprocity, consumption, and ritual respect. In fact, the local Garifuna community is reproduced through the same transnational networks that the Q'eqchi' see as serving foreign interests. At this transnational and abstract level of the global economy, emigration displaces human bodies and, through the return of hard currency, balances the exchange between what was once considered a consuming core and a drained periphery. But the Q'eqchi' see only difference. They envision globalized passersby who avoid making connections with the land and the Q'eqchi' community.

This inaccurate reading of the Garifuna may also be related to the visibility of the hustler street scene in Livingston, where (mostly young) men make false promises to naïve tourists. In sight are also the Garifuna living in the United States, who walk through town wearing shiny gold necklaces and clean expensive sneakers, carrying loud boom boxes, and bringing similar foreign luxury items to their loved ones. What the Q'eqchi' see, then, are the fruits, not the labor. Nor do they see how the Garifuna culture and morality is so similar to their own. They fail to understand how the Garifuna may have their own version of reciprocal exchanges that they use to define themselves and their community. They find only a living myth.

Two modes of production—a Q'eqchi' mode that involves local community exchange with owners and the land, and a Garifuna mode in which community is stretched and hidden through transnational networks of migration—create difference and confusion. Garifuna rituals are misperceived as wasteful and the Garifuna themselves are misconstrued as transnational sightseers—coming to Livingston for brief visits, avoiding connections with land or community, and displaying their inclination toward the consumption of foreign goods. And there is their skin color, which leads the Q'eqchi' to utilize an appropriate reference point of conflation— the mythical black Q'eq. They are thus imagined as cigar-smoking thieves who pilfer for foreign interests. Rather than bringing mythical loot to foreign landowners, however, the Garifuna earn dollars, buy American products, strengthen the U.S. economy, and mingle with pale-skinned tourists. Blocking compassion, negating what to some are obvious similarities, and explaining differences through a filter of historical and social exchanges, the Q'eqchi' identify the Garifuna as immoral and monstrous transgressors.

Digging deeper, one encounters even more irony in the way the Q'eqchi' categorize their Garifuna neighbors as criminally inclined foreigners. Nancie Gonzalez (1988:110) and numerous locals in Livingston propose that what precipitated Garifuna participation in a transnational network was actually the migration of the Q'eqchi'. Because the Q'eqchi' began to build homes and plant corn on much of the land that surrounds town, after the mid-century decline of the local economy the Garifuna could not return to agriculture. They had few economic options other than to migrate to the United States. Thus, it is believed by many that Garifuna migration was instigated and perpetuated by Q'eqchi' occupation of local land. If this is so, then the irony emerges from the fact that the Q'eqchi' create not only their own criminals, but their own foreigners. They take what the Garifuna reject and then renounce the alternatives they choose. They manifest immorality in the bodies of those engaged in global practices and morality in their own commitment to a localized mode of consumption and production. Q'eqchi' people position themselves as the producers, the consumers, and those consumed.

TODAY'S TRANSGRESSORS: THE STATE,
GUERRILLAS, AND THE Q'EQCHI'

There was a Garifuna man in Livingston who did not play by the rules of the community. I will call him Pablo. Everyone knew he was trouble—robbing homes, businesses, and tourists on a daily basis. He was murdered on the presidential inauguration night in 1995. It was bound to happen, for this is how justice works in a country where vigilantism and lynching are extremely common. The modernizing right-wing party, National Advancement Party (PAN), beat the Guatemalan Republican Front (FRG), an extreme right-wing party with deep ties to the military (there have since been two elections, the first won by FRG and the more recent by Gran Alianza Nacional [GANA]). I was glad that PAN's candidate, Arzú, won, although most of my Q'eqchi' friends were not. They had listened to FRG's charismatic leader Ríos Montt's political promises of bringing Guatemala back to the Guatemalans. They respected FRG's vehement stand on crime and foreign intervention. Consequently, because PAN won, they were afraid that foreign countries were going to invade Guatemala through military and economic means. Moreover, they feared a criminal uprising. For them, increased crime accompanies foreign intervention.

I heard that Pablo had been drunk on inauguration night. He was dancing, singing, and jumping around in ecstatic glee because PAN had won. He was now free to continue his crime spree. Alberto told me that Pablo was screaming and singing "Gracias a Dios que ganó PAN. Sí ganó FRG, iban a quitar todos los ladrones" (sp. Thank God PAN won. If FRG had won they would have kicked out all the criminals!). Later that night he was murdered.

Regardless of its accuracy, this Q'eqchi' version of events demonstrates how state politics intersects with the broad Q'eqchi' understanding of crime. Far from apolitical, their imagined world is firmly grounded in and influenced by contemporary national and international politics. Yet, their interpretation of the state is equally construed through their own perception of global economics and history. Rather than having an invisible authority that categorizes and castigates its subjects, the Q'eqchi' also construct the state—a criminalizing institution with foreign interests.[3] They create their own criminals.

The same can be said about another political figure—the guerrilla. Although most Q'eqchi' people now residing in Livingston did not directly witness the battles of the civil war, they were influenced by its practices. To them, the term "guerrilla" does not necessarily signify the political fighter of the Unidad Revolucionaria Nacional Guatemalteca (URNG), but rather simply means *un ladrón.* Being a liberal social scientist, I was surprised by this conflation of guerrillas with thieves. Didn't they realize, I wondered, that these soldiers were fighting for them? Yes, the Q'eqchi' were aware that URNG supported indigenous rights and land reform. They nonetheless would whisper to me that there were dangerous guerrillas in the area. Manuel told me that someone had killed a guerrilla on inauguration night, although not the bad kind—the type that only stole things like radios. (Pablo was not my image of a guerrilla.) Manuel also told me about a group of guerrillas who took over a bus in Semox and made everyone give them twenty quetzals. Manuel said his friend, who was on the bus, was upset because he had to give up his last twenty quetzals, leaving him without any means of returning home. What kind of help was that, he wanted to know?

Javíer tried to explain. He told me that in many villages guerrillas entered and made people give them food. They forced villagers to kill cows, turkeys, and chickens, and took food along with their collections of money. While consuming the village sustenance, the guerrillas promised the locals that they would fight for them and take care of them. But have they? How has life changed? In the eyes of many, the guerrillas simply came in and took what was not theirs. Q'eqchi' people typically are poor, and the loss of a cow or even a turkey can hurt a family economically. For them, the guerrillas are most definitely criminals, a sentiment similar to one revealed in war-torn areas of Guatemala where Mayan people find themselves caught between two armies (Stoll 1993). Moving covertly through the forest, consuming without producing, separated from their communities, and taking without permission, guerrillas, too, start to appear like monstrous transgressors.

If neither the state nor the rebels can protect you, who can? A Protestant pastor and his wife told me that Jesus is available. Because God's children are protected from all evils, they cannot be bitten by a snake nor killed by a guerrilla. This couple told me about another pastor who was preaching in a guerrilla-controlled area. Labeling him a troublemaker, the guerrillas decided that this pastor had to be assassinated. But when their leader went to shoot him, he could not remove his gun from the holster. His hand began to tremble and he was not able to lift his arm. He was frozen. The pastor was saved by God.

Unfortunately, not everyone is so intimate with Jesus. Guatemala continues, even after the signing of the peace accords, to be a violent country. It continues to be the number one car-napping country in the world. Over four hundred people were kidnapped in the first three months of 1997 (*Prensa Libre,* 5 April 1997) and public lynching is a routine form of justice. The year 2004 was named one the most violent years ever in Guatemala as a result of the alarmingly high number of homicides (*Prensa Libre,* 19 December 2004). The Q'eqchi' tell me that in order to reduce the crime, the government must find work for them. After the peace accords were signed, millions of dollars in foreign aid were sent to help Guatemala, but most people believe that the government is keeping this money for itself to purchase land. Felipe tells me that international support goes directly to the military and politicians who use it to buy mansions in the United States. "They want to own everything," he remarks. Still hidden and out of reach, foreign currency pours into Guatemala, secured not in mountains but in banks, foreign interest-minded owners keep it in their own hands. "The authorities do not help the people who need it; it is all for themselves," says Felipe. Q'eqchi' people complain about election promises that are never fulfilled and politicians who forget their platforms upon entering office. Even the president does not take the indigenous people into consideration; all he cares about is his friends. Not completing their end of the bargain, these political authorities of the state are emerging as the latest criminals. Although the peace accords support economic improvement, people have not seen more employment opportunities, lower prices, or accessible land. Things are getting worse. In fact, the government of Alfonso Portillo violated Convention 169 of the International Labour Organization (ratified in 1995) and granted further oil and mining concessions in Izabal to Canadian and United States companies. Various environmental and indigenous groups publicly denounced these concessions and condemned the violation of Convention 169 and the continued environmental devastation, but the government was unresponsive. The most recent government, that of Oscar Berger, is similarly accused and currently has an extremely low approval rating.

Things are so bad that people say the Q'eqchi' are beginning to steal. In a local village, Q'eqchi' *bandidos* raped a girl and stole thousands of quetzals from her mother. This same group was stealing cattle from an Italian-owned finca. They are considered extremely dangerous, and local finca owners now pay their laborers with checks rather than cash because they are afraid to carry large amounts of money in the bush. I heard various versions of these crimes and I do not know whether Q'eqchi' criminals actually were involved (although they likely were). What I do know is that previously this would have been unheard of. When I began fieldwork in 1994, Q'eqchi' people blamed only the Garifuna for the crime and violence in Livingston. A decade and a peace agreement later, Q'eqchi' are accusing each other.

What happened in the few years to bring about this switch is something about which I can only speculate. Accusations and the criminal act itself may be caused by national media reports of a violent crime wave that has been occurring in Guatemala since the signing of the peace accords. Accordingly, everyone in Livingston talks about the inordinate crime occurring in the country. Faith in the authority of the state diminishes daily. Most Q'eqchi' blame the government for the fluctuating price of corn, beans, and flour that only benefits the wealthy. Doubting their government's ability to help, the Q'eqchi' voice a concern raised as well by the Garifuna, thus unifying these people against the state. Mayan cultural revitalization also effects consensus. Coming to Livingston and proclaiming the equality of the Garifuna and the Q'eqchi', Mayan organizations emphasize similarities over differences, although few Q'eqchi' people have access to this rhetoric. A number of people did tell me that these organizations were beneficial because they taught the Garifuna that the Q'eqchi' are human. Equally, it demonstrates the same about the Garifuna for the Q'eqchi'. Under the law of the state, they are all indigenous people with rights to their own ethnic identities. Catholicism also helps to unify the two groups by promoting cultural equality.

As the economy slowly moves away from agriculture toward wage labor and the tourist industry, the Q'eqchi' value system is also adapting. The structure of the Q'eqchi' imaginary is transforming as it creates new myths and reacts to new economies and people. Still valuing a transcendental exchange with land and the community, the Q'eqchi' are also beginning to deal with national and foreign currencies, tourists, and luxury items. My older friends complain that the youth no longer tend to their milpas nor ask permission to cut down a tree. They say that the young are more concerned about buying clothes, sneakers, and radios. Desiring Tommy Hilfiger clothes, Air Jordans, and Barbie dolls, Q'eqchi' youth value foreign commodities carried through transnational networks. By purchasing homes, stores, boats, televisions, bicycles, and land, they are becoming owners themselves. The most dramatic impact on their concepts of community and identities may be this recent transference of ownership.

Nonetheless, there are plenty of people who still blame the morenos. They tell me that the crime in the villages is due to the fact the Q'eqchi' now take note of what the Garifuna do (sp. *les anotan*), learning from and copying their neighbors. This is why they now rape, steal, and scare people. As something learned, crime is not something they have intrinsically within themselves, as they claim for the Garifuna. Therefore, while the mythically and historically influenced image of Garifuna-as-criminals has not changed significantly, Q'eqchi' are now applying this identity to the youth and the budding capitalists among themselves. Politics, economics, and religion are fields of action that allow them to recreate imagined landscapes, innovate roles, and understand crime. These structures, though, are not rigid; they react to and are transformed by contemporary relations of power. Q'eqchi' Mayans experience various never-before-seen people and lifestyles by being active in the formation of cultural beliefs.

Crime has been a constant in Q'eqchi' history. Whether it be the Spanish stealing treasures, Q'eq' robbing eggs, morenos lifting watches, guerrillas demanding money, or politicians breaking promises, Q'eqchi' have continued to fit new circumstances into deeply embedded social and political categories. This, though, is not simply a color-coded racism or categorically driven process. This labeling of crime and criminals has to do with acts of morality—with what is and is not practiced. Criminals are defined by what they do, where they originate, who reaps the fruits of their labor, and with whom they collaborate or corroborate. Created through networks that stretch through time, across oceans, and through individual minds and collective histories, crime is naturalized through extrapersonal structures, internalized frameworks, cultural practices, mythical and historical narratives, and everyday social exchanges. Employing their mythical, historical, and social relationships as a filter of perception, Q'eqchi' people identify, justify, and explain the transgressors who fly through their imagined world laden with foreign goods on their way to somewhere else.

POSTSCRIPT

A friend visited me during the last few months of my fieldwork. We were walking to my house late one night when a machete-wielding youth jumped out from the shadows and demanded our money. With the blade pushed up against his neck, my friend handed over his keys rather than his wallet. I immediately grabbed the keys out of the thief's hands and began to scream. I yelled that I lived here and that we were walking home and that he would be sorry for picking on the wrong people! Friends who were lingering at the street corner heard my cries and ran to assist us. Even though the young man took off before my friends had the chance to identify him, they knew who it was. The next morning, a trail of people came to my house to tell me that they had spoken to him and that he was very sorry, that he did not know who I was. He thought we were tourists and sent me his apologies. Some asked if I wanted a hit put out on him.

There is an unspoken social rule that sanctions tourists as marks for crime. Tourists bring in dollars, disease, Western clothing, and lust, and give nothing back to the community. Many people insinuate that tourists deserve criminal violation. By robbing them, the people of Livingston have an opportunity to make the give-and-take bidirectional. Unfortunately, what happens when tourists are robbed is that the travel guides are filled with horror stories about Livingston's extreme crime rate and tourists stop coming, leaving a stagnant economy with no incoming source of revenue. Hotel and restaurant owners, who are predominantly Ladino or foreign, have formed an association to minimize crime and increase tourism. Many young Garifuna men, believing these hotel owners and outsiders are murdering known troublemakers in town, denounce the group as inherently racist, because the association indiscriminately targets only Garifuna youth accused of criminal acts. I had heard that the young man who threatened my friend and me was on the top of the association's hit list because not only did he try to rob us and other tourists, but he also victimized locals to supply his crack habit. Because we were white, he saw us as an easy and accepted mark. What he did not know was that I had become more than a tourist. As an ethnographer, I had become a peripheral member of the community. Like ritual kin, I was economically and morally bound to the community. Even though I could pack my bags and fly through the sky to my foreign home, I had obligations to the people of Livingston.

Ten

I AM A CAMERA

Vignettes of Ethnographic Vérité

VIGNETTE 1: QUEMÓ MI REY LEÓN?

The torrential rain echoed Tek's and my tears as we hugged during our first goodbye.[1] She feared it was our last. It was not. On a Sunday morning, almost two years after our initial tearful goodbye, I watched her husband stand motionless in the back room of their house. Roberto's body appeared to hang limp over his skeleton and his eyes were fearfully empty. He was lost. The house would normally be full of activity at this time of day, but Roberto stood frozen in the middle of the silent house. Then he moved toward the cardboard boxes that held the family's clothing. He rummaged through the boxes, but did not find what he was searching for. Other than what he was wearing, and the one pair of pants hanging on a rafter, all of his clothes were gone. She had burned them, taken his *cedula* (sp. identification papers), and run off to where no one knew. Tek had walked out on her husband and their children.

A few weeks earlier, when I had first seen Tek during one of my visits to Livingston, she had broken down crying. As she wept, Roberto explained to me that she had been feeling very sad the past few months. He looked at me, shaking his head as his wife's tears dripped onto my upper arm. I looked up, confused about my reception. Their children huddled up to me, assuming rightly that I brought them gifts from the United States. The next day I delivered a Barbie doll to the young daughter and a beautifully illustrated copy of Disney's *The Lion King* in Spanish to the young son. They were pleased. That day, Tek asked me if I could take her to the United States when I returned. Even though I wondered whether I was holding up my end of the reciprocal exchange, I told her no, that this was not possible.

The following Friday evening, Roberto lost his temper and hit Tek, supposedly because she attacked their eldest daughter. Tek marched up to my house where she showed me the black and blue mark under her eye, which provided her with a socially sanctioned rationalization to leave. She slept on sofa cushions in my house, while her husband took the children to their relatives' home in the aldeas. The following day, Tek was emotionally destroyed. I was afraid that she was suicidal. I went to speak with Roberto, who told me not to worry, that she had been threatening to kill herself for weeks.

Roberto and his children had heard that Tek was preparing to leave and that she had been burning clothes and papers. Martín, their youngest son, quietly approached me and tugged on my shorts. He looked up at me and asked *¿Quemó mi Rey León?* He was asking me if his mother had burned the picture book. He had already copied every picture into his school notebook with the crayons I had also delivered from the north. *¿Quemó mi Rey León?* His question touched me so deeply; its childlike simplicity rang pain through my body as its indexicality spoke clearly. I hugged him and told him that his mother would not do that. I could only hope this was true. (Her behavior had not been predictable.) On Sunday morning, when they were assured that she had left, though to where they did not know, the family returned home in single file to check out the damage. While Roberto desperately searched for any article of clothing his wife had not burned, Martín ran to the backpack where he had left the picture book. It was there.

The following day, Roberto and I were sitting outside his home. A woman came up and told Roberto that she had seen Tek at the market in Puerto Barrios. Roberto decided to go find her. He had not been paid recently, so I gave him fifty quetzals. The next morning he went to bring her home. I saw Tek later that same afternoon at the pila as she washed her clothing. I gave her a big hug and asked her how she was. She told me that she was not going to stay long and that she missed no one but me. Me? What about her children? Her husband? Her beloved turkeys? No, only me.

Tek had anticipated her next move. She intended to leave with me the following Sunday when I planned to go to Guatemala City. She would escort me to the Litegua bus station and then would stay in Puerto Barrios to work. She wanted to find employment in one of the *comedores* (sp. restaurants) at the market (although rumors speculated that Tek would get involved in prostitution). Nonetheless, at least her family knew where she was going. But this time it was me, the gringa, who was leading her away. It was me, the pale-skinned foreigner, with whom Tek's children saw their mother walking down the steps as we headed to the pier to find a motorboat to take us down the coast. I was furious at Tek. How dare she put me in such an awkward position! She knew I did not approve of her leaving, although she also knew that I could do nothing about it.

When we left, Roberto had tears in his eyes. He nodded his head at me. His children could barely look at me let alone give me a hug goodbye. Like organ- and baby-stealing gringos, I became fortified in their eyes as a foreign consumer. I was complicit in the removal of a maternal body. I was ashamed and sad. My so-called ethnographic neutrality and my sincere desire to help rather than harm a community felt like a sham.

VIGNETTE 2: THE COLLABORATIVE CONFLICT OF PROYECTO AJWACSIINEL

I should have realized what was happening at the second meeting in the small Catholic church in Crique Chino Barrio Nuevo. Agustin asked me what we would do if someone from another religion (i.e., an Evangélico) wanted to participate in the project. I told him that religion would not be a factor, that the community should unite rather than divide itself over this endeavor. I said that I would not refuse entry to any individual based upon religion, although the size of the project was adequate and we would not need to seek other participants.

One participant dropped out after a few months due to lack of interest. He felt that he was wasting his time because he had not seen any "fruits" of the project. I spoke to the others about this. I realized that one problem was the use of the word "proyecto." "Proyecto" implied work and rewards. Established foreign development projects and cooperatives with which Q'eqchi' people were acquainted offered medicine, schools, education, fertilizers, water systems, and bibles—i.e., tangible rewards for participation. Although we discussed the possibility of building a community center in Crique Chino Barrio Nuevo, their invested time and labor was not sufficiently rewarded. Even though I fed them, paid for passage on trips, and created a small Q'eqchi' library, I had not been reimbursing the Q'eqchi' for their time. They had agreed to this, although after a few months I saw that they had lost sight of the project's potential benefits. And this is when I began to realize the theoretical relevance of this methodology. For Q'eqchi' people, labor is part of a reciprocal relationship, and the project was not producing enough. The Q'eqchi' expected results for their participation. I needed to do something for them. I purchased a marimba for their church in Crique Chino Barrio Nuevo. I had once been wary about paying anthropological subjects, considering it commodification of a personal relationship. This is naïve. The Q'eqchi' people of Livingston needed, expected, and deserved payment of some sort. The marimba was sincerely appreciated, even though it later became a point of contention.

The congregation played the marimba during Masses and prayer gatherings. Then, one Sunday after I had left, musicians from Lampara, an aldea up-river, arrived at Mass. At the end of Mass they played *sones* (traditional Q'eqchi' songs) on the marimba. Agustin vehemently protested, complaining that their songs were worldly costumbre. He seized the hammers with which they were playing. Then, the following day he came and removed the marimba. He rationalized this decision by explaining that he and select others had participated the most in the video project and that they deserved the marimba. Those who did not do anything, or only suspected the project's intentions, were then reaping the benefits. Agustin explained that the others "solo quieren, quieren, quieren" (sp. they only want, want, want), but "no levantaron, no trabajaron, no pagaron, no ayudaron" (sp. they did not lift a finger, they did not work, they did not pay, they did not help at all). With the help of another man, he carried the marimba to his house where it slid into disrepair.

When I returned the following year, I was told what had occurred. I was surprised that the remaining participants were still interested in helping me with the project. New individuals even volunteered. I told them that I would now pay them for their time. Most refused payment. We did agree, however, that I should make a donation to the church to purchase musical instruments, such as a guitar or a harp. The entire congregation came to my house to pick up the donation, which ensured that the intended recipients were clearly defined—that it belonged to the collective congregation and not to an individual. Ownership of the marimba had not been clearly defined. I presented the marimba to the congregation in Crique Chino Barrio Nuevo, but I confusingly and mistakenly added that it was actually the video project that had purchased it because of all the members' hard work.

Q'eqchi' people understand ownership to be produced through action and labor. Agustin felt that he and a few others had done the most work. They, therefore, owned the marimba. It is all quite clear now. Nonetheless, I still find it ironic that Agustin played such a pivotal role in the balkanization of the community in Crique Chino Barrio Nuevo, considering how he so valued collaboration. Yet, that was exactly the problem. Agustin did not see the project as a form of collaboration. He felt that he put forth the most effort and that the others were not as dedicated to the project. He saw himself as a collaborator who acted-in-place and the others as betrayers who acted-out-of-place.

VIGNETTE 3: CH'ONA: THE MISTRESS OF THE PROJECT

Unlike Agustin, other project members found their participation worthy. But, even these individuals anticipated that eventually their active participation would turn into some sort of material reward.

> Well, like what I said that you are thinking that the project is to help the poor, right? For the indigenous, right? Well, thank God that you think to help us, like when the children are sick. (Videotaped interview with Juana)

> You are working, you are saying that you are going to provide a project. You say that you are going to help us. This is what you are doing. The people are very poor, and for this you have to help a little bit. For this you want to do the project. You want to help us because we are very poor. (Videotaped interview with Concepción, translated from Q'eqchi')

> As I said to my companions, let's work together, if we are united we will be able to advance. Because only if we are united can we reach further. This is the idea that I also have about the project. Because the project demands that we work together and that we develop together, we will advance and grow. (Videotaped interview with Agustin)

> Because, like we said, a project costs a bit because someone has to have a little time to dedicate to it. But, if someone has the interest, nothing costs too much. With interest, one can succeed. Because of this, we would like to continue in the project for the fruits it will bear in the future. (Videotaped interview with Armando)

Milpas and their cultural and economic productivity remain central to how Q'eqchi' imagine their worlds. It was no surprise then that the Q'eqchi' came to perceive the video project as a cornfield or a coffee plantation. Cornfields need to be tended, weeded, and worked. Coffee plants need labor for a bountiful harvest. Projects, too, need tending before they can produce. Q'eqchi' people thus spoke with agricultural references when we discussed the potential of the project. I myself began to understand the video project was like a cornfield or a coffee plantation. However, what I failed to recognize is that fincas and milpas have owners who must be

CONCEPCIÓN

respected, who must give permission for corn to grow and for concrete houses to be built. Of course, the Q'eqchi' people would use their cultural script, with its historical precedence of foreign providers, to categorize me as the owner of the project. Even though now obvious, this was my ethnographic epiphany.

It had been just over two months since I assembled the video project. An elder Q'eqchi' man came up to me, greeted me, and submissively nodded his head before me. "Ch'ona," he said. I was shocked. Ch'ona is a title of respect for elderly women, female foreign patrons, and female Tzuultaq'a. I was bewildered that he referred to me by using such an extreme title of respect. But then it came to make more sense. I, the foreign ethnographer, was categorized as the owner of this field. I was reincarnated as a German finca owner and the project was my plantation. I lived on top of the hill where Ferropazco, the German export company, had its residential and administrative seat decades before. I was a foreigner who could manage a few phrases in Q'eqchi' and I incidentally have blonde hair and blue eyes. Most of my Q'eqchi' friends knew that my father had been born in Germany. However, instead of a finca, I had the video project. Instead of little plots of land and concrete houses, I offered them community buildings and a marimba. I provided concern, monetary loans, medicine, and friendship. However, as a typical foreigner within the Q'eqchi' imaginary, I always had the capacity to harm, exploit, and plunder. With my camera, tape recorder, notebook, and computer, I stole images, histories, and cultural riches that I carried to foreign places, exporting ethnographic knowledge rather than coffee. I was a giver and a taker, self and other. I was Ch'ona.

I began to see how Q'eqchi' people put practically all relationships into a similar sort of structural discourse where respect is paid to outside owners and community members, both of whom reciprocate and provide. These relations do not need to be the traditional land-based or cosmological exchange between individuals, communities, and deities. Q'eqchi' people seem to fit novel historical and contemporary relationships into sets of moralized categories that structure how they think about themselves and others. By experiencing firsthand how Q'eqchi' people envisioned the video project (and the ethnographer), I was able to understand how these internalized categories emerge in practice. I began to see the metaphors and symbolism of a culturally structured imaginary in most everything Q'eqchi' people did. I saw it when they entered my house and when they went to church. I witnessed it when they built houses and fed their ancestors on Todos Santos. I viewed it when they spoke about robbers and guerrillas and when they expressed distrust of the government. Illness, ethnic relations, global and local economies, gender relations, religion, and collaborative video projects became clearly defined and comprehended within this moral structure that guided the profane as if it were sacred, and the sacred as profane.

No surprise, then, that I was asked to be a godparent. Outsiders have a long history of being *compadres* (sp. godparents) to the indigenous of Mexico and Central America, and the Q'eqchi' told me that Germans often served as godparents.[2] I was asked on two occasions. The first time, I was acquainted with the family, but not intimately. The mother of the child was working in Guatemala City, and it was the grandmother who cared for the baby and who requested that I be the godparent. I graciously refused. It felt inappropriate to have such a responsibility to a family I barely knew.

The second time was for the youngest son of my friend Martín, who had been killed in an automobile accident. You, the reader, have encountered the words of Martín in this book, although like a well-respected ancestor, he remains out-of-sight (since you have done nothing socially wrong, you can hear his words but not see his form). When Martín's widow asked me, I accepted with no hesitation. I am now the godmother to Eduardo Martín, a child who was still in utero when his father was killed on route to Guatemala City. Because Martín's father had shared with me his cultural knowledge, time, friendship, countless interviews, optimism, and generosity, I felt obligated and honored to accept his widow's offer to be a godparent. I became even more economically and morally bound to the Q'eqchi' of Livingston.

The *compadrazgo* system is a physical marking of a moral community[3]; it is a blueprint to the Q'eqchi' imaginary. It provides a model for interpersonal relationships of respect and a means to set them into action (Ravicz 1967:250). Compadrazgo fortifies vertical hierarchies and it reconstitutes and strengthens horizontal relations between godparents and the society (Mintz and Wolf 1950:348).[4] Likewise, the Q'eqchi' imaginary, encompassing a network of kin and non-kin, explains not only vertical social differences between owners and owned, but also horizontal differences between religions, ethnicities, genders, and nations. Outsiders and owners who provide become part of a kinship system where they are obliged to give loans, reward labor, and provide houses, corn, health, and enlightenment.

ETHNOGRAPHIC VÉRITÉ

> As soon as he aims the camera, the ethnologist disturbs the life he is recording. In *Moi Noir* the actors played their everyday existence in front of the camera. I did not hide in order to film them. We were partners. (Jean Rouch, in Ruby 2000:195)

I did not consciously use or espouse the direct style of Cinéma Vérité as an ethnographic method, even though there are obvious parallels between this active form of filmmaking and ethnographic fieldwork. These similarities are accentuated when utilizing a camera as an ethnographic tool. Commonly known through the filmic work of Dziga Vertov and Jean Rouch, Cinéma Vérité is a style of filmmaking that uses the camera as a protagonist, as a catalyst for action (Barnouw 1993:51–71). The interactive process of filming, and the camera itself, provoke subjects to reveal inner selves, emotions, and the invisible elements of culture (Ruby 2000:12). With an epistemology founded in "the possibility to render the ordinarily invisible visible to all" (Vertov, in Vaughan 1979:53), internalized feelings and the essences of social relationships are made evident through interference from the visible (MacDougall 1998:67).[5]

Our ethnographic methods and the camera itself were used to get at hidden perceptions, invisible knowledge, imagined worlds, and intangible identities. In this way, the video project clearly employed the notions set by Cinéma Vérité, as the collaborative use of the video camera was a stimulus for the revelation of embedded notions of practice. The project also overcame Cartesian perspectivalism where viewers consume and watch objects-as-others through visual surveillance and by constructing and consuming reified knowledge. We unsettled "the very divisions upon which such an epistemology is founded." Our techniques disrupted "the boundaries between the self and the world, mind and body, the mind's eye and the surveying eye" (Grimshaw 2001:91).

Cinéma Vérité is participatory and observational (Stoller 1992:2). Its interactive medium recreates theoretical fields, as did the video project in Livingston. It exposes a structural configuration where internalized sets of dispositions are expressed in practice. This revelation, however, can only be possible through the reflexive inclusion of the filmmaker or ethnographer (Winston 1988:25), who are—in addition to the camera and the interaction—catalysts for the expression of invisible culture. It was only through my participation and dialogue with the participants of Proyecto Ajwacsiinel and the community of Livingston that I was able to comprehend how they perceive themselves and others through internalized, practice-fortified categories. Because of my reflexive involvement—my necessary objective distance and my subjective intimacy—I was not only *A Woman with a Camera,* but I *was* a camera. As Dziga Vertov so concisely puts it, "I am kino-eye, I am a mechanical eye. I, a machine, show you the world as only I can see it" (in Ruby 2000:197).

As Ch'ona, I was, like the Q'eqchi' themselves, a composite, a hybrid montage of partiality, composed of the goodness provided by outsiders and the evil with which they drain life's riches. I was the partial gringa, an unlimited and fluid articulation that is only provided meaning through relations with multiple others—an entity that can be a target of deep-rooted anger and violence initiated by the same Mayan people who openly welcome gringa ethnographers and solidarity workers into their homes and communities as fictive kin (Nelson 1999:41). I was the nomadic subject

(Ong 1999:3), the translocal interlocutor who embodies explicitly readable global texts that span multiple nations and regimes of power. I was the archetypal ethnographic fieldworker who, depending on contexts, shifts back and forth between being insider and outsider, without ever firmly occupying one position or the other (Naples 1996). I was the oxymoronic participant observer who attempts the impossible and ironic task of subjectively objectifying (Tedlock 1992). I was a camera.

Being a positionless mediator was at times isolating, although it was also an advantage that allowed for deep cultural insight. My non-fixed roles (of benefactor, patron, researcher, friend, woman, confidant, foreign entity) assisted in an almost strategic slippage between outsiderness and insiderness (Naples 1996:142; Nelson 1999:41–73). I was a diasporic traveler, a displaced person shifting between cultural scenes. It was this movement that provided me with a "third eye" to see from within and without (Marks 2000:27; Rony 1996:4). Viewing culture as motion, as well as being an ethnographer-in-motion (and you potentially being a reader-in-motion) dissolves the distinctions between object and subject, self and other, and insider and outsider.

My "insiderout" position was further perpetuated by the disparate ethnographic methods I employed. I had the respect of many community members. I attended church with them. I provided marimbas and food. We laughed and joked. I was entrenched in the reciprocal exchange of their community. Yet, as an academic, I carried Westernized perspectives of knowledge. More so, I utilized a foreign apparatus that visually captured time and lives in bounded space. Within the Q'eqchi' imaginary, as a foreigner, I became the female patron of an ethnographic finca, a potentially harmful benefactor. As instruments in a foreign methodology, the camera I toted and the video project I initiated mimicked and recreated the hierarchical positions of power and sight within that imaginary.

An unbiased ability to survey, observe, gather data, inventory, and record was once considered the most valuable component of cameras in ethnographic research (Collier and Collier 1986:9–13; Prosser 1998:100–102). Margaret Mead, for example, suggested that cameras set upon tripods neutralize the particularities of individual anthropologists and expand upon their ability to see and record. She espoused viewing culture objectively from one distant point, suggesting the use of telephoto lenses to avoid disturbing or offending (Mead 1963:177). For Mead, cameras were tools of objectivity that efface the presence of anthropologist and filmmaker (Henley 1998:43). She was also convinced that film could be used for anthropological research by scholars who never even set foot in the field (Ruby 2000:47), since the objective methods of sight erased ethnographers and image-makers from photographic records.

Clearly, cameras "reproduce the world according to a set of perspectival conventions based on a single and unified point of view" (Henley 1998:42)—i.e., the patriarchal, colonizing, powerful and transcendental eye of the Enlightenment (Spanos 2000:14)—but this does not imply that cameras are objective mirrors to reality. They, like anthropologists and identities, shift back and forth between objectivity and subjectivity. They, too, are fluid articulations that embody webs of past and present relationships that are saturated with power. Even Margaret Mead, who adhered to the unbiased ability of the camera to record and observe, ironically considered the camera as a system of "note-taking" (1963:172–176), an overtly subjective form of interpreting culture.

This entrenched ambivalence is considered a "crisis in representation" (Ruby 2000:201) because it is firmly embedded in ethnographic methods, theories, texts, ways of thinking, pedagogical notions, images, and beyond. It is apparent in the anthropologists' traditional method par excellence, participant observation, which demands intimate (subjective) participation and distanced (objective) recording and observation. It is evident in the traditional opposing categories of home and field (Lavie and Swedenburg 1996:154), where home represents objective, centered analyzing and the field symbolizes marginal, subjective methods. It is a crisis because it causes cleavages in our dominant discourses and is an antithesis to our Westernized ideas of knowledge gathering, sight, power, and education.

Recent methodological and theoretical forms have embraced the decentering of traditional knowledge formation, at times through its fragmentation and hybridization or with an acceptance of the underlying ambivalence and lack of certainty. Displacement and movement have challenged reifications of knowledge, ways of seeing, and notions of truth. The once unquestioned categories of self, other, participant, observer, object, subject, center, and margin are now considered articulations, third timespaces where identities are not things but conjunctures that resist institutionalization (Lavie and Swedenburg 1996:168).

Ethnographers, with their training as intercultural producers of imagery and knowledge and their ability to move between identities and social positions, are capable of displacing traditional categories and challenging official histories and notions of truth (Marks 2000:24–28). Ethnographers view through a roaming third eye, which provides one with the ability to critically experience slippage between object and subject (Rony 1996:4–

5). Since movement of the third eye can lead to clarity of social mediation, it provides means to dig culturally deeper than traditional modes of
seeing and insight. It implodes the conjunctures in entities heavily reliant
upon the separation and inclusion manifest in hyphens, such as participant-
observer. Categorical distinctions can be dissolved and explored since the
new focus of academic inquiries are these constructed zones of articulation
(Lavie and Swedenburg 1996:171). To reveal how perception and intuition
emerge not from things but from movement and transitions (Merleau-
Ponty 2002 [1945]:320–321), ethnographers must embrace the complemen-
tary modalities of object and subject and accept individuals as concurrently
sensible and sentient.

Paul Stoller suggests we consider a "radically empirical anthropology"
that emphasizes the field experience and does not prioritize theory over
description, analysis over emotions, and sight over the other "lower" senses
(Stoller 1992:213–215). "It is an anthropology that recognizes blatant incon-
gruities, confounding ambiguities, and seemingly intolerable contradictions—the texture of life as it is experienced in the field" (Stoller 1992:213).
It is also the type of ethnographic and emotional commitment where scholars are compelled to return to the field year after year, a personal and professional engagement in which I clearly locate myself. Yet, although the
ethnographer must be an avid participator, this is not the participation
of "participant observation." Rather, "it means that anthropologists open
themselves to other worlds as they acknowledge their implication—their
entanglement—in networks of social relations" (Stoller 1992:214).

Ethnographic vérité challenges traditional academic constructs through
entanglement. While I, as ethnographic overseer, carried with me an objectifying recording mechanism, this apparatus, through its collaborative use,
could also explore the unseen and contribute to the dismantling of centered knowledge and sight from a dominant perspective. Collaboratively
sharing the video camera, and revealing multiple angles, different styles of
camera work, and various interpretations of what is aesthetic, even through
the use of a foreign piece of technology, was a step toward the creation of
a montage of identities, where boundaries—upheld through movement—
are vital to meaning and presentation. Through our collaborative methodology, not only does one see my Western-trained perspective and aesthetic
(along with all my identities), but one also sees all the participants' viewpoints on how they imagine themselves and others. Through the multiple
hands at work, traditional knowledge gathering, based upon vision from
one distanced point of view, is dismantled. Collaborative methods implode
hyphens and subsequently allow for the further exploration of them.

Likewise, ethnographic collaboration, whether manifested materially or more theoretically, returns the senses to representations of culture and identities; it mimics the flows and textures of life. Through the use of a technological tool that does not necessarily permanently freeze images, but rather represents them optically as movements of be-ing, temporality, dimensionality, and auditory processes, emotional elements can be actively restored to processes of identification and to the representations of these processes (whether video footage or written text). Yet, one does not need to implement a visual collaborative video project in order to explore the senses or to envision identities as spatial and temporal; one must analyze and hear from subjects from a multiplicity of encounters and positions within far-reaching networks of translocal exchanges (Clifford 1997; Marcus 1995; Rodman 1992). Actually, for me, collaboration is more a philosophy of motion than a method; it is a form of process-oriented knowledge that emerges from the inclusion of difference and movement rather than a bounded domain. Viewers and readers hear, see, and move through the eyes of multiple subjects instead of one primary (dominant, seeing, stationary) informant. Ethnographic vérité is a radically empirical anthropology, one that engages multiple subjects and viewers and reconceptualizes ideas of images, the field, and identities as articulating processes of active and strategic practice.

Collaboration, however, does not necessarily imply harmony. Even Jean Rouch, who through Cinéma Vérité observed and participated, had foes and friends in the field (Stoller 1992:47). The Oxford Concise English Dictionary [tenth edition] defines the term "collaborate" in two ways: to "work jointly on an activity or project" and to "cooperate traitorously with an enemy." These two disparate understandings of a term represent the somewhat slippery process of ethnographic collaboration, in all the various understandings of the word. Collaboration, like the gringa interlocutor, and similar to all ethnographic endeavors, provides us with multiple significations that blur boundaries between peaceful coexistence and somewhat strained political relations. It is ironic that anthropologists have embraced the term "collaboration," and the ideas behind it, when it ambivalently implies a cooperative interaction and a somewhat sinister covert deal. Or perhaps it is not ironic at all. Like identities, collaboration might represent the shifting montage of be-ings that individuals access and pull upon in strategic ways. Perhaps it also exemplifies the subjects of ethnographic inquiry that in the past have been assumed to be harmony-creating processes. Most anthropological research on kinship, for example, fails to mention how it can be a divisive thing, that kinship is supported by antipathy and gossip (Strathern and Edwards 2000:151).

The video project in Livingston was not necessarily harmonious; our collaboration led to dissent and envy among the "community." Reciprocity and exchange do not necessarily make things socially equitable, but rather maintain difference and social distance (Weiner 1992:66). Collaboration is not always about coalescence. Further, some may claim that what we did in the field was far from collaborative, since "for a production to be truly collaborative, parties involved must be equal in their competencies or achieved equitable division of labor" (Ruby 2000:208). An outsider who donates a camera or arranges for video production does not escape the ethical implications of intervention (Turner 2002:78). And because most of the editorial power still lies in hands of the anthropologist and filmmaker, I could be accused of providing the participants of the projects with an illusory power (Ruby 2000:204).

However, I do not think ethnographic collaboration presents only chimeras of shared authority. Clearly it has the potential to overcome ethical and representational dilemmas,[6] but it also allows ethnographers to "speak with" rather than "speak for" (Ruby 2000:195–219). It challenges traditional modes of knowledge production. Because ethnographic methodologies where locals are handed cameras produce cultural representations that are multi-local and multi-temporal, video collaboration can display the many facets of culture and its manifestations.[7] The final ethnographic product is not strictly the ethnographer's, but rather a representation of the cooperative process between the anthropologist and the individuals with whom she or he works. Interpersonal codes are practiced, articulations are embraced rather than ignored, and the slippery and porous borders between subjects and objects are exposed.

Think about the name of the video project— *Proyecto Ajwacsiinel*. Ajwacsiinel means "one who stirs up, rouses, or lifts." The project, with its microcosmic mimicry of a field of action, made cultural scripts and unseen culture rise up to the ethnographic surface. Through collaboration and ethnographic epiphany, I could understand how the Q'eqchi' conceptualize their world. *Intau ru.* I understand. It is in front of my face. I intimately experienced and lived through the relationships that structure Q'eqchi' perception and practice. And since Q'eqchi' people define themselves through these imaginary webs, they understand themselves as a conglomeration of all the subjects to which they have related today and through history. They embody the transnational network that crosses time and space, from pre-

Columbian deities to twenty-first-century tourists. Because the relations of this imaginary continuously shift, and power is transferred between subjects, identities and difference are not about dichotomies, but instead about multiplicity, montage, and movement.

Ethnographic vérité provokes subjects into revealing the emotions and subtleties of unobservable culture. Collaboration not only mirrors internal and external structures, but is also the protagonist that reveals their relative existence. It is a phenomenological method that allows objects and subjects to be brought out as composites (Merleau-Ponty 2002 [1945]:80) and articulations within greater fields of action. It is no coincidence, then, that Dziga Vertov, the original practitioner of Cinéma Vérité, had the task for *Kino-Nedelia* (Film Weekly) in Moscow to assemble fragments of incoming bits of film into organized and meaningful wholes (Barnouw 1993:52). Just as people create identities, cameras create images, and as anthropologists conceptualize culture, Vertov created montages—whole, composite texts that appeared as bounded domains, but were actually fragments of reality from shifting positions in transnational networks.

With this said, it must also be stated that, while social imaginaries are models that guide practice and perception, they are also dynamic networks in which people organize and recreate themselves. Tek's vignette, for example, demonstrates how cultures exist within and also beyond structures and how individuals strategize and manipulate cultural models idiosyncratically through their own personal relationships. Cultural scripts are not impenetrable and culture can be transformed from within interpersonal relationships and from one generation to the next. Consider Tek's children. They have seen their mother shatter a cultural script by acting-out-of-place while concurrently seeing a benevolent gringa remove their maternal body. They witnessed the intimate transmission and transformation of the fluid entity we call culture, and they encountered how concordance and continuity can emerge equally from intimacy and broader structuring relations. And you, the reader, did the same. From within this emotional montage of histories, individuals, hearts, and souls, through collaboration and ethnographic vérité, you too have experienced how individuals succumb to social structures and also how they reduce them to scrap.

Eleven

ENDINGS AND BEGINNINGS

As I conclude this exploration into the Q'eqchi' imaginary and its embodiment in practice and perception, I reflect on the multiple and multifaceted fields of action through which internalized culture reveals itself in observable manifestations. I contemplate how metaphors of visibility, reciprocity, consumption, respect, and ownership are symbolic acts of morality that forge and maintain the Q'eqchi' imaginary. I consider the primacy of ethnographic vérité, the intimate links between the global and local, the merging of method with theory, and the role of vision in maintaining power, authority, and cultural imaginaries. I pore over engaged types of ethnographic research that can challenge academic ways of seeing by understanding how cohesion can emerge from difference. Wandering through the more than a decade of memories I have with the people of Livingston, I think of my friends and family, emotional attachments, cultural idiosyncrasies, and the ethnographic insights encountered during fieldwork. Thus, it is not surprising that endings also lead to beginnings.

The first time I went to Central America was in 1990, when I participated in an archaeological field school in northern Belize. During the day, we excavated ancient Mayan structures in search of artifacts, while at night we interacted with our Yucatec- and Spanish-speaking hosts and coworkers, bridging the contemporary and past as archaeologists do so well. I vividly recall the breezy afternoon in April when I uncovered a pre-Columbian cache of jade, shells, pottery, and beads, left some 1,500 years ago as a private, in-home offering to deities or ancestors. I prayed, quite aware of the "unobservable"—the respectful hands that once lay the precious objects in their resting place. With my own undeserving hands being the next to touch them, I handled them with respect, gratitude, awe, and fear.

Disjointedly, I am also reminded of the first week of that same archaeological field school, riding in a dugout canoe on the river with my bunkmate, Marla, being paddled by two young Yucatec Mayan men. I felt, naïvely, as though I had entered the "Heart of Darkness," traversing the course of time, civilization, and self-realization, sensing cultural isolation and mysterious fortitude as we quietly glided under thick mangroves. Then, without warning, our Mayan guides began singing word-for-word what Marla claimed were lyrics from Metallica (a heavy metal band popular in the 1980s and early 1990s). Culturally shocked out of my romantic rapture—similar to how the Q'eqchi' family described in Chapter 1 jolted me out of my trance during Ash Wednesday—I experienced the in-my-face necessity to understand Mayan people in their contemporary worlds, as people influenced by present webs of significance, as individuals looking to the future, and as be-ings embodying structures of longevity. Mayan people are not mere reflections of the past, even if these mirrors of continuity do emerge in fields of action.

The Q'eqchi' Mayan people of Livingston live within a community constructed by relationships that span the local and global. It is no coincidence that the people at the service desk of the Bloomington, Indiana Wal-Mart know me as the woman who sends Moneygrams to Guatemala. Just last month I sent money to Blanca and to my godson, Eduardo (I am due to send money to the video project participants). Transnational networks, electronic money transfers, and international corporations are fluidly incorporated into the Q'eqchi' imaginary. The Q'eqchi' habitus is firmly global (Nash 2001); it is far from isolated and native only to a local environment. The Q'eqchi' imaginary is constructed through transnational networks that stretch across the continents, from Asia, Germany, England, New York, Los Angeles, to Belize, Honduras, Alta Verapaz, Guatemala City, and Livingston. From global networks, past and present, imaginaries and moralities emerge, explain, and self-perpetuate through practice. And I am far from the only individual to recognize this.

> Because one day the time will come when they are not going to have corn. They will have to request corn from the United States and how much will that cost? Rather, growing it here, I say yes. For this reason, things are getting worse because there is no corn. There is no rice. There are no beans. People are not working very hard. We are losing many things. It is not like before. Before, we Q'eqchi's did not use things like we use today, plastic things. Before, we used only ceramic pots. The women made pots and *comales,* all things. But today, we have electric frying pans, electric pots, all of this stuff.

> And it is expensive! And it is from the United States! Before,
> no way! Before, they had to make their *comales* out of clay,
> pots from clay. And soap too. They made soap. Now, now we
> have to buy Zest and who the hell knows where that is from!!
> (Videotaped interview with Mariano)

Mariano offered an illustrative allegory of globalization and dependency. Q'eqchi' people see foreign nations supplying Guatemalans with products they are unable to supply themselves. They see their money heading afar and they see themselves and others in Guatemala getting poorer while the foreigners get richer. Mariano, like many people in Livingston, blamed the authorities for the problems in Livingston, even for the drugs and crime usually associated with the Garifuna. Mariano said that the Garifuna people also have nothing because foreigners and the Guatemalan authorities are the only ones gaining wealth and power. Q'eqchi' people in general say that the Garifuna have no choice but to rob people even though they have one extreme advantage over the Q'eqchi'—they have Western Union sending them checks every month. Incoming dollars are the most significant distinguishing factor between the Q'eqchi' and the Garifuna. Because of their more direct involvement in the U.S. economy, the Garifuna have a different system of (invisible) values.

Nonetheless, except for their immediate transnational connection to wired dollars, the Garifuna are not very different from the Q'eqchi', particularly in regard to their sentiments about the authorities. Both the Q'eqchi' and Garifuna people do not trust the Guatemalan government that tends to forget their isolated town on the Caribbean. Because this kind of suspicion is not only a local phenomenon but a national one, people's concerns about the government will pose a significant problem in the further implementation of the peace accords, in which people have no faith. If authorities are seen as criminals, how will they ever represent a social system that provides? How will Q'eqchi' people and others ever trust them? This is a major social problem. Until the authorities reciprocate by providing employment, water, electricity, paved roads, and titles to land, among other political promises, Q'eqchi' people and others in Guatemala will continue to have their misgivings about the government. This national distrust sadly was expressed on 16 May 1999, when the citizens of Guatemala voted down constitutional reforms that would have restructured the government and the military, and federally acknowledged the twenty-three indigenous groups in Guatemala. The *Latin American Caribbean and Central America Report* claims that only 18.5 percent of the registered voters turned out, attributing the negative results to "a lack of information and mistrust of the political system" (June 1999:4). Like the Spanish who duped the Mayans of Guatemala into trading precious gold for mirrors, spoons, and files, and like Q'eq who eats eggs and steals shoes for his German owner, Guatemalan authorities are conceived as indiscriminately consuming wealth supplied by the poor.

Yet, one might ask, since cultures and communities are filtered through global fields from the past and present, how are we still able to find cohesive forces within communities and through histories? In a world where meaning emerges from multiple voices and various positions, how can we observe oneness in cultural values, beliefs, and practices? Admitting and celebrating the subjectivity in ethnographic fieldwork, as I do, can potentially place ethnographers in a difficult situation, making it questionable whether we can justify any representation of culture that is envisioned as collectively shared and powerfully influential.

I propose that we are capable of imagining a compelling, objectifying collective in culture, even within this world of hybridity and movement. However, it is imperative that we understand that this unobservable facet of culture made visible is only manufactured and reproduced by individuals who do not exist exclusively as object or subject. People, their identities, and their shared imaginaries—like images—are unquestionably transmitted while they are concurrently reformulated in various times and across space. As objects and subjects, we create images of ourselves and others.

When I began my research in Livingston, I fully expected to find heterogeneity rather than a homogenizing doxae. I had no idea that I would encounter through practice the unobservable framework that tied Q'eqchi' people together, to themselves, and to me. What I learned was that homogeneity emerges from difference. Social and historical structures link people to one another, to deities, and to near and ancient ancestors, though they are able to do so only through encounters of multiplicity, through movement, and through the cohesion that emerges from conflict. Psychic unity and a doctrine of diversity are not contradictory dogmas (Tambiah 1990:112).

To find cohesion from a history of connections, researchers must use methods that accept multiplicity as a cohort to collectivity. Ethnographers should traverse the multi-sited structures that create filters through which practice and perception emerge. The body and its senses ought to be viewed as embodying the residue of historical relations. Fieldworkers must encounter the type of ethnographic intimacy made possible through collaboration and engaged ethnography. Traditional dichotomies and academic categories of knowledge must be challenged, questioned, and considered as transitions rather than stable entities. Ethnographic vérité can accomplish this.

Further, through multi-sited, sensory-oriented, and intimate ethnography, one can experience how vision is more than an optical process that involves physical and material objects, how it explores the less tangible politics of authority, knowing, and controlling. Ethnographic vérité is our *ilob'aal,* the quartz tool that allows readers and researchers, like shamans, to probe deep into intangible realms. In turn, I propose that visual theory can and should be applied to non-visual culture, such as internalized relationships. Most scholars of culture consider that physicality is an attribute that must be visible at some level. However, the methods of ethnographic vérité reveal that physicality need not be visualized by the naked or mechanized eye to be considered within reach. Nonphysical culture also is tangible. Made visible through intimate ethnography, practice, and collaboration, relations of power surface as the girders of internalized imaginaries.[1]

Through ethnographic vérité and a radically empirical anthropology, we can reach the invisible undercoating of cultural processes when we allow for the materialization of metaphysical relations. In this book, I present the reader with these abstract theories and relations through real physical behavior and images. In this way, this book is a reinterpretation of what is physical. Relations are real objects that are saturated with power and personal agency. Ethnographic vérité brings them in front of your face. The reader has thus traversed the same relationships that Q'eqchi' people use to understand themselves and others. You have "seen" more than is visible.

This reinterpretation of what is visible and tangible challenges the marginalization of images and image-based research (Prosser 1998:97–112). The traditional academic perspective uses vision and ocular metaphors as means of surveillance, proof, and controlling rather than as forms of expression. Ethnographic vérité conceptualizes images and words as equals, just as it imagines parity between method and theory, self and other, home and field. Images carry the potential to embody and explore theory, to incite emotion, and to engage the viewer intellectually. This is why I integrate images into the text rather than marginalizing them to separate pages, and why the images have limited or no supporting verbal subtext. Images speak on their own.

Images take time and capture it (even if it is a lived pace such as with video), putting it on display for observation and engagement. This brings the textures of culture to viewers, strives to represent how identities are montages of motion, endeavors to make the unseen tangible and mean-

ingful, and records and observes culture. Images and words are like identities. They appear as stable objects, although they are interpreted differ-
ently by various subjects across time and space. They can also embody and
signify cultural logic that objectifies them in such a way that they signify
similar things to different people and that defines them temporally as objects maintained through action and exchange. Through their ability to
record and evoke, images and their verbal counterparts represent the many
porous divides that partially exist and are only reified through practice and
perception.

Identities, however, are not tangible apart from the relationships from
which they emerge. Even intimate relationships, where people transfer
knowledge, ideas, and symbolic meaning to other people, friends, neighbors, and kin, are grounded in far-reaching webs where political economies and transnational channels traverse and connect faraway regions and
individuals. This was evinced in Tek's vignette, in Chapter 10, which de-
tailed how our personal relationship was governed by broader, globalized
networks of power. Her story also demonstrates that individuals have mo-
ments of agency and that it is far too easy to reduce everything to shared
cultural constructs.

I was humbled by watching Roberto and his family search through their
belongings that Sunday morning. It refocused my analytical concern to the
personal relations within a family, between siblings, between lovers, and
even to friendships between anthropologists and locals. The intimate idiosyncrasies—the messiness of culture—reveal how individuals share ideological and cultural thoughts with each other. Yet, equally at this personal
level, we experience the global, the transnational, and the transmission of
culture. A woman, a family, and a little back room in Livingston can become a house of mirrors that reflect the personal and the socially and globally shared.

Global- and structural-oriented academic perspectives have the potential to ignore the fact that culture emerges and changes, often drastically, at
an interpersonal level. Culture arises from individuals interacting among
one other, from people practicing and reinforcing ideology, from people
sharing ideas and belief systems, and from individual experience. Culture,
like personal, national, and ethnic identities, is ultimately forged through
both intimate and global relationships. When we think of culture, we tend
to think about bounded systems and structures of longevity that fluidly
transform while remaining resolute. However, Tek demonstrated how easy
it is for an individual to break the mold.

Tek and her family have personal histories that dictate whether she remained content as mother or opted to shatter cultural values and leave her husband and children. Relations between spouses and between parents and children are intimately distinctive and subjective all the while they are practiced in historic and social fields that create coherency through structural endurance. Nonetheless, even intimate and idiosyncratic phenomena mirror translocal connections. Tek and her family adhere to a hybridized and transnational imaginary. I, with my Disney Lion King picture books, am a broker that represents another discursive web of power and action. Tourists symbolize another. German finca owners and the Garifuna people offer various worldviews. The governments of Guatemala and Belize, the Mayan Revitalization Movement, and Tek's Protestant Church, all represent different cultural fields. Like a house of mirrors, Tek's breakdown and rebellion was a nexus of all these cultural contexts that she bounced about in the definition of herself. And here is where power enters the intimate scenes of cultural transmission, through all these mirrored reflections of cultural and personal ideologies. While global and regional politics create different arenas where voices are fortified by structures and various means of power, it is Tek who either reinforces them through practice or ignores them. Clearly influenced by transnational and personal mirrors, she is the one who ultimately transforms culture and transmits this to her family. We must not ignore the individual within personal relationships as a reproducer and practitioner of societal norms. Intimacy distinguishes anthropology from other social sciences, because emotional engagement does not need to be disqualified as unobjective messiness. Personal bonds can be explored alongside professional revelations. In fact, I affirm that I cannot separate them; the professional and personal, like selves and others, are fused into processes of being.

My relationship to the people of Livingston extends far beyond an academic connection of ethnographer and subject. I continue to visit Livingston regularly, and I frequently talk with Lola and my neighbor Blanca on the telephone. I send money to my godson and others as often as possible. A strong emotional link transcends the telephone, the wire transfers, the occasional letter. Livingston is part of me, and I cannot extract it from my being, nor do I want to. I dream of Livingston, where I find myself in Lola's home, comfortable as ever, swinging in a hammock or making tortillas, and always laughing, smiling, joking. I imagine myself cleaning fish and sipping coffee with Blanca. I recall my own young son jumping alongside his "brother" on Eduardo's small bed in Livingston. All these memories and dreams are tangibly real and represent the strong links that keep me tied to my friends and colleagues in Livingston. As a trained ethnographer, friend, provider of technology, powerful eyes, and foreign owner, I admit that I was indispensable to this research. I was pulled into the global imaginary of the Q'eqchi', where I comfortably remain. I certainly sense the obligation of a ritual kin and community member of Livingston. I carry this physical, ethical, and spiritual responsibility with me throughout my days.

The Q'eqchi' of Livingston shared their lives. They revealed themselves and they opened their homes. I can sit in front of my computer, thousands of miles from Livingston, and sense the relationships I have forged and uncovered. The field seeps into my home, the past into the present, other into self, theory into method, invisibility into visibility. I travel through the network of relations that stretches across regions, histories, individuals, and nations. I see the years merge, the technology change, the buildings develop, the roads become paved, and the children grow. I watch how relationships remain firm, how endings lead to beginnings, and how object-subject and selfother are upheld through practice, in perception, and always in motion.

NOTES

CHAPTER 1

1. For glossing Q'eqchi' words, I use the abbreviation *q.*, and for Spanish words, I use the abbreviation, *sp.* I gathered most of the Q'eqchi' translations I provide from Spanish terms from Q'eqchi' speakers in Livingston, which I then translated into English. For further translations, I used the Q'eqchi' dictionaries of Sedat (1993 [1955]) and Sam Juárez and Stewart (1997).

CHAPTER 2

1. Like the Yucatan Peninsula, which lies directly north of Livingston, this area sits on a karst limestone bed. This provides the high cliffs and local caves, but it also means the soil layer is very thin and is easily leached by heavy rainfall. Erosion is a problem. Altitude ranges from sea level to 1,310 meters above. There are two seasons, *invierno* (sp. winter) and *verano* (sp. summer), which correspond to the dry and the rainy seasons. The rainy season lasts from approximately June through November with the dry season running from December to May (as in most areas of Guatemala, the beginning and end of these seasons are contestable). Temperatures range from 20.4°C to 35.6°C and the humidity often reaches 100 percent. Only during rare nights in December, January, or February will you find people wearing jackets or using blankets on their beds.

2. Throughout this book, "Livingston" refers to the town of Livingston rather than the municipio. I will clearly state when I am discussing the municipio or the general area.

3. According to Sapper (1985 [1936]:16), these Chol people lived near what is now Puerto Barrios and were known locally as the *Loqueguas*.

4. Hernán Cortéz was in the area in 1525 in search of supplies (Mejía 1997:89).

5. *Reducción* was a Spanish policy of "gathering scattered settlements into nucleated centers" (Lovell and Lutz 1995:173).

6. See González (1988:15–73) for a complete ethnohistory.

7. The penal codes that Edward Livingston had created for Louisiana were adapted and adopted by the republic of Guatemala in 1836. Interestingly, they had been rejected by the Louisiana Legislature in 1826 (Woodward 1990:60).

8. See Náñez Falcón (1970) for more on the German owner of Ferropazco, Erwin Paul Dieseldorff.

9. In 1955, the port at Santo Tomás de Castilla, just south of Puerto Barrios, began operation as the main free port and now handles 70 percent of Guatemala's international maritime commerce (Stanley 1994:79).

10. The Río Dulce region was designated a National Park in 1955, and CONAP (*Consejo Nacional de Áreas Protegidas*) devised a master plan for its zoning, use, and management in 1992. However, a loophole in the agreement allows certain individuals and institutions to buy land and build houses and marinas in protected areas, so development and deforestation continues today (Mejía 1997: 134).

11. Ladinos in Guatemala are non-Mayan and non-European. Specific to Guatemala, Ladino is a term akin to *Mestizo,* a descriptive category that refers not only to biological blending but also to cultural and social practices.

12. In January 2004, a Q'eqchi' teacher named Miguel Rax became the first indigenous person to be elected mayor of Livingston. I have not been to Livingston since his election, so I have very little information about his personal background, political philosophies, and local support.

13. Sadly, Bibi was among several Livingston residents tragically killed in a bus accident in 2004. This horrendous accident was a devastating loss to the entire community.

14. An interesting side note is that most of the schools in the aldeas are taught using PRONEBI, a bilingual education program that promotes the use of early education in Mayan languages. The first two years of school in the aldeas are taught in Q'eqchi', the third in both Q'eqchi' and Spanish, and the fourth through sixth predominantly in Spanish. However, my research indicates that many parents prefer school to be taught in Spanish rather than Q'eqchi' and therefore believe that their children receive a better education in Livingston where schools are taught only in Spanish. See Richards and Richards (1996) for further discussion on PRONEBI.

15. I stayed from September 1995 through July 1996, for two months in 1997, for three weeks in 1998 and 1999, and for one week in 2003.

16. For differing viewpoints on participant observation, see Behar (1996:1–33), Bernard (1994:136–164), Collier and Collier (1986:19–28), Jackson (1987:63–78), Minh-ha (1991:64–78), and Tedlock (1991).

17. Viewing and then discussing video was an extraordinary elicitation tool, a chance to bring up multiple viewpoints. I showed all native-made footage and my own videotapes to the participants in the video project and their families, and occasionally videotaped the lively discussions interjected during and after the viewing. Altogether, we shot over forty-five hours of footage.

18. See note 1, Chapter 1.

CHAPTER 3

1. The Q'eqchi' language originated from a Proto-Mayan language spoken some 4,000 years ago. It broke off from the Quichean branch circa 600 B.C.E. (Cahuec del Valle and Richards 1994:2).

2. Northern influences were felt from Teotihuacan, the Pipil, Toltec, and Chichimec (Estrada Monroy 1979:12; King 1974:14).

3. Scholars continue today to speculate about the karst cave system in the area, particularly a cavernous opening at Semuc, as a possible entrance to Xibalba, the mythical Mayan underworld described in the *Popol Vuh* (Pope and Sibberensen 1981:54; Tedlock 1996:256).

4. *Encomienda* was a colonial "award that entitled the recipient, an *encomendero,* to receive tribute in goods and services from a designated number of Indians" (Lovell and Lutz 1995:174). However, unlike in other parts of Guatemala, the encomienda system failed here because the Q'eqchi' people fled, returning to their homes in the mountains (Estrada Monroy 1979:16).

5. These settlements were mainly pre-Columbian centers that were Christianized by adding a saint to their name. For example, Chamelco became San Juan Chamelco and Cahabón became Santa María Cahabón (Schackt 1986:13). Q'eqchi' were also taught to read, write, count, play the flute, and help during Mass, which was given in Q'eqchi' (King 1974:21).

6. Over the next 150 years, Catholic missions were sent to control and convert the Chol, Lacandón, Mopan, and Itzá. The Q'eqchi', most of whom had already been converted, became the recipients of non-Christian enemy attacks. In 1628, a group of Lacandón attacked a town twenty-five kilometers from Cobán. By the end of the seventeenth century the Spanish had completed their mission to control the Chol, who had already begun mixing with the Q'eqchi' of Alta Verapaz.

7. Cochineal is a red dye derived from cultivation of insects that live on the leaves of the nopal cactus (Jones 1994:147).

8. Whether there was communal land at this time is a point of debate. Scholars such as McAnany (1995:92) and Wilk (1991:51) contend that communal land was a colonial or even a nineteenth-century innovation.

9. Barrios offered a *caballería* (109.8 acres) for as little as fifty pesos, equivalent to one dollar (Stanley 1994:7).

10. For ethnographic research on the Q'eqchi' of Belize, see Howard (1975), Rambo (1962), Schackt (1986), and Wilk (1991).

11. One manzana equals 1.7 acres.

12. One cuerda is approximately forty-six yards. Fincas would pay as little as five cents per day (Gordon 1983:53).

13. Because it still lives in memories, I am concerned that in regards to its economic role in forming a model of morality, this time period may be artificially inflated.

14. David Stoll (personal communication) states that this inequality in land-ownership is not descriptive of the regions of Quiche, Solola, Huehuetenango, Chimaltenango, and Totonicopan.

15. See Dosal (1993) for a political history of the UFC in Guatemala, and Stanley (1994) for a more sympathetic view of this company.

16. For further research on this topic see Fried et al. (1983), Galeano (1967), Schlesinger and Kinzer (1982), and Smith (1990).

17. In 1960, then President Miguel Ydígoras announced that all remaining federal land would be divided among the military (Brockett 1992:8).

18. Brockett (1992:3) writes that indigenous people did not support the Agrarian Reform to the extent that the government had hoped for, and that they preferred the more conservative policy of the nineteenth century, before the growth of the coffee industry, that granted them titles to communal land.

19. See Bastos and Camus (1995) for more on Mayan migrants in Guatemala City.

20. It has been suggested that North American planes taking off from Panama dropped napalm (Galeano 1967:69).

21. For further discussion on the war in Guatemala, see Manz (1988, 2004), Carmack (1988), Smith (1990), Stoll (1993), and Wilson (1991). In Chapter 9, I discuss what the peace accord of 29 December 1996 means to the Q'eqchi' of Livingston and how violence and guerrillas influence their understanding of themselves and others in Livingston.

22. According to a Guatemalan sociologist conducting research in Crique Maya, an aldea upriver from Livingston, the Q'eqchi' residents there openly discuss the violence that forced them from their homes in Alta Verapaz. But these people do not live in Livingston. Their reasons for remaining in the aldeas may be related to politics and fear, but this is an ethnographic question in itself. Further, in some more politically torn areas, silence sets up documentary immunity for the theorist (David Stoll, personal communication).

23. See Carey (2001) for Kaqchikel Mayan perspectives on history.

24. It is no coincidence that many of these contemporary deities are considered owners (Thompson 1970:262–274). It is also significant that the term *batab* means "axe-wielder" in Yucatec Maya. Ancient and contemporary rain gods (including mountain spirits) are often depicted carrying axes of red lightening. They also symbolically manifest as bright, red lights, as does the eastern Chac deity representing the red planet Venus.

25. Relations with foreigners were what originally constructed the colonial cargo system, and they were also what subsequently maintained it. Wolf's (1957) ideas about the closed corporate community are useful in understanding how outside relations can maintain a closed moral community.

CHAPTER 4

1. There is no plural form of Tzuultaq'a in Q'eqchi'. I thus use Tzuultaq'a in both singular and plural references to the mountain spirits, distinguishing between the two forms with the use of singular and plural pronouns. Also, because of their dual gender or bisexuality (Humberto Ruz 1992:224), I use "s/he" to refer to Tzuultaq'a in the singular.

2. A belief in spirits of the earth is not unique to the Q'eqchi' Maya. Other Mayan groups revere mountain spirits that, however particular their manifestations, names, and relations, all have similar qualities. They exist in numerous areas of Guatemala, southern Mexico, Yucatan, and Belize. Mam speakers call them Witz (Watanabe 1992:74–76) while K'iche' people of Momostenango refer to them as Juyubtak'aj (Tedlock 1992:262). They are 'Anhel in Tzotzil (Laughlin 1969:177), Yumtzilob among the Yucatec (Villa Rojas 1969:217), and Hitz-hok for the Mopan Maya of Belize (Humberto Ruz 1992:224; Schackt 1984:58). Pan-Mayan attributes include the ability to be both male and female, an association with snakes, manifestation as a light-skinned individual, and large plantations inside the cavernous homes. They are considered the true owners of the land as they control springs, mountains, caves, lakes, corn, and animals. Individuals must receive the mountain spirit's permission before planting, building, digging, or somehow altering the sacred earth. That most Mayan people revere similar mountain spirits leads one to assume that Tzuultaq'a evolved from a pan-Mayan deity. Consequently, the contemporary Mayan revitalization movement employs the mountain spirits and their sacred earth as key symbols of a pan-Mayan ethnic identity and as evidence of cultural continuity (Tedlock 1992:213). While continuity from the past is a polemic academic, social, and political issue (Hervik 1999:91–95; Warren 1989:188–193), evidence that Tzuultaq'a has pre-Columbian roots, even with its foreign personification, is quite substantial.

3. Thirteen has significance in contemporary and past Mayan cultures, as in the thirteen days of the divinatory calendar, thirteen layers of the Mayan universe, and their thirteen corresponding deities (Thompson 1970:195).

4. According to B. Tedlock (personal communication 1998), gender determination of Tzuultaq'a is also influenced by the gender of the individual speaking.

5. Hans Sieber (1999:86) breaks down what he calls "the contract" between Q'eqchi' people and their Tzuultaq'a. The three elements of this contract are respect, sacrifice, and thanks, which are integral, according to Sieber, in all Q'eqchi' ritual.

6. Envisioning a patron-as-provider is part of the more reciprocal patron-client bond as theorized by moral economists (Foster 1953; Popkin 1979; Sahlins 1972; Scott 1976). Rather than unequal and exploitative, moral economists envision the patron-client bond as a matter of filial relations, parents caring for their children who pay them back with due respect. Capitalism is what supposedly tears this

family relation to shreds and brings it to new exploitative levels. I would add that these scholarly viewpoints regarding the ambiguity of patrons/owners should not be based simply on whether they are engaged in capitalist or pre-capitalist modes of production. I believe these theories prioritize capitalism by envisioning only two opposing economic systems.

7. Catholic Action is a Catholic-sponsored orthodox missionary movement that defines traditional Mayan ritual and beliefs as pagan practices or *mundial* (sp. worldly).

8. For Pierre Bourdieu, this internalized framework of dispositions is the *habitus,* which he defines as "history turned into nature" (1977:78). Habitus is "necessary in order for those products of collective history, the objective structures (e.g., of language, economy, etc.) to succeed in reproducing themselves more or less completely, in the form of durable dispositions" (Bourdieu 1977:85).

9. According to Bourdieu and Wacquant, fields are "systems of objective relations which are the product of the institution of the social in things or in mechanisms that have the quasi-reality of physical objects" (1992:127). Fields are "frames of social life" (Holland et al. 1998:7) or "figured worlds" that are "socially and culturally constructed realms of interpretation" (1998:52). Fields are the contexts where the internalized, symbolic categories forge practice, perception, and the positioning of selves and others. "Figured worlds" imply a shared social reality— such as the art world, the economic field, the literary field, or romance—where symbolic ordering is shared by actors and manifest in practice. These social contexts activate the practiced embodiment of internalized scripts and also reproduce them through social action and the manner by which individuals conceive of themselves within these "systems of relations" (Bourdieu and Wacquant 1992:106). Once actively engaged within a field, actors proceed, all in line with tacit codes, to position themselves strategically through their practices and perceptions (Bourdieu and Wacquant 1992:99).

10. For anthropological studies on morality, see Anderson et al. (1997), Benedict (1989 [1946]), Brandt (1954), Howell (1997), Kluckhohn and Strodtbeck (1961), Kluckhohn (1948), Read (1955), and Smith (1994).

11. Q'eqchi' morality is not a primordial characteristic, and although it uses concepts of reciprocity and exchange, it is not intrinsically linked with a more natural economy. In fact, I assume, as Annette Weiner suggests (1992:66), that reciprocity is not the homogeny-creating mechanism that so many social scientists assume. Instead, it is a creator of difference between participants whose identities are formed through the establishment of this difference.

12. I thank Don Pollock for helping me formulate this idea of Q'eqchi' morality as action-in-place.

13. The realization that communities are not coherent entities is not a novel idea (Mintz 1998:124). Even so, many scholars now question the applicability of the traditional anthropological terms of "community" and "culture." Like Mintz, I maintain that we need not hastily disregard these concepts as long as we acknowl-

edge the global political economies from which communities and cultures emerge. Even in this world where communities are split across nations, cultural practices and ideas of self and community are effectively shared. What we ought to focus on is how culture is communicated in such fragmented and localized spaces. In many ways, this is exactly what I am attempting to do in this book—to analyze how shared ideology is effectively transmitted, reproduced, and reformulated.

14. See Harvey (1989:218–222) for more on imagined landscapes and spaces of representation.

CHAPTER 5

1. Most of these individuals are *Criollos,* Guatemalan elite who have pale skin and are ethnically, culturally, and economically connected to Europe. Criollos are outsiders to the Q'eqchi' community in Livingston.

2. As an active process, this type of consumption is quite distinct from the more passive early twenty-first-century consumption of products, media, signs, and symbols.

3. The term *Q'eq* can be either singular or plural, used to refer to a character ("It is Q'eq flying by when the wind whistles . . .") or to a type of creature ("Q'eq are owned by and submissive to the German finqueros . . ."). Unlike the dual-gendered Tzuultaq, Q'eq is always masculine ("half-man, half-animal").

4. Q'eqchi' perceive the Garifuna people of Livingston as hyper-sexualized beings, and use the Q'eq myth to comprehend and explain their black neighbors' behavior (see Chapter 9).

5. It is not clear exactly what mode of transportation is used by the Q'eq. While some people say that Q'eq flies like an airplane, others say he runs as fast as an automobile.

6. A *rancho* is the typical thatched-roof hut with mud flooring used by most Mayan people in Guatemala.

7. Yucatec Maya of Chan Kom have stories of a similar mythological creature, which they call *Uay kot.* This half-human, half-animal being is an evil force who flies around at night and enters people's home to poison their food, thus causing illness and even death to non-Christian souls. In Chan Kom, Uay kot is always associated with store owners and businessmen (Re Cruz 1996:69).

8. *Susto,* an illness of fright that attacks the senses, is associated with foreign difference (see Chapter 7).

9. Maximon, the religious icon revered by many Guatemalan highland Mayan people, is also a hyper-sexualized being. Likewise, his foreignness is evident by his Ladino appearance.

10. Although I heard that both God and Tzuultaq'a are the recipients of prayer and reverence during uk'iha, most people tell me it is God who is the recipient of their prayer.

11. Because there is no permanent market in Livingston, opportunities for growing cash crops are significantly reduced.

12. Interestingly, seventy quetzals in 1996 and one hundred quetzals in 2005 both equaled approximately twelve U.S. dollars.

13. The fact that many Q'eqchi' men consider milpa agriculture as risky challenges traditional economic theories. Classic economic theories tend to explain risk-aversion as the reason for horticulturists maintaining their subsistence methods rather than switching to cash crops. In the case of the Q'eqchi', milpa agriculture is seen as more risky than involving oneself in the local economy through wage labor or running a small business.

CHAPTER 6

1. Evangélicos would never support the Deer Dance because they consider it the work of the devil.

2. This is the same pipeline that was blown up by guerillas sometime in the early 1990s (Sieber 1999:35). I did not hear about this from locals in Livingston.

3. Other dances with pre-Columbian origins include El Palo Volador, La Culebra, El Rabinal Achí, and La Paach (García Escobar 1989:6–15; Mace 1970:9–13).

4. While many researchers have tended to call these figures conquistadors, the Q'eqchi' people referred to them as *reyes*. One Ladino woman, I recall, described the dancers as *moros* (sp. Moors), yet another local description of these obviously foreign figures.

5. See Comaroff and Comaroff (1992:18–31) for more on historical, enduring structures.

6. Jaguars may even represent a pre-Columbian "totemic military order" (Bricker 1981:143).

7. In ancient times, deer were sacrificed to Tohil, the K'iche rain god (Mace 1970:56), in a manner similar to how contemporary Q'eqchi' people were sacrificed to Tzuultaq'a for the sake of foreign commerce in El Estor.

8. While most Q'eqchi' people tell me they do not know why the dance is named Katarina (Catherine in English), I understand the title to be derived from the Catherine Wheel, a type of pinwheel lined with firecrackers that represents the instrument used to torture Saint Catherine. Because the finale of the dance involves firecrackers being lit on the back of the Devil Bull, I firmly believe the origin of the name, although not the dance, is with Saint Catherine, martyr of Alexandria. Clearly, this dance is of Hispanic origin (García Escobar 1989:17–18).

9. As Victoria Bricker (1981:129–150) points out in her study of Zinacantan, Chiapas, a performer can symbolize multiple historical figures.

10. Q'eq, who supports foreigners by harassing cattle and locals alike, finds his way into many Mayan dances and performances (Bricker 1981:130–138; García Escobar 1989:18).

11. Stoll (1988) points out that this rhetoric was used not only by Catholic Action, but by the World Church, a Protestant missionary church, to distinguish between opposing qualities of good and evil. In the 1970s, the World Church dramatically and forcefully entered Guatemala with the assistance of then President Ríos Montt as their most famous, vocal, and effective convert.

12. Perhaps colonists and missionaries sensed the power of this invisible community and considered it an attack on their authority. Subsequently, they labeled any custom that paid reverence to something less tangible than God as paganism or as devil's work.

13. The fact that they have more than one identity is vital and I discuss this again in Chapter 8 when I conclude the section on Q'eqchi' identity.

14. Although the Q'eqchi' community in Livingston is far from a "traditional society," Wolf's (1957) "closed corporate community" is still a useful analogy to understand how external networks play a role in the maintenance of corporate-orientated societies.

15. See Chapter 10 for more on indigenous video projects.

CHAPTER 7

1. Although in Livingston I heard only that ancestors were with God. In contrast, Carlson and Eachus write that upon death, ancestors enter the residence of Tzuultaq'a (1977:48–49).

2. Multi-faceted souls have been discussed as occurring among other Mayan groups such as the K'iche of Momostenango (Cook 1986:146–151), the Tzotzil of Chamula (Gossen 1974:210–211), and the Mam-speakers of Santiago Chimaltengo (Watanabe 1992:85–87).

3. Surprisingly, and happily, I knew of no Q'eqchi' person who died while I was in Livingston (both Martín and Mariano died later while I was in the United States). I attended numerous Garifuna and Ladino funerals but not a Q'eqchi' one. All the information in this section was obtained through interviews with various people. Martín and Matilde were extremely patient in helping me understand Q'eqchi' practices that surround death. Because much of my description comes from their assistance, this image of death is predominantly Catholic.

4. Clearly, ancestors require the items of clothing and other material objects that are placed in their grave, although reasons offered as to why relatives must place personal belongings in the coffin vary. Many say that it is to respect and please the dead person so that they do not become restless and come back to earth to bother the living. Others explain that they do this so ancestors have something to wear in heaven (sp. *cielo*), although many people laugh at this because they say that spirits do not wear clothes. Equally, people claim that these objects are offerings to God so that he grants permission for the deceased to enter his realm in the sky. If the latter is true, it is the most precious and personal items that

are given to God, thus indicating the highest amount of respect to the supreme owner.

5. After Spain entered the New World, a more legal and word-oriented concept of ownership was most likely imposed as Q'eqchi' people were removed from their "unowned" land.

6. Karl Marx describes ownership in pre-capitalist economic systems as the relationship between worker and the "objective conditions of his labour" (1964 [1857–8]:67). He envisions pre-capitalist economics and collective property as first emerging from being a member of a tribe or community. Ownership, therefore, was initially organized communally, before becoming the exclusive mode of capitalism (Marx 1964 [1857–8]:90–91).

7. Día del Guadalupe is an exception to this. See Chapter 8.

8. This discussion centers on Catholic conceptions of death and ownership. While many Evangélicos feel exactly the same way, they tend to de-emphasize the practice of burning clothes and hammocks. Lola told me that she does not believe in this practice, that she would not waste clothing like that. Meanwhile, her eldest son whispers in my ear that clothes do come back to haunt people. Javiér says that when his mother died, they placed her clothes in a cardboard box where they remain today. He says women in his family cannot wear his mother's corte but after one year, others are allowed. In these cases, Evangélicos differ from Catholics but they both recognize that ownership is not simply transferred at death.

9. Even the Q'eqchi' word for silence, *ch'anam,* stems from the word *chanabaank,* which means "to stop doing."

10. See Lowenthal (1985) for more on spatialized history.

11. I thank Dennis Tedlock for clarifying this non-grammatical concept.

12. Because elderly people are the closest living individuals who represent the historical phase, they too are respected and revered for their knowledge of myths, costumbres, and ritual.

13. These developmental phases of Mayan chronology may correlate with the two past grammatical tenses and the third formless realm.

14. In Crique Chino Barrio Nuevo, a woman placed salt upon the altar during Todos Santos for the ancestors who mediate between historical spaces.

15. To cure an infant's ojo, a curer (often the midwife who delivered the baby) must pass an egg over the entire body of the child thus making the sign of the cross. Babies are often bathed in a bath of rue. Rubbing the egg equally over the body returns the equilibrium to the baby's body. The egg may be left on the belly of the baby for some time and then cracked open to see if a foamy liquid emerges. If so, it signifies that the ojo has been properly removed.

16. Time is defined through exchanges, as it has no meaning in and of itself; it only gains significance by relating to something else. Figures who control time, therefore, also symbolically control relationships.

17. León-Portilla discusses time as a powerful attribute of pre-Columbian Mayan deities (1988:35–55).

18. By representing culture and people, cameras automatically lend authorship and authority to the individual who turns the video camera on or presses the shutter. But the videographer is not alone in the production of imagery. Filmed subjects define and direct; they influence the final product as much as do the camera and the individual behind it. A tripartite relationship exists between the subject matter (whether person, performance, or thing), the camera (method), and the individual author of the image. This complex relationship is then read/looked at by the reader/viewer who becomes an additional fourth subject in the complex process of cultural representation (Eco 1982:32–33). Because the viewer, too, comes to images with preconceived ideas and personal histories and biases, the viewer does more than passively consume.

CHAPTER 8

1. Día de Guadalupe, 12 December, is a festive and sacred day in Guatemala, Mexico, and much of Latin America. Throughout the Americas, different groups of people attach various meaning to the image of Guadalupe (Castillo 1996, Poole 1995, Wright 1995, Wolf 1958). She symbolizes ethnic blending, feminism, indigenous rights, freedom, and nationalism to indigenous, Criollos, Ladinos, Mestizos, and Chicanas. In Guatemala, as in Mexico, this day also emphasizes the *mestizaje* (blending of Ladino and indigenous cultures) in the national culture where Criollos and Ladinos celebrate Día de Guadalupe by dressing their children in huipil and corte and going to Mass. As with most national traditions, Livingston has its own way of venerating Guadalupe.

2. To my knowledge, there is no connection between the Pororo dance and the Poro secret dance societies in West Africa.

3. See Castillo (1996), Poole (1995), and Wolf (1958) for English texts on the Virgin of Guadalupe. Poole questions whether Juan de Zumárraga was ever involved in the construction of the chapel.

4. See Bricker (1981), Friedlander (1975), Gossen (1993), Hawkins (1984), Martinez Peláez (1994 [1971]), and Warren (1989), for examples of how foreigners, particularly Ladinos, have shaped an indigenous identity.

5. Yet, like the feeding of Tzuultaq'a, Q'eqchi' women control the consumption by commodifying and renting their own traje.

6. For further discussion of the differences and similarities between the cultural organizations of the Mayan and Garifuna people, see Chapter 9.

7. Indeed, this belief was recently strengthened by Catholic Action's stress on the separation of spiritual soul from physical blood (Annis 1987; Warren 1989).

8. See Fanon (1952), Hawkins (1984), Linker (1983), and Silverman (1992) for identity as a psychological process of opposition within unequal power relations.

9. For examples of binary thinking in the conceptualization of Mayan identities see Bricker (1981), Brintall (1979), Friedlander (1975), Gossen (1999:1–30),

Hawkins (1984), Re Cruz (1996), Stavenhagen (1977), Warren (1989), and Watanabe (1992).

10. Hale 1996; Hernández Castillo 2001; Hervik 1999; Leyva Solano and Ascencio Franco 1996; Montejo 2002; Nash 2001; Nelson 1999; Smith 1995; Thompson 2001; Wasserstrom 1983; among others—the critical research of Demetrio Cotjí Cuxil, Jan Rus, and Richard Wilk comes to mind.

CHAPTER 9

1. I refer the reader to the work of Diane Nelson for more on the political symbolism of this violence acted upon a gringa body (Nelson 1999:41–73).

2. As David Stoll reminds me, this is still no excuse for the decisions made by the Pokomchí Mayans involved in this attack, who continued to beat June Weinstock even after the missing child reappeared without harm.

3. See Nelson (1999) for more on the porous boundary between the state and individual in Guatemala.

CHAPTER 10

1. Because of the personal nature of this vignette, I have changed the names of the individuals involved.

2. Travel writer John Lloyd Stephens (1856) details how he unknowingly became the godparent to a Carib child in Punta Gorda, British Honduras in 1839. George Collier (1975:147) discusses how Indians of Chiapas formed ties of ritual kinship to their ranch owners or foremen, who would sponsor children's baptisms. George Foster (1953:5–10) reports that the indigenous people of Middle America commonly choose a Ladino or Mestizo (of mixed descent) godparent as a means of forging social ties to fulfill social and economic needs of the young child and family.

3. *Compadrazgo,* the practice of naming compadres, has been extensively addressed by scholars of Mesoamerica (Collier 1975; Foster 1953; Mintz and Wolf 1950; Nash 1958; Paul 1942; Ravicz 1967; Redfield and Villa Rojas 1962 [1934]). Most often, the term designates "the particular complex of relationships set up between individuals primarily, though not always, through participation in the ritual of Catholic baptism" (Mintz and Wolf 1950:341). Weddings, family rituals, funerals, and moral and social council are other responsibilities of the compadre.

4. Compadrazgo and culturally scripted morality are also similar in that they are ultimately connected to economics and the land. Mintz and Wolf (1950:343–352) trace compadrazgo back to changes in medieval European relationships between serfs and feudal lords. Because it was a means of gaining control of land,

parents used compadres as a means of reorganizing the vertical relationships between the socioeconomic classes. Compadrazgo was an adaptive mechanism.

5. This style of image production, with its emphasis on non-visual components of culture, parallels the contemporary anthropological interest in things that
cannot be seen (MacDougall 1998:121). Although, due to the camera's visible technical priorities, the representation of unseen culture through filmic vision can be
problematic (Ruby 2000:51).

6. For more on filmic collaboration and visual methods, see Asch (1992), Barbash and Taylor (1997), Burns (1993), Elder (1995), Ginsburg (1995), MacDougall
(1994), Pink (2001), and Stoller (1992).

7. For discussions on indigenous video projects see Burns (1993), Chalfen
(1992), Ewald (1993), Ginsburg (1995), Turner (1991), and Worth and Adair (1972).

CHAPTER 11

1. Intimate ethnography also demonstrates that these structural relations of
sight and authority do not strictly involve one subject feeding off the production of
another. Producers, too, control consumption. The Q'eqchi' people of Livingston
do just this. Through practice and reinforcement of a shared ideological substrate,
they control the feeding of authorities and they govern the feeding of themselves.

GLOSSARY

Aquardiente   (sp) firewater

Ahijidos   (sp.) godchildren

Aj eechal   (q.) owner

Aj ilonel   (q.) curer, shaman; translates literally as "one who sees"

Aj pop   (q.) indigenous leader; translates literally as "one of the mat"

Aj waclisiinel   (q.) the sower

Aj wacsiinel   (q.) one who stirs up, rouses, or lifts

Aldea   (sp.) outlying village

Alemanes   (sp.) Germans

Asustar   (sp.) to frighten, to cause *susto*

Atole   (sp.) sweet, thick drink usually made from corn, served hot; the Garifuna
make atole from ripe bananas

Awas   (q.) a variety of illnesses acquired by a child in utero, occurs when the
mother breaks a social rule; translates literally as "bad luck," "sorcery," or
"taboo"

Baile de Katarina   (sp.) traditional dance in which the dancers carry a ring of
lighted firecrackers; believed to originate from the Catherine Wheel—a
pinwheel lined with firecrackers that represents the instrument used to
torture St. Catherine of Alexandria

Barrios   (sp.) neighborhoods

Batab   (Yucatec) Postclassic indigenous leader; translates literally as "yielder of
the axe"

Boleto de solvencia   (sp.) solvency ticket carried during the late nineteenth and
early twentieth century to prove that an individual was free of debt

Boleto de trabajo   (sp.) working papers

Cabecera   (sp.) head town of the *municipio*, where government offices are
located

Caciques   (sp.) indigenous leaders

Campesino   (sp.) peasant

Cayucos   (sp.) canoes, usually made by hand from tropical hard woods

Chac   (Yucatec) Classic Mayan gods of rain

Ch'olwiinq   (q.) mythico-historical beings who reside deep in the jungle; translates literally as "wild men" or "men of heart"

Ch'ona   (q.) term of respect used in reference to female *Tzuultaq'a,* female patrons, and other female figures of authority

Chugu   (gar.) Garifuna ritual of ancestor worship

Cofradía   (sp.) religious brotherhood

Comal   (sp.) griddle placed over hearth where tortillas are cooked

Compadrazgo   (sp.) practice of defining social networks by naming godparents

Corte   (sp.) traditional Mayan woven skirt

Costumbre   (sp.) custom, often juxtaposed with *tradición*

Difuntos   (sp.) ancestors, the deceased

Dueño, Dueña   (sp.) owner (male and female)

Encomienda   (sp.) colonial award that gave an individual (the *encomendero*) the right to receive tribute in services and goods from a certain number of indigenous people

Evangelicos, Evangelicas   (sp.) Protestants (male and female)

Ferropazco   local name for German export company Empresa Ferrocarril Verapaz S.A.

Finca   (sp.) plantation

Finqueros   (sp.) finca owners, patrons

Frutera, La   (sp.) local name for the United Fruit Company

Habilitaciones   (sp.) cash advances

Hindoos   local name for people of East Asian descent

Huipil   (sp.) traditional Mayan female blouse

Ilabil   (q.) the evil eye; same as *ojo*

Ilob'aal   (q.) quartz crystals used by shamans for divining and providing insight; translates literally as "view" or "something that provides vision"

Inna' Inyuwa'   (q.) my mother, my father

Ixim   (q.) corn

K'ajb'ak   (q.) a sowing ritual; to pray, perform ritual

Kux   (q.) young sweet corn

Ladino, Ladina   (sp.) ethnic and social term (male and female) that designates mixed indigenous and European ancestry, specific to Guatemala

Ladrón   (sp.) criminal

Lancheros   (sp.) motorboat conductors

Loma, La   (sp.) the hill, a neighborhood in Livingston

Loq'inkil   (q.) to respect one's community and kin; also to buy, to revere, or to be saintly

Mandamiento   (sp.) government policy that forced indigenous people to work on plantations and public works to ensure the provision of the necessary work force

Manzana   (sp.) 1.7 acres

Mayahaac   (q.) Q'eqchi' ritual paying respect and goods to *Tzuultaq'a,* often practiced to ensure a good harvest

Milpa   (sp.) cornfield

Monte   (sp.) the bush, jungle

Moreno   (sp.) term used in Livingston to refer to the Garifuna; translates literally as "brown"

Mozo   (sp.) worker, serf

Mu   (q.) shadow, spirit, soul

Muelle   (sp.) pier

Mundial   (sp.) worldly, pagan

Municipio   (sp.) region governed by local government

Ojo   (sp.) eye; refers to the disease known as the evil eye; same as *ilabil*

Paab'ankil   (q.) to respect a foreign owner, outsider

Paisanos   (sp.) country people, often used to refer to indigenous Q'eqchi' people, thought by some to be derogative

Paseando   (sp.) walking, hanging out

Pedida   (sp.) ritual of asking permission to marry; translates literally as "request"; same as *tz'aamank*

Pila   (sp.) community wash area and water source

Poch   (q.) small corn tamale

Pom   (q.) copal incense

Poot   (q.) traditional Q'eqchi' embroidered blouse worn by women

Primaria   (sp.) elementary school

Puros   (sp.) cigars

Q'eq   (q.) mythico-historical deviant half-man/half-animal who is owned by the foreign *finqueros;* translates literally as "black one"

Quetzal   the Guatemalan currency

Rancho   (sp.) thatched-roof home with mud floor

Reducciones   (sp.) sixteenth-century villages to which the Spanish relocated indigenous people

Sangre fuerte   (sp.) strong blood; a condition associated with foreigners and social deviants

Sembrar   (sp.) to sow

Sones   (q.) traditional Q'eqchi' songs

Sumlaac   (q.) wedding

Susto   (q.) fright; illness involving soul loss

Testiig   (q.) witness

Todos Santos   (sp.) All Saints' Day, 1 November

Tohil   K'iche rain god

Tradición   (sp.) tradition, often juxtaposed with *costumbre*

Traje   (sp.) refers to traditional Mayan attire, as opposed to *vestido*

Tz'aamank   (q.) ritual of asking permission to marry; translates literally as "request"; same as *pedida*

Tzuultaq'a   (q.) Q'eqchi' mountain spirit; translates literally as
    "mountain-valley"
UFC   United Fruit Company
Uk'   (q.) traditional Q'eqchi' woven skirt
Uk'iha   (q.) a wedding ritual; translates literally as "drinking of the water"
Vestido   (sp.) refers to typical Ladino attire, western clothing, as opposed to
    traje
Wa   (q.) tortilla
Waacax Diab'   (q.) Devil Bull Dance
Xeel   (q.) leftovers
Yo' yo   (q.) alive

BIBLIOGRAPHY

Abrahams, Roger D. 1983. *The Man-of-Words in the West Indies: Performance and the Emergence of Creole Culture.* Baltimore and London: Johns Hopkins University Press.

Abrahams, Roger D. and Richard Bauman. 1978. "Ranges of Festival Behavior." In *The Reversible World: Symbolic Inversion in Art and Society,* Barbara Babcock, ed., 193–208. Ithaca and London: Cornell University Press.

Adams, Richard N. 1965. *Migraciones Internas En Guatemala: Expansión Agraria de los Indígenas Kekchíes hacia El Petén.* Guatemala: Jose de Pineda Ibarra.

Adams, Richard. 1990. "Ethnic Images and Strategies." In *Guatemalan Indians and the State: 1540–1988,* Carol A. Smith, ed., 141–162. Austin: University of Texas Press.

Agar, Michael. 1996. *The Professional Stranger.* New York: Academic Press.

Altman, Patricia B. and Caroline West. 1992. *Threads of Identity: Maya Costume of the 1960s in Highland Guatemala.* Los Angeles: Fowler Museum of Cultural History.

Anderson, Benedict. 1983. *Imagined Communities: Reflections on the Origin and Spread of Nationalism.* Revised Edition. London and New York: Verso.

Anderson, E. N., T. A. Wong, and Lynn Thomas. 1997. *Good and Bad Person: The Construction of Ethical Discourse in a Chinese Fishing Community.* Unpublished manuscript.

Andrews, Anthony P. 1983. *Maya Salt Production and Trade.* Tucson: University of Arizona Press.

Annis, Sheldon. 1987. *God and Production in a Guatemalan Town.* Austin: University of Texas Press.

Arrivillaga Cortés, Alfonso. 1989. "Expresiones Culturales Garífuna de Guatemala." *La Tradición Popular* 75:1–12.

Asch, Tim. 1992. "The Ethics of Ethnographic Film-making." In *Film as Ethnography,* Peter Ian Crawford and David Turton, eds., 196–204. Manchester: Manchester University Press.

Bakewell, Liza. 1998. "Image Acts." *American Anthropologist* 100(1):22–32.

Barbash, Ilisa and Lucien Taylor. 1997. *Cross-Cultural Filmmaking: A Handbook for Making Documentary and Ethnographic Films and Videos.* Berkeley: University of California Press.

Barnouw, Erik. 1993. *Documentary: A History of the Non-fiction Film.* New York and Oxford: Oxford University Press.

Barry, Andrew. 1995. "Reporting and Visualising." In *Visual Culture,* Chris Jenks, ed. London and New York: Routledge.

Barthes, Roland. 1981. *Camera Lucida: Reflections on Photography,* Richard Howard, trans. New York: Hill and Wang.

Bassie-Sweet, Karen. 1991. *From the Mouth of the Dark Cave: Commemorative Sculpture of the Late Classic Maya.* Norman: University of Oklahoma Press.

Bastos, Santiago and Maneula Camus. 1995. *Los Mayas de la Capital: un estudio sobre identitdad étnica y mundo urbano.* Guatemala: FLACSO.

Battaglia, Debbora. 1995. "Problematizing the Self: A Thematic Introduction." In *Rhetorics of Self-making,* Debbora Battaglia, ed., 1–15. Berkeley: University of California Press.

Behar, Ruth. 1989. "Sexual Witchcraft, Colonialism, and Women's Power: Views From the Mexican Inquisition." In *Sexuality and Marriage in Colonial Latin America,* A. Laurin, ed., 178–206. Lincoln: University of Nebraska Press.

————. 1996. *The Vulnerable Observer: Anthropology That Breaks Your Heart.* Boston: Beacon Press.

Benedict, Ruth. 1989 [1946]. *The Chrysanthemum and the Sword: Patterns of Japanese Culture.* Boston: Houghton Mifflin Company.

Benz, Stephen Connely. 1996. *Guatemalan Journey.* Austin: University of Texas Press.

Bernard, Russell. 1994. "Methods Belong to All of Us." In *Assessing Cultural Anthropology,* Robert Borofsky, ed., 168–179. New York: McGraw Hill.

Bhabha, Homi. 1984. "Of Mimicry and Man: The Ambivalence of Colonial Discourse." *October* 28:125–133.

Bourdieu, Pierre. 1977. *Outline of a Theory of Practice.* Richard Nice, trans. Cambridge: Cambridge University Press.

————. 1990. *The Logic of Practice.* Stanford: Stanford University Press.

Bourdieu, Pierre and Loïc J. D. Wacquant. 1992. *An Invitation to Reflexive Sociology.* Chicago: University of Chicago Press.

Brandt, Richard B. 1954. *Hopi Ethics: A Theoretical Analysis.* Chicago: University of Chicago Press.

Bricker, Victoria. 1981. *The Indian Christ, The Indian King: The Historical Substrate of Maya Myth and Ritual.* Austin: University of Texas Press.

Brigham, William T. 1887. *Guatemala: The Land of the Quetzal.* New York: Charles Scribner's Sons.

Brintall, Douglas E. 1979. *Revolt Against the Dead: The Modernization of a Mayan Community in the Highlands of Guatemala.* New York: Gordon and Breach.

Brockett, Charles D. 1992. "Transformación agraria y conflicto político en Guatemala, 1944–1986." In *500 Anos de Lucha Por La Tierra: Estudios Sobre Propiedad Rural y Reforma Agraria en Guatemala,* Vol. 2, J. C. Cambranes, ed., 1–38. Guatemala: FLACSO.

Brown, Michael F. 1996. "On Resisting Resistance." *American Anthropologist* 98(4):729–735.

Bunzel, Ruth. 1952. *Chichicastenango: A Guatemalan Village.* New York: J. J. Augustin.

Butler, Mary. 1940. "A Pottery Sequence from the Alta Verapaz, Guatemala." In *The Maya and Their Neighbors,* C. L. Hay, et al., eds., 250–267. New York: D. Appleton-Century Company.

Burns, Allan. 1993. "Everybody's a Critic: Video Programming with Guatemalan Maya Refugees in the United States." In *Anthropological Film and Video in the 1990's,* Jack R. Rollwagen, ed., 105–129. Brockport: Institute Press.

Cabarrús, Carlos Rafael. 1979. *La Cosmovision K'ekchi' en Proceso de Cambio.* San Salvador: Universidad Centroamericana.

Cahuec del Valle, Eleuterio and Julia Becker Richards. 1994. "La Variación Sociolinguística del Idioma Maya Q'eqchi'." *Boletín de Lingüística* 43–44:1–13.

Cambranes, J. C. 1985. *Coffee and Peasants: The Origins of the Modern Plantation Economy in Guatemala, 1853–1897.* Woodstock, Vt.: CIRMA, Plumsock Mesoamerican Studies.

Campos, Sara and John Marshall. 1997. "New Law Threatens Guatemalans in the U.S." *Report on Guatemala* 18(2):6–7,11–13.

Cancian, Frank. 1965. *Economics and Prestige in a Maya Community: The Religious Cargo System in Zinacantán.* Stanford: Stanford University Press.

Carlson, Ruth and Francis Eachus. 1977. "El Mundo Espiritual de los Kekchíes." *Guatemala Indigena* 3:39–72.

Carey, David, Jr. 2001. *Our Elders Teach Us.* Tuscaloosa: University of Alabama Press.

Carmack, Robert M., ed. 1988. *The Harvest of Violence.* Norman: University of Oklahoma Press.

Carter, William. 1969. *New Lands and Old Traditions: Kekchi Cultivators in the Guatemalan Lowlands.* Gainesville: University of Florida Press.

Castañeda, Quetzil E. 1996. *In The Museum of Maya Culture: Touring Chichén Itzá.* Minneapolis: University of Minnesota Press.

Castillo, Ana. 1996. *Goddess of the Americas: La Diosa de las Américas.* New York: Riverhead Books.

Chalfen, Richard. 1992. "Picturing Culture Through Indigenous Imagery: A Telling Story." In *Film as Ethnography,* Peter Ian Crawford and David Turton, eds., 222–241. Manchester: Manchester University Press.

Chang Sagastume, German Rolando. 1995. *Guía de Historia y Geografía del Departamento de Izabal.* Guatemala City.

Chow, Rey. 1994. "Where Have All the Natives Gone?" In *Displacements: Cultural Identities in Question,* 125–151. Bloomington: Indiana University Press.

Christman, John. 1994. *The Myth of Property: Toward an Egalitarian Theory of Ownership.* New York and Oxford: Oxford University Press.

Clifford, James. 1997. *Routes: Travel and Translation in the Late Twentieth Century.* Cambridge and London: Harvard University Press.

Clifford, James and George E. Marcus. 1986. *Writing Culture: The Poetics and Politics of Ethnography.* Berkeley: University of California Press.

Collier, George A. 1975. *Fields of the Tzotzil: The Ecological Bases of Tradition in Highland Chiapas.* Austin and London: University of Texas Press.

Collier, John, Jr. 1995 [1975]. "Photography and Visual Anthropology." In *Principles of Visual Anthropology,* Paul Hockings, ed., 235–254. Berlin and New York: Mouton de Gruyter.

Collier, John, Jr. and Malcolm Collier. 1986. *Visual Anthropology: Photography as a Research Method.* Albuquerque: University of New Mexico Press.

Comaroff, Jean. 1985. *Body of Power, Spirit of Resistance.* Chicago and London: University of Chicago Press.

Comaroff, Jean and John Comaroff. 1992. *Ethnography and the Historical Imagination.* Boulder: Westview Press.

Comaroff, John. 1996. "Ethnicity, Nationalism, and the Politics of Difference in the Age of Revolution." In *The Politics of Difference: Ethnic Premises in a World of Power,* Edwin N. Wilmsen and Patrick McAllister, eds., 162–183. Chicago: University of Chicago Press.

Cook, Garrett. 1986. "Quichean Folk Theology and Southern Maya Supernaturalism." In *Symbol and Meaning Beyond the Closed Community: Essays in Mesoamerican Ideas,* Gary Gossen, ed., 139–153. Albany: Institute for Mesoamerican Studies.

Corbey, R. 1988. "Alterity: The Colonial Nude, Photographic Essay." *Critique of Anthropology* 8(3):75–92.

de Certeau, Michel. 1984. *The Practice of Everyday Life,* Steven F. Randall, trans. Berkeley: University of California Press.

DeChicchis, Joseph. 1986. *The Kekchi and Their Language in Guatemala and Belize.* Unpublished field report.

Dessaint, Alain Y. 1983. "Land and Labor after Independence." In *Guatemala in Rebellion: Unfinished History,* Jonathan L. Fried, et al., eds., 25–28. New York: Grove Press, Inc.

De Vos, George A. and Lola Romanucci-Ross, eds. 1995. "Ethnic Identity: A Psychocultural Perspective." In *Ethnic Identity: Creation, Conflict, and Accommodation,* 349–379. Third Edition. Walnut Creek: Altamira Press.

Dosal, Paul J. 1993. *Doing Business with the Dictators: A Political History of United Fruit in Guatemala, 1899–1944.* Wilmington, Delaware: Scholarly Resources, Inc.

Douglas, Mary. 1966. *Purity and Danger: An Analysis of Concepts of Pollution and Taboo.* London: Routledge and Kegan Paul.

———. 1982 [1970]. *Natural Symbols: Explorations in Cosmology.* New York: Pantheon Books.

Drummond, Sandra Lewis. 1987. *Analisis Historico Urbano de Livingston y Propuesta para La Valorizacion del "Viejo Puerto."* Tesis de Arquitectura: Universidad Rafael Landivar.

Durkheim, Emile. 1976 [1915]. *The Elementary Forms of the Religious Life,* Joseph Ward Swain, trans. London: George Allen & Unwin.

Eco, Umberto. 1982. "Critique of the Image." In *Thinking Photography,* Victor Burgin, ed., 32–38. London: Macmillan.

Elder, Sarah. 1995. "Collaborative Filmmaking: An Open Space for Making Meaning." *Visual Anthropology Review* 11(2):94–101.

Escobar, Alonso de. 1841. "Account of the Province of Vera Paz, in Guatemala, and of the Indian Settlements or Pueblos established therein." *Journal of the Royal Geographic Society* 11:89–97.

Escobar, Arturo. 1997. "Cultural Politics and Biological Diversity: State, Capital, and Social Movements in the Pacific Coast of Colombia." In *The Politics of Culture in the Shadow of Capital,* Lisa Lowe and David Lloyd, eds., 201–226. Durham and London: Duke University Press.

Estrada Monroy, Agustin. 1979. *El Mundo K'ekchi' de la Vera-Paz.* Guatemala: Ministerio de la Defensa Nacional y el Museo de Cobán.

———, Agustin. 1990. *Vida Esotérica Maya-K'ekchi.* Guatemala: Ministerio de Cultura y Deportes.

Ewald, Wendy. 1993. *Retratos y Suenos: Portraits and Dreams: Photographs by Mexican Children.* An exhibit at The George Eastman House, Rochester, New York, 12 June to 5 September, 1993.

Fabian, Johannes. 1983. *Time and the Other: How Anthropology Makes Its Object.* New York: Columbia University Press.

Fanon, Frantz. 1952. *Black Skin, White Masks.* London: Pluto Press.

Foster, George. 1953. "Cofradía and Compadrazgo in Spain and Spanish America." *Southwestern Journal of Anthropology* 9:1–28.

Foster, Robert. 1997. "Commercial Mass Media in Papua New Guinea: Notes on Agency, Bodies and Commodity Consumption." *Visual Anthropology Review* 12(2):1–17.

Foucault, Michel. 1977. *Discipline and Punish: The Birth of a Prison,* Alan Sheridan, trans. New York: Vintage Books.

———. 1980. "The Eye of Power." In *Power/Knowledge: Selected Interviews and Other Writing,* C. Gordon, ed., 146–165. New York: Pantheon.

Freidel, David, Linda Schele, and Joy Parker. 1993. *Maya Cosmos: Three Thousand Years on the Shaman's Path.* New York: William Morrow and Company.

Fried, Jonathan L., et al., eds. 1983. *Guatemala in Rebellion: Unfinished History.* New York: Grove Press, Inc.

Friedlander, Judith. 1975. *Being Indian in Hueyapan: A Study of Forced Identity in Contemporary Mexico.* New York: St. Martin's Press.

Galeano, Eduardo. 1967. *Guatemala: Occupied Country.* New York and London: Modern Reader Paperbacks.

García Escobar, Carlos René. 1989. "Panorama de las Danzas Tradicionales de Guatemala." *La Tradición Popular* 71:1–24.

Geertz, Clifford. 1973. *The Interpretation of Cultures: Selected Essays.* New York: Basic Books.

Ginsburg, Faye. 1995. "Production Values: Indigenous Media and the Rhetoric of

Self-determination." In *Rhetorics of Self-making,* Debbora Battaglia, ed., 121–138. Berkeley: University of California Press.

Goldin, Liliana R. and Brenda Rosenbaum. 1993. "Culture and History: Subregional Variation among the Maya." *Comparative Studies in Society and History* 35(1):110–132.

González, Nancie L. 1988. *Sojourners of the Caribbean: Ethnogenesis and Ethnohistory of the Garifuna.* Urbana: University of Illinois Press.

Gordon, Max. 1983. "A Case History of U.S. Subversion: Guatemala, 1954." In *Guatemala in Rebellion: Unfinished History,* J. L. Fried, et al., eds., 45–68. New York: Grove Press.

Gossen, Gary. 1974. *Chamulas in the World of the Sun: Time and Space in a Maya Oral Tradition.* Cambridge: Harvard University Press.

———. 1993. "The Other in Chamula Tzotzíl Cosmology and History: Reflections of a Kansan in Chiapas." *Cultural Anthropology* 8(4):443–475.

———. 1996. "Maya Zapatistas Move to the Ancient Future." *American Anthropologist* 98(3):528–538.

———. 1999. *Telling Maya Tales: Tzotzíl Identities in Modern Mexico.* New York and London: Routledge.

Goubaud Carrera, Antonio. 1949. *Notes on San Juan Chamelco, Alta Verapaz.* Microfilm Collection of Manuscripts on Middle American Cultural Anthropology. No. 23. University of Chicago Library. Chicago, Il.

Green, Linda. 1999. *Fear as a Way of Life: Mayan Widows in Rural Guatemala.* New York: Columbia University Press.

Grimshaw, Anna. 2001. *The Ethnographer's Eye: Ways of Seeing in Anthropology.* Cambridge: Cambridge University Press.

Gudeman, Stephen and Alberto Rivera. 1990. *Conversations in Columbia: The Domestic Economy in Work and Text.* Cambridge: Cambridge University Press.

Hale, Charles. 1996. "Introduction to Mestizaje." *Journal of Latin America Anthropology* (Special Issue) 2(1):2–3.

Hall, Stuart. 1989. "Ethnicity: Identity and Difference." *Radical America* 23(4):9–20.

Halperin, Rhoda H. 1994. *Cultural Economies: Past and Present.* Austin: University of Texas Press.

Hamilton, Nora and Norma Stoltz Chinchilla. 1991. "Central American Migration: A Framework for Analysis." *Latin American Research Review* 26(1):75–110.

Handy, Jim. 1990. "The Corporate Community, Campesino Organizations, and Agrarian Reform: 1950–1954." In *Guatemalan Indians and the State: 1540–1988,* Carol Smith, ed., 163–182. Austin: University of Texas Press.

Hannerz, Ulf. 1996. *Transnational Connections: Culture, People, Places.* London: Routledge.

Hartmann, Wolfram, Jeremy Silvester, and Patricia Hayes. 1999. *The Colonising Camera: Photographs in the Making of Namibian History.* Athens: Ohio University Press.

Harvey, David. 1989. *The Condition of Postmodernity: An Enquiry into the Origins of Cultural Change.* Oxford: Basil Blackwell.

Hawkins, John. 1984. *Inverse Images: The Meaning of Culture, Ethnicity and Family in Postcolonial Guatemala.* Albuquerque: University of New Mexico Press.

Hendrickson, Carol. 1995. *Weaving Identities: Construction of Dress and Self in a Highland Town.* Austin: University of Texas Press.

———. 1996. "Women, Weaving, and Education in Maya Revitalization." In *Maya Cultural Activism in Guatemala,* Edward F. Fisher and R. McKenna Brown, eds., 156–164. Austin: University of Texas Press.

Henley, Paul. 1998. "Film-making and Ethnographic Research." In *Image-based Research: A Sourcebook for Qualitative Researchers,* Jon Prosser, ed., 42–59. London: Falmer Press.

Hernández Castillo, Rosalva Aída. 2001. *Histories and Stories from Chiapas: Border Identities in Southern Mexico.* Austin: University of Texas Press.

Hernández Castillo, Rosalva Aída and Ronald Nigh. 1998. "Global Processes and Local Identity among Mayan Coffee Growers in Chiapas, Mexico." *American Anthropologist* 100(1):136–147.

Hervik, Peter. 1999. *Mayan People Within and Beyond Boundaries: Social Categories and Lived Identity in Yucatán.* Amsterdam: Harwood Academic Publishers.

Hervik, Peter and Hilary E. Kahn. 2006. "Scholarly Surrealism: The Persistence of Mayanness." *Critique of Anthropology* 26(2):209–232.

Holland, Dorothy, William Lachicotte Jr., Debra Skinner, and Carole Cain. 1998. *Identity and Agency in Cultural Worlds.* Cambridge and London: Harvard University Press.

hooks, bell. 1992. *Black Looks: Race and Representation.* Boston: South End Press.

Howard, Michael C. 1975. *Ethnicity in Southern Belize: The Kekchi and The Mopan,* University of Missouri Museum Briefs. No. 21. Columbia: University of Missouri.

Howell, Signe, ed. 1997. *The Ethnography of Moralities.* London and New York: Routledge.

Howes, David. 1991. "Sensorial Anthropology." In *The Varieties of Sensory of Experience: A Sourcebook in the Anthropology of the Senses,* David Howes, ed., 167–191. Toronto: University of Toronto Press.

Humphreys, S. C. 1981. "Death and Time." In *Mortality and Immortality: The Anthropology and Archaeology of Death,* S. C. Humphreys and Helen King, eds., 261–283. London: Academic Press.

International Organization for Migration. 2004. *National Survey on the Impact on Family Remittances on Guatemalan Households 2004.* Guatemala.

Ivic de Monterroso, Matilde. 1995. "Arqueología y Etnohistoria." *Identidad* 6:6–7, supplement to *Prensa Libre,* 17 June 1995.

Jackson, Bruce. 1987. *Fieldwork.* Urbana: University of Illinois Press.

Jackson, John L., Jr. 2004. "An Ethnographic *Filmflam:* Giving Gifts, Doing Research, and Videotaping the Native Subject/Object." *American Anthropologist* 106(1):32–42.

Jay, Martin. 1988. "Scopic Regimes of Modernity." In *Vision and Visuality*, Hal Foster, ed., 3–27. Seattle: Bay Press.

Jenkins, Carol L. 1998. "Ritual and Resource Flow: The Garifuna Dugu." In *Blackness in Latin America and the Caribbean*, Vol. 1, Norman E. Whitten Jr. and Arlene Torres, eds., 149–167. Bloomington: Indiana University Press.

Jonas, Susanne. 1997. "Guatemalan Peace Accords: An End and a Beginning." *NACLA: Report on the Americas* XXX(6):6–10.

Jones, Grant D. 1989. *Maya Resistance to Spanish Rule: Time and History on a Colonial Frontier*. Albuquerque: University of New Mexico Press.

Jones, Oakah L. 1994. *Guatemala in the Spanish Colonial Period*. Norman and London: University of Oklahoma Press.

Kane, Stephanie. 1998. *AIDS Alibis: Sex, Drugs, and Crime in the Americas*. Philadelphia: Temple University Press.

Kearney, Michael. 1996. *Reconceptualizing the Peasantry: Anthropology in Global Perspective*. Boulder: Westview Press.

Kelly, John D. and Martha Kaplan. 1990. "History, Structure, and Ritual." *Annual Review of Anthropology* 19:119–150.

Kerns, Virginia. 1998. "Structural Continuity in the Division of Men's and Women's Work among the Black Carib (Garífuna)." In *Blackness in Latin America and the Caribbean*, Vol. 1, Norman E. Whitten Jr. and Arlene Torres, eds., 133–148. Bloomington: Indiana University Press.

King, Arden R. 1974. *Coban and the Verapaz: History and the Cultural Process in Northern Guatemala*. New Orleans: Middle American Research Institute of Tulane University.

Kluckhohn, Clyde. 1948. *Personality in Nature, Society, and Culture*. New York: Alfred A. Knopf.

Kluckhohn, Florence and Fred L. Strodtbeck. 1961. *Variations in Value Orientations*. Evanston, Ill.: Row, Peterson and Company.

Kondo, Dorinne K. 1990. *Crafting Selves: Power, Gender, and Discourses of Identity in a Japanese Workplace*. Chicago and London: University of Chicago Press.

Kopytoff, Igor. 1988 [1986]. "The Cultural Biography of Things: Commoditization as Process." In *The Social Life of Things: Commodities in Cultural Perspective*, Arjun Appadurai, ed., 64–91. Cambridge: Cambridge University Press.

Lacan, Jacques. 1977. *Ecrits: A Selection*, Alan Sheridan, trans. New York: Norton.

Las Casas, Bartolomé de. 1992 [1552]. *In Defense of the Indians*. Stafford Poole, trans., De Kalb: Northern Illinois University Press.

Lash, Scott and John Urry. 1994. *Economies of Signs and Space*. London: Sage.

Laughlin, Robert M. 1969. "The Tzotzil." In *Handbook of Middle American Indians: Volume 7, Ethnology, Part I*, Robert Wauchope, ed., 154–194. Austin: University of Texas Press.

Lavie, Smadar and Ted Swedenburg. 1996. "Between and Among the Boundaries of Culture: Bridging Text and Lived Experience in the Third Timespace." *Cultural Studies* 10:154–179.

León-Portilla, Miguel. 1988. *Time and Reality in the Thought of the Maya.* Norman: University of Oklahoma Press.

Leyva Solano, Xochitl and Gabriel Ascencio Franco. 1996. *Lacandonia al Filo del Agua.* Hidalgo y Matamoros: Centro de Investigaciones y Estudios Superiores en Antropología Social.

Linker, Kate. 1983. "Representation and Sexuality." *Parachute* 32:12–23.

Lovell, George. 1985. *Conquest and Survival in Colonial Guatemala: A Historical Geography of the Cuchumatán Highlands: 1500–1821.* Montreal: McGill-Queen's University Press.

Lovell, George and Christopher H. Lutz. 1995. *Demography and Empire: A Guide to the Population History of Spanish Central America, 1500–1821.* Boulder: Westview Press.

Lowenthall, David. 1985. *The Past is a Foreign Country.* Cambridge: Cambridge University Press.

Lumb, Judy. 1989. "San Antonio Deer Dance." *Belize Currents* Winter 1989:10–13.

MacDougall, David. 1992. "Whose Story Is It?" In *Ethnographic Film Aesthetics and Narrative Traditions,* Peter I. Crawford and Jan K. Simonsen, eds., 25–42. Oslo: Intervention Press.

———. 1994. "Whose Story Is It?" In *Visualizing Theory: Selected Essays from V.A.R. 1990–1994.* Lucien Taylor, ed., 27–36. New York and London: Routledge.

———. 1998. *Transcultural Cinema.* Princeton: Princeton University Press.

Mace, Carroll Edward. 1970. *Two Spanish-Quiché Dance Dramas of Rabinal.* New Orleans: Tulane University.

Malkki, Lisa. 1992. "National Geographic: The Rooting of Peoples and the Territorialization of National Identity among Scholars and Refugees." *Cultural Anthropology* 7(1):24–45.

Manz, Beatriz. 1988. *Refugees of a Hidden War: The Aftermath of Counterinsurgency in Guatemala.* Albany: State University of New York Press.

———. 2004. *Paradise in Ashes: A Guatemalan Journey of Courage, Terror, and Hope.* Berkeley: University of California Press.

Marcus, George E. 1995. "Ethnography in/of the World System: The Emergence of Multi-sited Ethnography." *Annual Review of Anthropology* 24:95–117.

Marks, Laura. 2000. *The Skin of the Film: Intercultural Cinema, Embodiment, and the Senses.* Durham, N.C.: Duke University Press.

———. 2002. *Touch: Sensuous Theory and Multisensory Media.* Minneapolis: University of Minnesota Press.

Martinez Peláez, Severo. 1994 [1971]. *La Patria Del Criollo.* Mexico City: EEM.

Marx, Karl. 1964 [1857–8]. *Pre-capitalist Economic Formations,* Jack Cohen, trans., E. J. Hobsbawm, ed. London: Lawrence & Wishart.

Mauss, Marcel. 1954 [1950]. *The Gift: Forms and Functions of Exchange in Archaic Societies,* Ian Cunnison, trans. Glencoe, Ill.: Free Press.

McAnany, Patricia A. 1995. *Living with the Ancestors: Kinship and Kingship in Ancient Maya Society.* Austin: University of Texas Press.

McCreery, David. 1990. "State Power, Indigenous Communities, and Land in

Nineteenth-Century Guatemala, 1820–1920." In *Guatemalan Indians and the State: 1540–1988,* C. Smith, ed., 96–136. Austin: University of Texas Press.

———. 1993. "Hegemony and Repression in Rural Guatemala, 1871–1940." In *Plantation Workers: Resistance and Accommodation,* B. V. Lal, D. Munro, and E. D. Beechert, eds., 17–39. Honolulu: University of Hawaii Press.

———. 1995. "Wage Labor, Free Labor, and Vagrancy Laws: The Transition to Capitalism in Guatemala, 1920–1945." In *Coffee, Society, and Power in Latin America,* William Roseberry, Lowell Gudmundson, and Mario Samper, eds., 206–231. Baltimore: Johns Hopkins University Press.

Mead, Margaret. 1963. Anthropology and the Camera." In *The Encyclopedia of Photography,* Vol. 7, Willard D. Morgan, ed., 166–184. New York: Greystone Press.

Mejía, Marco Vinicio. 1997. *Memorial del Golfo Dulce: Ecología Política y enclaves en Guatemala.* Guatemala: La rial academia.

Merleau-Ponty, Maurice. 1968. *The Visible and the Invisible,* Alphonso Lingis, trans. Evanston, Illinois: Northwestern University Press.

———. 2002 [1945]. *Phenomenology of Perception,* Colin Smith, trans. London and New York: Routledge & Kegan Paul.

Minh-ha, Trinh T. 1991. *When the Moon Waxes Red: Representation, Gender, and Cultural Politics.* New York and London: Routledge.

Mintz, Sidney. 1998. "The Localization of Anthropological Practice: From Area Studies to Transnationalism." *Critique of Anthropology* 18(2):117–133.

Mintz, Sidney and Eric Wolf. 1950. "An Analysis of Ritual Co-parenthood (Compadrazgo)." *Southwestern Journal of Anthropology* 6:341–368.

Mitchell, Timothy. 1988. *Colonising Egypt.* Cambridge: Cambridge University Press.

Mitchell, W. J. T. 1994. *Picture Theory: Essays on Verbal and Visual Representation.* Chicago and London: University of Chicago Press.

Montejo, Victor. 2002. "The Multiplicity of Mayan Voices: Mayan Leadership and the Politics of Self-representation." In *Indigenous Movements, Self-representation, and the State in Latin America,* Kay B. Warren and Jean E. Jackson, eds. 123–148. Austin: University of Texas Press.

Morrison, Andrew R. and Rachel A. May. 1994. "Escape From Terror: Violence and Migration in Post-revolutionary Guatemala." *Latin American Research Review* 29:111–140.

Mulvey, Laura. 1989. *Visual and Other Pleasures.* Bloomington: Indiana University Press.

Náñez Falcón, Guillermo. 1970. *Erwin Paul Dieseldorff, German Entrepreneur in the Alta Verapaz of Guatemala, 1889–1937.* Ph.D. dissertation, Tulane University.

Naples, Nancy. 1996. "The Outsider Phenomenon." In *In the Field: Readings on the Field Research Experience,* Carolyn D. Smith and William Kornblum, eds., 139–149. Westport, Conn.: Praeger Press.

Narayan, Kirin. 1993. "How Native is a 'Native' Anthropologist?" *American Anthropologist* 95:671–686.

Nash, June. 1993. *We Eat the Mines and the Mines Eat Us: Dependency and Exploitation in Bolivian Tin Mines.* New York: Columbia University Press.

———. 2001. *Mayan Vision: The Quest for Autonomy in an Age of Globalization.* New York: Routledge Press.

Nash, Manning. 1958. *Machine Age Maya: The Industrialization of a Guatemalan Community.* Chicago and London: University of Chicago Press.

Nelson, Diane. 1991. "The Reconstruction of Mayan Identity." *Report on Guatemala.* 12(2):6–7, 14.

Nelson, Diane M. 1999. *A Finger in the Wound: Body Politics in Quincentennial Guatemala.* Berkeley: University of California Press.

Neruda, Pablo. 1970. *Pablo Neruda: Selected Poems.* Boston: Houghton Mifflin Company.

Ong, Aihwa. 1999. *Flexible Citizenship: The Cultural Logics of Transnationality.* Durham: Duke University Press.

Orellana, Sandra L. 1987. *Indian Medicine in Highland Guatemala: The Pre-Hispanic and Colonial Periods.* Albuquerque: University of New Mexico Press.

Ortner, Sherry B. 1989. *High Religion: A Cultural and Political History of Sherpa Buddhism.* Princeton: Princeton University Press.

———. 1995. "Resistance and the Problem of Ethnographic Refusal." *Comparative Studies in Society and History* 37(1):173–193.

Otzoy, Irma. 1996. "Maya Clothing and Identity." In *Maya Cultural Activism in Guatemala,* Edward F. Fischer and R. McKenna Brown, eds., 141–155. Austin: University of Texas Press.

Pacheco, P. Luis. 1988. *Tradiciones y Costumbres del Pueblo Maya Kekchi: Noviazgo, Matrimonio, Secretos, etc.* San José, Costa Rica: Editorial Ambar.

Parra Novo, José C. 1993. *Aproximacion Cultural a la comunidad Q'eqchi' de Santa Maria Cahabon: Reflexiones en Torno al Desafío la Inculturación.* Guatemala: Facultad de Teologia, Universidad Francisco Marroquin.

Paul, B. D. 1942. *Ritual Kinship: With Special Reference to Godparenthood in Middle America.* Ph.D. dissertation, University of Chicago.

Pedroni, Guillermo. 1991. *Territorialidad Kekchi: Una Aproximación al Acceso a la Tierra: La Migración y la Titulación.* Guatemala: FLACSO.

Pink, Sarah. 2001. *Doing Visual Ethnography: Images, Media and Representation in Research.* London: Sage Publications.

Pinney, Christopher. 1992. "The Parallel Histories of Anthropology and Photography." In *Anthropology and Photography: 1860–1920,* Elizabeth Edwards, ed., 74–95. New Haven and London: Yale University Press.

Poignant, Roslyn. 1992. "Surveying the Field of View: The Making of the RAI Photographic Collection." In *Anthropology and Photography: 1860–1920,* Elizabeth Edwards, ed., 42–73. New Haven and London: Yale University Press.

Poole, Stafford. 1995. *Our Lady of Guadalupe: The Origins and Sources of a Mexican National Symbol, 1531–1797.* Tucson: University of Arizona Press.

Pope, Kevin O. and Malcom B. Sibberensen. 1981. "In Search of Tzultacaj: Cave Explorations in the Maya Lowlands of Alta Verapaz, Guatemala." *Journal of New World Archaeology* 4(3):17–54.

Popkin, Samuel L. 1979. *The Rational Peasant: The Political Economy of Rural Society in Vietnam*. Berkeley: University of California Press.

Portes, Alejandro, Luis Guarnizo, and Patricia Landolt. 1999. "The Study of Trans-nationalism: Pitfalls and Promise of an Emergent Research Field." *Ethnic and Racial Studies*. 22(2):217–237.

Prosser, Jon. 1998. "The Status of Image-based Research." In *Image-based Research: A Sourcebook for Qualitative Researchers*, Jon Prosser, ed., 97–112. London: Falmer Press.

Rambo, A. T. 1962. "The Kekchi Indians of British Honduras: An Ethnographic Study." *Katunob* 3:40–48.

Ravicz, Robert. 1967. "Compadrinazgo." In *Handbook of Middle American Indians: Volume 6, Social Anthropology*. Manning Nash, ed., 238–252. Austin: University of Texas Press.

Read, K. E. 1955. "Morality and the Concept of the Person among the Gahuku-Gama." *Oceania* XXV(4):233–282.

Re Cruz, Alice. 1996. *The Two Milpas of ChanKom: Scenarios of a Maya Village Life*. Albany: SUNY Press.

Redfield, Robert. 1941. *The Folk Culture of Yucatan*. Chicago: University of Chicago Press.

Redfield, Robert and Alfonso Villa Rojas. 1962 [1934]. *Chan Kom: A Maya Village*. Chicago and London: University of Chicago Press.

Richards, Julia Becker and Michael Richards. 1987. *A Historical, Cultural, Linguistic and Sociolinguistic Overview of the Four Major Language Regions of Guatemala*. Ministerio de Educación, Dirección Socio Educativo Rural, Programa Nacional de Educación Bilingue Republica de Guatemala.

————. 1996. "Maya Education: A Historical and Contemporary Analysis of Mayan Language Education Policy." In *Maya Cultural Activism in Guatemala*, Edward F. Fischer and R. McKenna Brown, eds., 208–221. Austin: University of Texas Press.

Rodman, Margaret C. 1992. "Empowering Place: Multilocality and Multivocality." *American Anthropologist* 94(4):640–655.

Rojas Lima, Flavio. 1988. *La Cultura del Maiz en Guatemala*. Guatemala: Ministerio de Cultura y Deportes.

Rony, Fatimah Tobin. 1996. *The Third Eye: Race, Cinema, and Ethnographic Spectacle*. Durham, N.C.: Duke University Press.

Root, Deborah. 1996. *Cannibal Culture: Art, Appropriation, and the Commodification of Difference*. Boulder: Westview Press.

Rorty, Richard. 1980. *Philosophy and the Mirror of Nature*. Princeton: Princeton University Press.

Rose, Jacqueline. 1988. "Sexuality and Vision: Some Questions." In *Vision and Visuality,* Hal Foster, ed., 115–130. Seattle: Bay Press.

Roseberry, William. 1989. *Anthropologies and Histories: Essays in Culture, History, and Political Economy.* New Brunswick: Rutgers University Press.

Rouse, Roger. 1991. "Mexican Migration and the Social Space of Postmodernism." *Diaspora* Spring 1991:8–23.

Royce, Anya P. 1982. *Ethnic Identity: Strategies of Diversity.* Bloomington: Indiana University Press.

Roys, Ralph. 1972. *The Indian Background of Colonial Yucatan.* Norman: University of Oklahoma Press.

Rubel, Arthur J., Carl W. O'Nell, and Rolando Collado-Ardón. 1985. *Susto: A Folk Illness.* Berkeley: University of California Press.

Ruby, Jay. 1980. "Exposing Yourself: Reflexivity, Anthropology, and Film." *Semiotica* 30(1/2):153–179.

———. 2000. *Picturing Culture: Explorations of Film and Anthropology.* Chicago and London: University of Chicago Press.

Ruz, Mario Humberto. 1992. "Los Mayas de hoy: pueblos en lucha." In *Del Katún al siglo: Tiempos de colonialismo y resistencia entre los mayas,* María del Carmen León, Mario Humberto Ruz, and José Alejos García, eds., 191–267. Mexico: Consejo Nacional para la Cultura y las Artes.

Saguil Castillo, Jose Luis. 1991. *La Ensenanza en Espanol a Ninos Hablantes del Idioma Q'eqchi.* Quetzaltengo, Guatemala: Universidad Rafael Landívar.

Sahlins, Marshall. 1972. *Stone Age Economics.* Chicago: Aldine.

———. 1985. *Islands of History.* Chicago: University of Chicago Press.

Said, Edward. 1978. *Orientalism.* New York: Vintage Books.

Sam Juárez, Miguel and Stephen Stewart. 1997. *Diccionario Q'eqchi'.* Guatemala: Proyecto Lingüístico Francisco Marroquín.

Sanchiz Ochoa, Pilar. 1993. "Sincretismos de Ida y Vuelta: El Culto de San Simón en Guatemala." *Mesoamérica* 26:253–266.

Sapper, Karl. 1985 [1936]. *The Verapaz in the Sixteenth and Seventeenth Centuries: A Contribution to the Historical Geography and Ethnography of Northeastern Guatemala.* Los Angeles: Institute of Archaeology, University of California.

Schackt, Jon. 1984. "The Tzuultak'a: Religious Lore and Cultural Processes among the Kekchi." *Belizian Studies* 12(5):16–29.

———. 1986. *One God—Two Temples: Schismatic Process in a Kekchi Village.* Oslo: Department of Social Anthropology.

Schlesinger, Stephen and Stephen Kinzer. 1982. *Bitter Fruit: The Untold Story of the American Coup in Guatemala.* New York: Anchor Books.

Scott, James. 1976. *The Moral Economy of the Peasant: Rebellion and Subsistence in Southeast Asia.* New Haven: Yale University Press.

———. 1985. *Weapons of the Weak: Everyday Forms of Peasant Resistance.* New Haven: Yale University Press.

Scott, James C. 1990. *Domination and the Arts of Resistance: Hidden Transcripts.* New Haven and London: Yale University Press.

Sedat, Guillermo. 1993 [1955]. *Nuevo Diccionario de las Lenguas K'ekchi' y Española.* Guatemala: Centro Editorial VILE.

Seremetakis, C. Nadia. 1994. "The Memory of the Senses: Historical Perception, Commensal Exchange, and Modernity." In *Visualizing Theory: Selected Essays From V.A.R. 1990–1994,* Lucien Taylor, ed., 214–229. New York and London: Routledge.

Sharer, Robert. 1994. *The Ancient Maya.* Fifth Edition. Stanford: Stanford University Press.

Sieber, Hans. 1999. *"We Are the Children of the Mountain," Creolization and Modernization among the Q'eqchi'es.* Amsterdam: CEDLA.

Silverman, Kaja. 1992. "Histoire d'O: The Construction of a Female Subject." In *Pleasure and Danger: Exploring Female Sexuality,* Carol S. Vance, ed., 320–349. Boston: Routledge and Kegan Paul.

Smith, Carol, ed. 1990. *Guatemalan Indians and the State: 1540–1988.* Austin: University of Texas Press.

———. 1990a. "Origins of the National Question in Guatemala: A Hypothesis." In *Guatemalan Indians and the State: 1540–1988.* Austin: University of Texas Press.

Smith, Carol A. 1995. "Race-Class-Gender Ideology in Guatemala: Modern and Anti-Modern Forms." *Comparative Studies in Society and History* 37(4):723–749.

Smith, Michael French. 1994. *Hard Times on Kairiru Island: Poverty, Development, and Morality in a Papua New Guinea Village.* Honolulu: University of Hawaii Press.

Sobchack, Vivian. 1992. *The Address of the Eye: A Phenomenology of Film Experience.* Princeton: Princeton University Press.

Spanos, William V. 2000. *America's Shadow: An Anatomy of Empire.* Minneapolis and London: University of Minnesota Press.

Stallybrass, Peter. 1999. "Worn Worlds: Clothes, Mourning, and the Life of Things." In *Cultural Memory and the Construction of Identity,* Dan Ben-Amos and Liliane Weissberg, eds., 27–44. Detroit: Wayne State University Press.

Stanley, Diane K. 1994. *For the Record: The United Fruit Company's Sixty-six Years in Guatemala.* Guatemala: Centro Impresor Piedra Santa.

Stavenhagen, Rodolpho. 1977 [1963]. *Clases, Colonialismo, y Aculturacion: Ensayo sobre un sistema de relaciones interétnicas en Mesoamérica.* Second Edition. Guatemala: Editorial "Jose De Pinada Ibarra," Ministerio de Educación.

Stephens, John L. 1856. *Incidents of Travel in Central America, Chiapas, and Yucatan.* New York: Harper & Brothers.

Stoll, David. 1988. "Evangelicals, Guerillas, and the Army: The Ixil Triangle under Ríos Montt." In *Harvest of Violence,* Robert Carmack, ed., 90–116. Norman: University of Oklahoma Press.

———. 1993. *Between Two Armies in the Ixil Towns of Guatemala.* New York: Columbia University Press.

Stoller, Paul. 1989. *The Taste of Ethnographic Things: The Senses in Anthropology.* Chicago: University of Chicago Press.

—————. 1992. *The Cinematic Griot: The Ethnography of Jean Rouch.* Chicago: University of Chicago Press.

—————. 1997. *Sensuous Scholarship.* Philadelphia: University of Pennsylvania Press.

Strathern, Andrew. 1981. "Death as Exchange: Two Melanesian Cases." In *Mortality and Immortality: The Anthropology and Archaeology of Death,* S. C. Humphreys and Helen King, eds., 205–223. London: Academic Press.

Strathern, Marilyn. 1988. *The Gender of the Gift.* Berkeley: University of California Press.

—————. 1991. "Partners and Consumers: Making Relations Visible." *New Literary History* 22:581–601.

Strathern, Marilyn and Jeanette Edwards. 2000. "Including Our Own." In *Cultures of Relatedness: New Approaches to the Study of Kinship,* Janet Carsten, ed., 149–166. Cambridge: Cambridge University Press.

Strauss, Claudia and Naomi Quinn. 1997. *A Cognitive Theory of Cultural Meaning.* Cambridge: Cambridge University Press.

Swetman, John. 1989. "What Else Did Indians Have to Do with Their Time? Alternatives to Labor Migration in Prerevolutionary Guatemala." *Economic Development and Cultural Change* 38(1):89–112.

Tambiah, Stanley J. 1990. *Magic, Science, Religion, and the Scope of Rationality.* Cambridge: Cambridge University Press.

Taube, Karl A. 1992. *The Major Gods of Ancient Yucatan.* Washington, D.C.: Dumbarton Oaks Research Library.

Taussig, Michael. 1980. *The Devil and Commodity Fetishism in South America.* Chapel Hill: University of North Carolina Press.

—————. 1987. *Shamanism, Colonialism, and the Wildman.* Chicago: University of Chicago Press.

—————. 1993. *Mimesis and Alterity: A Particular History of the Senses.* Routledge Press.

Tax, Sol. 1937. "The Municipios of the Midwestern Highlands of Guatemala." *American Anthropologist* 40:584–604.

Tedlock, Barbara. 1991. "From Participant Observation to the Observation of Participation: The Emergence of Narrative Ethnography." *Journal of Anthropological Research* 47(1):69–94.

—————. 1992. *Time and the Highland Maya.* Second Edition. Albuquerque: University of New Mexico Press.

Tedlock, Dennis. 1983. *The Spoken Word and the Work of Interpretation.* Philadelphia: University of Pennsylvania Press.

—————. 1993. *Breath on the Mirror: Mythic Voices and Visions of the Living Maya.* San Francisco: Harper Collins.

—————, trans. 1996. *Popol Vuh: The Definitive Edition of the Mayan Book of the Dawn of Life and Glories of Gods and Kings.* Revised Edition. New York: Simon and Schuster.

Thompson, Charles D. 2001. *Maya Identities and the Violence of Place: Borders Bleed.* Aldershot and Burlington: Ashgate.

Thompson, J. Eric. 1938. "Sixteenth and Seventeenth Century Reports on the Chol Mayas." *American Anthropologist* 40:584–604.

———. 1970. *Maya History and Religion.* Norman: University of Oklahoma Press.

Turner, Victor. 1995 [1969]. *The Ritual Process: Structure and Anti-structure.* New York: Aldine de Gruyter.

Turner, Terence. 1991. "Representing, Resisting, Rethinking: Historical Transformations of Kayapo Culture and Anthropological Consciousness." In *Colonial Situations,* George Stocking, ed., 285–313. Madison: University of Wisconsin Press.

———. 2002. "Representation, Politics, and Cultural Imagination in Indigenous Video." In *Media Worlds: Anthropology on New Terrain.* Faye D. Ginsburg, Lila Abu-Lughod, and Brian Larkin, eds., 75–89. Berkeley: University of California Press.

Vaughan, Dai. 1979 [1960]. "The Man with the Movie Camera." In *The Documentary Tradition,* Lewis Jacobs, ed., 53–59. Second Edition. New York and London: W. W. Norton and Company.

Villacorta, J. Antonio. 1929. "Arqueología Guatemalteca-Pokomá, Cak-yú, Chamá, Chajcar, Panzamalá, Chisec, Puruljá, Chacjual, etc." *Anales de La Sociedad de Geografía E Historia* 1:52–71.

Villa Rojas, Alfonso. 1969. "Maya of Yucatan." In *Handbook of Middle American Indians: Volume 7, Ethnology, Part I.* Robert Wauchope, ed., 244–275. Austin: University of Texas Press.

Wagner, Regina. 1987. "Actividades Empresariales de los alemanes en Guatemala: 1850–1920." *Mesoamérica* 13:87–123.

———. 1996. *Los Alemanes en Guatemala: 1820–1944.* Guatemala: Afanes.

Warren, Kay. 1989. *The Symbolism of Subordination: Indian Identity in a Guatemalan Town.* Second Edition. Austin and London: University of Texas Press.

Wasserstrom, Robert. 1983. *Class and Society in Central Chiapas.* Berkeley: University of California Press.

Watanabe, John M. 1992. *Maya Saints and Souls in a Changing World.* Austin: University of Texas Press.

Weiner, Annette B. 1992. *Inalienable Possessions: The Paradox of Keeping-While-Giving.* Berkeley: University of California Press.

Werbner, Pnina. 1997. "Essentialising Essentialism, Essentialising Silence: Ambivalence and Multiplicity in the Constructions of Racism and Ethnicity." In *Debating Cultural Hybridity: Multi-cultural Identities and the Politics of Anti-Racism,* Pnina Werbner and Tariq Modood, eds., 226–254. London and New Jersey: Zed Books.

Wilk, Richard. 1991. *Household Ecology: Economic Change and Domestic Life among the Kekchi Maya in Belize.* Tucson: University of Arizona Press.

Wilmsen, Edwin N. 1996. "Premises of Power in Ethnic Politics." In *The Politics of Difference: Ethnic Premises in a World of Power,* Edwin N. Wilmsen, ed., 1–25. Chicago and London: University of Chicago Press.

Wilson, Richard. 1991. "Machine Guns and Mountain Spirits: The Cultural Effects of State Repression among the Q'eqchi' of Guatemala." *Critique of Anthropology* 11(1):33–61.

———. 1995. *Maya Resurgence in Guatemala: Q'eqchi' Experiences.* Norman and London: University of Oklahoma Press.

Winston, Brian. 1988. "Documentary: I Think We Are in Trouble." In *New Challenges for Documentary,* Alan Rosenthal, ed., 21–33. Berkeley: University of California Press.

———. 1998. " 'The Camera Never Lies': The Partiality of Photographic Evidence." In *Image-Based Research: A Sourcebook for Qualitative Researchers,* J. Prosser, ed., 60–68. London: Falmer Press.

Wolf, Eric. 1957. "Closed Corporate Peasant Communities in Mesoamerica and Central Java." *Southwestern Journal of Anthropology* 13(1):1–18.

Wolf, Eric R. 1958. "The Virgin of Guadalupe: A Mexican National Symbol." *Journal of American Folklore* 71:34–39.

———. 1999. *Envisioning Power: Ideologies of Dominance and Crisis.* Berkeley: University of California Press.

Woodward, Ralph Lee. 1990. "Changes in the Nineteenth-Century Guatemalan State and Its Indian Policies." In *Guatemalan Indians and the State: 1540–1988,* C. Smith, ed. 52–71. Austin: University of Texas Press.

Worth, Sol and John Adair. 1972. *Through Navajo Eyes: An Exploration in Film Communication and Anthropology.* Bloomington: Indiana University Press.

Wright, Pamela. 1995. "The Timely Significance of Supernatural Mothers or Exemplary Daughters: The Metonymy of Identity in History." In *Articulating Hidden Histories: Exploring the Influence of Eric R. Wolf,* Jane Schneider and Rayna Rapp, eds., 243–261. Berkeley: University of California Press.

INDEX

Note: Transcripts of interviews are indexed in italics; photographs and illustrations are noted in bold.